Sleep-Tight Money

A Guide to
Managing Your Money
Safely and Achieving
Financial Peace of Mind

LAWRENCE A. KRAUSE

SIMON AND SCHUSTER
NEW YORK, LONDON, TORONTO, SYDNEY, TOKYO

Published by Simon and Schuster
A Division of Simon & Schuster, Inc.
Rockefeller Center
1230 Avenue of the Americas
New York, NY 10020

SIMON AND SCHUSTER and colophon are registered trademarks
of Simon & Schuster, Inc.

Designed by Irving Perkins Associates
Manufactured in the United States of America

10   9   8   7   6   5   4   3   2   1

Library of Congress Cataloging-in-Publication Data

Krause, Lawrence A.
  Sleep-tight money.

  Includes index.
  1. Finance, Personal.   2. Investments.   I. Title.
HG179.K664   1987   332.024   87-14806

ISBN 0-671-64023-2

Portions of this book were previously published in *The Money-Go-Round*
by Lawrence Krause.

Acknowledgments

I had a lot of fun writing this book; but no book is created in a vacuum. A great deal of help came from many people. I owe a special debt of gratitude to the thousands of people who have written me or called me on the radio or on television. They helped me to understand the need to present personal financial planning in a manner that everyone can understand and enjoy. This book belongs to all of you.

I also am indebted to a large number of people from the financial planning community, the financial services industry and various schools throughout the country. Their need to utilize a commonsense financial planning book in the classroom and for lectures, and their praise and constructive criticism have helped make this book happen. Books, like life, are enhanced by good criticism and some praise, and for both of these I am thankful.

I thank too, my many friends and clients who gave me their stories. Though they must remain anonymous, I really cannot thank them enough for their willingness to share their experience.

I must also thank Art Garcia, my good friend, as well as *California Business* magazine. Without Art and his continuing support, you would not be reading this book today. Were it not for his introduction to America's largest regional business magazine and almost nine years of writing monthly columns, you would probably be reading nothing more provocative than a business letter.

Then there's Richard Wollack, who originally suggested I base my book on some of my columns. I have learned that the awesome power of suggestion must first be present before the power of the word processor can exist. Thank you.

I am indebted to Robert Stanger, Harold Gourgues, Jr., and Alexandra Armstrong. They are consummate financial and investment planning professionals who clearly influenced my thinking. I offer my sincere gratitude.

And I will always thank Loren Dunton, founder of the International Association for Financial Planning, the College of Financial Planning, *The Financial Planner* magazine, and the National Center for Financial Education. Committed to the consumer, Loren continues to teach me about people and their needs.

Thank you, Shelley—Shelley Berman—for your encouragement, your humor and love.

And thank you, Ronn—Ronn Owens—for your inspiration, interest, and enthusiasm.

I would also like very much to thank Marcella Smith and my editor, Fred Hills, both from Simon and Schuster, for believing in me, my ideas, and for making this book a reality.

How can I ever thank Donna, my wife, my love, my friend, my partner, my editor, my sounding board, my greatest supporter? She would often say, "If you want someone to talk with, to listen . . . or simply to be there, you can count on me." That says it all.

And finally, my good fortune continues due to my daughters, Alexis and Danielle, ages six and eleven. While their technical assistance amounted to "Are you finished yet?" they have nonetheless demonstrated patience and understanding well beyond their years. Being as quiet as mice yet desiring to be close, they would often bring their sleeping bags into "Daddy's work-study" to sleep while I worked late into the night. And now it's my turn to bring my sleeping bag into their rooms.

This book is dedicated to my mother, Sylvia, a very wise, loving, sensitive, yet strong woman. I'm proud as I can be to call her "Mom."

Contents

PART FOUR: GUARDING YOUR ASSETS

Introduction

You and Your Money—
The Anxiety of It All

Most people (and you are probably one of them) want to be free to enjoy their lives without worrying about where the money is coming from to pay the bills. They want to be free to be themselves, to take good care of their kids, to quit their jobs if they so desire, to slow down, or to enjoy retirement without continually fretting about money matters. They want to build that little "nest egg" for the future. And they don't want to lose what they have accumulated. In short, most people want enough money to be happy. But these same people (and as a professional financial planner I see a lot of them) worry so much about money that they live in a state of perpetual *un*happiness.

I don't believe you have to suffer to be happy. I think it was Dr. Scholl who once said, "The longest journey starts with a single bunion." As the first step on your own journey toward a worry-free financial future, you must overcome your anxiety about money.

You may be lucky enough to have good earning power, intelligence, imagination and a realistic attitude about life. But you probably have not been as fortunate with your money education. And that's the primary reason you feel as you do about money. I know you probably *believe* you are reasonably well informed. After all, your training probably started from the time you were small. You may have initially learned how to make it on your own by mowing lawns, delivering newspapers or through a baby-sitting job. As you grew older, you may have worked as a waiter or waitress, clerked in a department store or slaved away in your parents' business.

Then came the formal training on how best to spend and invest your earnings. Courses in school were the answer. You took economics, accounting and . . . well, your best classroom was really all around you. All you had to do was turn on the radio or TV or pick up a magazine or newspaper to become a world-class economist. If you were fortunate enough to catch the stock market report on a particularly wild day, you might have heard something like this: "On Wall Street today, news of lower interest rates sent the stock market up, but then the expectation that those rates would be inflationary sent the market down, until the realization that lower rates might stimulate the sluggish economy pushed the market up, before it ultimately went down on fears that an overheated economy would lead to a reimposition of higher interest rates." (Could someone please interpret that message for me?)

When it came to other courses on investments, there was certainly no lack of information. As a matter of fact, part of the beauty of being alive is that total strangers are more than happy to share their financial knowledge: the cab driver, a bank teller, the computer salesperson sitting next to you on the plane, an insurance agent, a part-time actor (who waits on tables by day) or a fellow sufferer at the dentist's office.

Then there are those who really know you who are happy to provide a higher level of financial education: your barber or beautician, Uncle George, your next-door neighbor, your golf and bridge partners or your fellow commuter. Not to worry. If you needed *impartial* professional advice on how to develop a financial strategy, there was always the stockbroker, the real estate agent, the antique or coin dealer and, last but not least, your doctor.

Rounding out the picture, you probably have sought advice from an accountant. After all, what better person to turn to for developing future tax strategies? He was anxious to help and all you had to do was take the initiative. "Ask away," he said. "If you have specific questions dealing with the taxes you've *already* paid, I'll be happy to answer them." "Gee, thanks . . . what a deal."

Then, fully educated, you were ready to strike out on your own. You knew the world was full of crossroads and temptations. You were willing to take the risk. After all, it made a lot of sense to imitate your rich friends by investing to reduce the burden of taxes. It was simply bad luck the IRS disallowed your four-to-one tax deduction in that not too surprisingly unprofitable project in techniques of growing corn at the North Pole. And if only the price of oil had gone to $50 a barrel as it was supposed to, your letter of credit for the drilling deal would not have been called and you would not have had to sell other assets to meet that call. Oh, yes, let's not forget that the Peruvian gold mine recommended by Harley Greed, a friend from your country club, was a mistake. (Lord, protect us from our friends.)

It's not that you're a bad money manager. As a matter of fact, it was you who decided to purchase those 30-year tax-free bonds at an unbelievable 10 percent yield. All the economists hosting shows on TV said the economy could not tolerate higher interest rates. So they were a little bit wrong. Though the bond market value plummeted for a while, you hung on, and today you're a hero.

But on the other hand, there was that inside information that Big Mom's Microchip Company was going to be bought out at a substantial premium over current share price. Seymour Doe, your neighbor, "got the word" from Big Mom's second husband's son by a previous marriage (they're squash partners). You bought as many shares as you could reasonably afford; "A short-term killing guaranteed," Doe said. Well, it may still be a good long-term investment, but you will probably sell once you get even. (Lord, protect us from our neighbors.)

It has been said that there are two areas in one's life where no formal training can be found: how to succeed at marriage and how to be a good parent. I will add another: how to take care of your money. The assumption has always been that handling money is so complicated, so risky, that you need to plot and scheme continually to get ahead. The *reality* is that all you really need is a basic understanding of how you can easily accumulate enough money to do what you want, when you want, as long as you live. You can learn how to know when enough money is enough, how to hold on to what you've got, and still get a good night's sleep.

It is with that single purpose in mind that I have written this book— not only to give you a better understanding of what is happening to you financially, but also what you can do to improve your financial situation. To accomplish that, I will show you how to evaluate your present financial picture and put it into perspective. Then I will offer you practical advice in the two areas in which you may be spending the most amount of money: your home and the cost of higher education. And finally, you will learn how to manage your money, with the degree of risk that is appropriate to you, to achieve your future financial goals.

I can't promise you financial miracles—just the sweet dreams that come with knowning how to spend, save and invest your money with self-confidence and good common sense.

> Give a man a fish and you feed him for a day;
> Teach a man to fish and you feed him for a lifetime.
>
> —A Chinese proverb

PART ONE

The Predictable
and the Unpredictable

Chapter 1

Financial Security—
Making That Dream Come True

As a professional financial planner, I work with many clients: all types of people, but mostly people like you. Sure, some are millionaires, even multimillionaires. Others are "squeaking by" on incomes of $250,000 a year. But a recurring theme I hear from *all* my clients is that having or making a lot of money does not guarantee peace of mind. Quite the opposite. It seems the more money you have, the less serenity you can enjoy. You worry constantly about losing it. You worry that you are not smart enough to handle relatively large sums of money or wise enough to choose from among the diverse investment possibilities now open to you (indeed, more choices plant in you a suspicion that you are not obtaining the best return on your money). You worry that the responsibility of having money is too much for you, that people will like you for the wrong reasons. You even worry if you're not worried.

Whether you have a lot of money or would like a lot (more), I understand your frustrations and your anxieties. You are not alone. Though you are a unique person, of course, you suffer the same money fears as millions of others. A private study reveals that the more people earn, the greater their insecurity. Four out of five people whose incomes exceed $50,000 feel insecure when making personal financial decisions. Look at the following list of the twelve most common reasons people come to see me, or any financial planner. You'll probably find yourself identifying with one or more of them.

1. I don't have the time to handle my personal financial situation properly. (I'm too busy being successful to think about money.)

2. I'm confused by all the investment choices, by what I feel about our economy and by all these tax-law changes. (It's getting too complicated and I don't know how to sort it all out.)
3. I don't have an actual financial plan—nine out of ten people don't—and I'm tired of reacting, I've decided I want to act. (Tell me what to do.)
4. Everyone is just trying to sell me something. (I don't know a lot about investments, yet I want to buy the right thing—from someone I can trust.)
5. I feel as though I should do something. (I know I must make changes today just to stay in place.)
6. I'm paying—or am I paying?—too much in taxes. (I've bought my last $600 toilet seat for the Pentagon.)
7. I'm not interested in personal financial matters. (It's boring.)
8. Numbers confuse me. (I break out in hives when I look at a ruler.)
9. I want someone to tell me what to do and when to do it. (And maybe even do it for me.)
10. I'm not a money plotter and schemer. I just want to accumulate enough to do what I want. (I really don't know what I want.)
11. I want to become or know I am financially secure. (How secure is secure?)
12. I'd like to have some financial perspective. (I can't figure it out. Can you?)

If none of these reasons applies to you, then you are qualified, or may think you are qualified, to open your own financial planning practice. Either way, I wish you well—as long as you open your office somewhere else.

Seriously, if one of the reasons mentioned above strikes a familiar chord, then you are reading the right book because its aim is to deal with your financial fears and worries. Read on and soon you will be able to put those fears and worries to rest. You will learn how to calculate your financial needs and determine what will best meet those needs. I am not going to bore you with minutia—leave that to the textbooks. Though I believe I am providing you with practical information, you undoubtedly are reading this book because you want to know what time it is, not how to build a watch.

In case you missed my message, let me restate it. I am going to be very candid about money. This book is plain-speaking, easy (yes, and I hope fun) to read and you will see that I believe, if put in its right place, money can be fun, too. My goal is to show you not only that financial planning is not complicated, but also that it is really easy. I will help you establish a framework within which to make the financial decisions that are right for you and I provide concrete recommendations. But no matter what I or anyone else says, the success of your personal financial planning ultimately depends not on me but on you. It's still your money, your life, your family's future. Not mine. And *no* one else can do it for you.

Now, sit back and relax, and you will probably discover that the financial decisions you have already made are better than you thought. You just worry too much. Financial decision-making is neither intimidating nor perplexing. And money, after all, is just money. Whether it's earmarked for spending or saving, there's no mystery about it. The problem is that anxiety sets in once you stop to think too much about financial decisions that are really nothing more than common sense—decisions that enable you to sleep well rather than wake up with nightmares.

Have you ever heard the story of the ant and the centipede? The ant stopped the centipede and asked him how he knew which leg he was going to move next—after all, he had so many. The centipede said he never thought about it. But once he did, for the first time he was unable to move; he couldn't figure out which leg to move next. You probably have a similar problem. You think of money in terms of dollars and cents rather than what it is meant to accomplish.

When buying a pair of shoes, it is important to determine their quality, but it is senseless to count the number of stitches in the soles and uppers. You are purchasing the shoes because you need them to protect your feet and to complement your clothing. You will never know if you have selected the perfectly made shoe, even if you count the number of steps taken or hours worn compared to other shoes. So it is with your money. You determine its purpose, study what you can buy with it to achieve that purpose, get advice, shop around a little to determine if you're going to feel comfortable with that purchase. If you are, then buy. If the shoe fits, wear it.

Financial planning doesn't have to be any more complicated than that. Because in the final analysis, no one I know has ever chronicled his or her investment record to the point where he or she saw, or even felt, what the return of those extra-hard-fought 1 or 2 percentage points achieved over a long period of time. Have you? When was the last time you placed money in a 25-year account that was unaffected by inflation or taxes—an account that continually maintained that 2 percent edge? Usually, the time you might spend playing interest-rate tag would be better spent on your job or with your family. You would probably make as much money and find yourself less exasperated. Life itself is a series of trade-offs, and the world of personal financial decisions is no different.

Of course, I suggest you monitor your investment performance from time to time (see Chapter 9) and make adjustments when necessary. But I'm fully aware there is no such thing as a right decision. After you make a decision, through the monitoring process, you then make it right. You should treat your portfolio of investments like a good pair of shoes; you don't throw it (them) out unless it no longer functions as it was meant to function, or takes too much time or money to repair.

So step back and view your money from a different, less frightening perspective. And stop blindly believing all you read and hear, too. At this moment I am looking at a 1984 *Wall Street Journal* article about a respected money manager who warned, "The financial system should produce horrendous inflation by 1985 or 1986." In anticipation of spiraling prices, he was advising clients to immediately invest heavily in gold, silver and oil that typically do well under such circumstances. Consider yourself fortunate that you missed that article. Most of the time the values of each of the three have been substantially lower. The sleep you saved was your own.

How Comfortable Are You with Risk?

Will Rogers said it best: "Forget about a return *on* my investment. What I want is a return *of* my investment."

In other words, his first priority was to avoid losing money. And I'm sure you feel the same way. For most people, the fear of loss is far greater than the greed for gain. Loss aversion is a surprisingly powerful emotion; so much so, that often our own quirks interfere with what would otherwise be a rational decision. A group of students were invited to wager on a hypothetical coin toss: Heads, you win $150; tails, you lose $100. Though the potential payoff is 1½ times the possible loss, most students refused to bet. Maybe they thought it was the old "heads, I win/tails, you lose" routine. Nevertheless, despite the outsize reward for taking this risk, a majority of the population is put off by a 50 percent chance of losing.

A research study by two Israeli-born psychologists, Daniel Kahneman, of the University of California at Berkeley, and Amos Tversky of Stanford, as reported in *Fortune's 1987 Investor's Guide,* demonstrates this point further: If *you* had a 100 percent chance to win $3,000 or an 80 percent chance to win $4,000, which would you choose? (Please answer before you read on.) When asked this question, most people went for the sure thing and chose the guaranteed $3,000, even though in the long run you come out ahead by making the second choice consistently (80 percent times $4,000 is $3,200.) But most people were anxious about the 20 percent chance of getting nothing in the second choice.

You have another chance. Now which would you choose: a certain loss of $3,000 or an 80 percent chance of losing $4,000 and a 20 percent chance of losing nothing? Answer: Most people will take the second choice, which offers a 20 percent chance of winning, even though there is greater risk (80 percent of $4,000 is $3,000). In other words, their fear of loss is so great that it leads them to make poor investment decisions.

What is *your* risk tolerance? It is early in the morning and you are about to leave for work. Your job requires you to attend an important meeting first thing on this day, and although you believe there is enough fuel in your car for your trip, there is the possibility you may run out of gas. Which of the following thoughts is most likely to be uppermost in your mind as you leave the house?

1. I must make that meeting at all costs. The gauge reads empty, but I can't be out of gas. Gas gauges are usually wrong. So, it's full steam ahead!
2. Even though the gauge reads empty, it's happened before. So I'll stretch my luck again and take a chance by going to work without stopping for gas.
3. I can't risk being stranded without gas. Who knows what else might happen? Someone could come along and sideswipe me. I'm going to have to stop for gas despite the fact that I'll be late for the meeting.
4. I would feel foolish if I ran out of gas. On the other hand, this meeting is important and I wouldn't want to be late unnecessarily. So I'll compromise by driving somewhat slower than usual, conserve gas and be only slightly late for the meeting.

If your reaction was:

1. You are an uninformed risk-taker. Your eye is on your destination, with little or no thought about how you get there.
2. You like to take risks.
3. You have an aversion to risks.
4. You are willing to take calculated risks when the potential reward justifies it.

Of course, there are many degrees of risk tolerance—depending on what is at risk. If it's money—your money—the way you feel about risk will—and should—influence every investment decision you make.

Money Is All Relative

Money has enormous emotional and symbolic meaning. And money is all relative. Though I've asked you not to get too caught up in details, let me just ask whether you have ever thought about this: your attitude toward money and its emotional impact on you.

Before you can map out a financial plan, you first must understand your emotional relationship to money, because your investment life follows your psychological makeup. Money is both an economic and an emotional commodity. It pays for our basic needs, as well as our services in the workplace. Yet money is also experienced as an adult's way of looking at emotional supply and demand. When we don't have enough real money, we may not be able to buy food or clothing. When we don't have enough emotional money, we may feel we're not getting enough love and attention. Money doesn't come with a set of written instructions, but instead with tacit directives that we received from our parents. More than 90 percent of the people I see tell me that money was never discussed in their homes. However, if their parents were inside their heads, they would each be saying something about how their kids handled their money. To illustrate, think of one incident that typifies your father's style of spending or saving. Think of one incident that typifies your mother's money style. Now, where do you fit in?

Couples bring such hidden messages and an inability to discuss money to their relationships. Today, many couples admit it is harder to talk about money than sex (and less fun, too). That is why money is the most frequent cause of family arguments. It also explains why spending and investment patterns tend to be polarized as the partners push each other to extremes.

Are you a woman? How you invest your money is generally different from how a man invests. If you are married and have a family, you will tend to be hesitant to accept risk. Your primary financial goal is to protect the home and family, whereas the male is inclined to take greater financial risk. If you are a woman, you tend to invest more cautiously, gauging the investment more rationally and logically, whereas most men are oriented toward the "bottom line" and may take a full-steam-ahead approach to get there.

Step back and take a look at yourself. What are your money attitudes and where did they come from? Does money make you feel powerful; or because you are not the wage-earner, is it a case of "matri-money" management? Do you see money as a means of buying freedom, or are you a slave to it? Are you reluctant to reveal how much you make, how much is in the bank or how much the house cost? Are you a product of the Great Depression, or do you feel you must get rid of money? Are you a compulsive bargain hunter? Do you know how to spend and enjoy money, or are you a saver, afraid to let go of your cash no matter what?

Why is this important?

Unless you know how you feel about your money, you will always have anxiety. You will always feel worried about financial matters, and they will always seem out of control. By understanding your money meshugas, you will then better understand that you aren't missing out on some great get-rich-quick stock or bond, and that the way you invest is probably just fine and that performance can be improved completely within the confines of what makes you comfortable. You don't have to step outside your comfort zone to achieve your financial goals.

I have a client, a single, 44-year-old tailor, who has squirreled away $600,000 in bank CDs and money market funds. He works seven days a week, rents his apartment and owns few material goods. He was constantly saving money because he lived in fear that he would lose his job, might not find another and had no one to turn to. He never knew when he might need as much cash as he could accumulate. As interest rates were declining, he turned to a professional advisor because he wanted to increase his rate of return with no increase in risk. Though he also questioned whether he should buy a condominium rather than rent, he could not part with his money.

Though he sought and received recommendations for investments with higher returns, he rejected them all because they were outside his comfort level. He could not alter the comfort-level habit he so long ago formed. He "knew" he should be exploring other avenues, and part of his anxiety came from a belief that he was supposed to reposition his money. After all, that is what he had read. But articles do not account for people's differing needs, desires and comfort levels, and he remained on his one-way street. But once he (and I) recognized the fact that his tolerance for risk was low, he was able to accept my recommendation to purchase sequential maturity CDs, which are a continuous succession of CDs (see Chapter 14). Later he replaced the CDs

with sequential (insured) municipal bonds. Both were low-risk investments well within his comfort level.

Just recognizing that you are unable or don't care to change your
attitude about money will not only help you take that first step toward
lowering your anxiety, but also help you become a better investor in
the process. As Thoreau once said, "That man is richest whose plea-
sures are the cheapest." If you conclude that your threshold of risk is a
30-month certificate of deposit (see Chapter 14) yielding 8 percent, so
be it. At the moment, in fact, such a return might still put you well
ahead of inflation. Most important, your capital would be safe. You
may not get rich, but you will have peace of mind.

I am reminded of a story told by one of my clients. He is in his
eighties, a high achiever who hates losing, but he knows himself so
well he can repeat a story of lost opportunity with good humor. About
sixty years ago, as an insurance claims agent, it seems he paid $5,000
to a claim recipient in Lake Tahoe, California. The recipient said he
was going to use the money to buy ten lakefront lots at $500 apiece.
My client considered making the same investment but chose not to.
Today he says that was one of his best financial decisions ever. Had
he purchased similar lots, he figures he would probably have sold
them after they had doubled or tripled in value, and he would have felt
terrible once they rose in value to more than $1 million apiece. How-
ever, he now has no regrets because he never owned them in the first
place.

Like this fellow, you need to gain perspective about yourself. If you
find you can't, ask a friend of the same sex, age and socioeconomic
level to help out. Ask what he or she understands or recognizes about
your financial attitudes. You will find this discussion enlightening—
perhaps even exhilarating.

The next step is to find out where you stand financially. Obviously,
you must determine where you are before you can figure out how far
you have to go and how to get there. A plane isn't a very good choice
of transportation if your destination is only fifteen miles away.

What You Have

Now for a bit of paperwork. You have to know what you have before
you can tailor a financial plan that fits your life and matches your goals.
Determining your net worth—the amount by which your assets ex-

ceed your liabilities—as well as your monthly income and expenses, is the first step. You can go to a bank and ask for a net worth statement or just use a blank sheet of paper.

List what you own and what you owe. Make sure you distinguish your *personal* assets from your *investment* assets. Your home, a painting, a classic car and a diamond ring may all be worth a lot of money, but they're as worthless as old shoes unless you plan to sell them to put food on the table. True, they can be considered investments of last resort—you will sell them to flee from dire political unrest, for example—but if your need for cash is that desperate, you can expect to receive a lot less for personal assets than you paid for them or what they may actually be worth. When determining what assets can be counted upon to provide normal financial security, therefore, only investment assets are used.

List expected tax refunds, the cash value of your life insurance, the real value of your real estate and limited partnerships, any equity in your business, your bank accounts, securities, bonds, trusts, retirement plans (yes, they do have a specific value at a specific point in time), money owed to you by relatives, and so on—every investment asset you can think of should be counted. The same is true for your debts or liabilities. Don't be overwhelmed by the following list. Its completeness is simply meant to remind you of possible assets or liabilities that may have slipped your mind.

INVESTMENT ASSETS *(WHAT I/WE OWN)*	*LIABILITIES* *(WHAT I/WE OWE)*
Current assets	Current bills due
Checking	Credit cards
Savings	Medical/dental bills
Money market accounts	Other
Certificates of deposit	Estimated tax liabilities
Treasuries	Gains
U.S. agency	Real estate
Securities	Federal/state
Stocks	Other debt and installment loans
Bonds	Auto
Mutual funds	Home improvement
Real estate	Education
Income property	Margin accounts
Miscellaneous	Bank
Foreign accounts	Mortgages

INVESTMENT ASSETS (WHAT I/WE OWN)	LIABILITIES (WHAT I/WE OWE)
Limited partnerships	Other notes
Inheritance (near-term)	Child support
Insurance	Letters of credit
Cash value	Known future expenses
Annuities	Miscellaneous
Single-premium life	
Universal life	TOTAL: _____
Retirement plans	
Pension	
Profit sharing	
IRAs	
Keogh	
401(k)	
Other	TOTAL ASSETS: _____ minus
Business interest(s)	
Miscellaneous	TOTAL LIABILITIES: ____ equals
TOTAL: _____	NET WORTH: _____

Please don't assume this list is definitive. You may have items I have not included. Remember, too, to list assets for both you and your spouse. If you have children, create a separate list of their assets. Now subtract your liabilities from your assets. The result is your net worth. You should end up with a number greater than zero: that's called a positive net worth. And I'm positive you will not be pleased if you have a negative net worth.

What does your net worth tell you? A lot. At a glance, you can see whether you have put your money to good use. You may find, for example, that the debt you've been taking on is unreasonable, that your insurance is not keeping pace with the growing value of your property, that your emergency cash fund (usually three to six months' gross income, which has been placed in an interest-bearing account for emergency purposes) is too low for your income or that you can't seem to save. A personal financial statement such as the one you have just completed can do much more than indicate immediate deficiencies. It gets you thinking and provides a guide for your financial future.

The next step is to make a similar list of your monthly income and expenses using the following guide:

MONTHLY INCOME

Take-home earnings from employment or self-employment
Profits from business
Interest, dividends, rent, royalties, fees
Child support or alimony received
Social Security, pensions, annuities
Other

MONTHLY EXPENSES

Basic life-style expenses
    Mortgages on residential and investment property/rent
    Loan, note or installment payments
    Federal, state and local tax payments, not withheld (broken down as if made monthly)
    Residential and investment real estate tax payments (broken down into monthly payments)
    Food at home
    Household supplies and maintenance
    Transportation (include car maintenance and insurance, taxis, bus fares, commutation, etc.)
    Insurance premiums
    Unreimbursed doctor, hospital, health care costs
    Education and child care
Variable expenses
    Eating out
    Clothes
    Entertainment, recreation, vacations
    Contributions, donations, gifts
    Personal expenditures
    Other

Now add it up and weep. Almost every one of my clients goes into a state of shock when he or she realizes how much is really spent. If you're past the "budgeting" stage, you probably spend a great deal more money than you think you do. This is because you are in the "cash flow" era, which means cash flows into one pocket and right out the other. You spend money without thinking too much about it. Once you add up what you really spend during the course of a year, you begin to realize how much money is possibly wasted.

Are you gaining or losing ground? You could be spending more than you are earning without even knowing it. You might be consuming assets—selling stock whose proceeds are not reinvested, but instead used for the purchase of material goods. Perhaps a tax refund never made it into the asset column. Maybe you used credit to make up a shortfall. Simply to assume that your expenses equal your income, less taxes, less savings (if any), might be a serious error on your part.

On the other hand, do you have more money than you need for everyday expenses? If so, do you spend it anyway, or do you save it? Are you expecting an increase or decrease in your income? Could you (still) cut unnecessary or marginal expenses in order to invest some money and thus achieve your financial goals?

To determine your financial goals, ask yourself, "Where do I want to be in five years? Ten years? Beyond that, say, twenty or thirty years? What do I want to achieve in life during those periods? Do I intend to stay in the same profession or job? Will my family be larger, or will they have moved away? Will my children want to go to college? Am I approaching or considering an early retirement, or do I plan to retire or slow down in twenty or twenty-five years?" You may think it's silly to think about these events so far in advance, but then again, you know very well that Social Security won't meet all your needs. Be sure to determine whether your desires coincide with those of your family.

Obviously, these particular financial goals may not apply exactly to your situation. They may not even be close. You may have little desire for material things, you may be childless, or you may have so much money that you needn't worry about retirement funding or education costs. But the principle is the same: Planning allows you to make the future a little more predictable, a little less threatening. Thinking positively about your financial future and the steps you need to take to achieve your goals places you in control of your money rather than the other way around.

Know Where You Are Going

Yogi Berra said it best: "If you don't know where you're going, you'll probably end up someplace else."

In the 1950s the graduating class of a well-known university was asked to complete a survey. Only about 3 percent of that class had written financial goals and a plan for achieving them. Twenty years later the surviving graduates were again surveyed. The 3 percent who had written financial goals had achieved most of them. In addition, this small group of graduates was worth more money than the remainder of their classmates put together.

My experience in consulting with individual investors is that few have stated goals. Even fewer have written goals and a written plan for achieving them. Yet precisely written goals are a key to success. You know where you are going.

When I begin to work with a new client, we talk about goals for a long time. We have a freewheeling discussion often lasting two or three hours (and you can do the same thing with your "significant other" or with friends). Usually it's only after that first hour that we get down to what the client *really* wants. That's how out of touch most of us are with our basic desires and deepest goals. They *are* there: It's just a matter of finding them. Don't stop digging until you're certain of what you want from life, and (if applicable) be sure to include your family in the discussion.

You then commit your goals to paper. You could call it your "wish list." Write down everything that you would like to happen in your life. Pretend that you have no limitations. Just start wishing. Don't waste time thinking about whether you really want something or not, or whether you will be able to afford it. Put it down on paper and keep on writing until there is nothing left.

When you finish writing, look over each item on your "wish list." Then decide when you want to achieve each goal and write the date beside it. Now divide the long-term future into five-year segments, later breaking the first two segments (intermediate-term) into even shorter (one- to two-year) segments.

Now rewrite each of your goals so that they are positive and specific. Goals such as "I want to quit my job" program your mind to focus on the negative aspects of the situation: not happy in your present position. Instead, state your goals positively, such as "I want to start a new career as a financial planner" (that's a positive?). Then make it even more specific: "In two years, I will become a financial planner."

Once you know *where* you want to go, by breaking your long-term goals down into shorter time frames, you will then be able to take the next step, which will help you decide *how* to get there. Meanwhile, you will be plotting a route that also takes your major long-term goals into account. If you want to become a financial planner, you have to determine what courses you must take and how long it will take. You will also have to plan for lower income during your early years as a planner by building up other sources of income (such as your savings) if you wish to maintain your standard of living. Let's take a more complicated example, make it a "real-life" situation so you can better follow it, and then draw up a financial road map.

Hadmour Gelt is 42 years old, his wife Mary is 40, and they have two teen-age children, Mai and Grant. The family lives together in a house with a big mortgage, and both parents work. Hadmour may be transferred soon by his company, but he isn't sure when, if ever. Mary works half-time as a free-lance writer. Mai is doing well in school and is intent on getting her driver's license. Grant, a young history buff, is dying to go to Europe. Each member of the family has different things on his or her mind, and Hadmour—who manages the household finances—must make sense of all their goals. So first he lists in order of importance a framework within which the smaller dreams will fit. After talking it over with Mary, he establishes a long-term wish list on paper. He then modifies it by making sure these goals are specific and positive. Finally, he rearranges them into five-year periods. Since Hadmour is a frustrated doodler, his written goals might look like this:

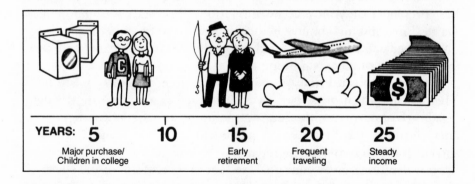

YEARS:	5	10	15	20	25
	Major purchase/ Children in college		Early retirement	Frequent traveling	Steady income

To Hadmour, five years—let alone twenty-five years—sometimes seems a long way off, lost in the haze of the future. But he now realizes that committing pencil to paper actually helps him put into focus things he hasn't been able to relate to. In addition, the written (or doodled) word will act as a reminder, something for Hadmour (or you) to keep in the back of his head to inform, if not influence, his current financial decisions. But Hadmour needs to improve even further the quality of his planning decisions, so he now creates a chart (or list of goals) with a narrower focus. Having gained a sense of the overall, he is now ready to chart his more immediate goals in detail.

Hadmour wants to buy, at her urging, a used car for Mai. He also wants to take his family on a European vacation, partly as a gift to Grant but mostly because the family has never traveled abroad to-

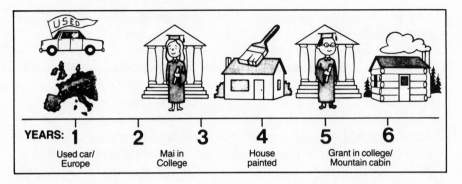

gether. Other large expenses are looming: the house needs painting and Mary—who loves cross-country skiing, camping, fishing and general peace and quiet—has suggested buying a mountain cabin, or a time-share with another couple. Hadmour creates another chart with those goals in mind.

Hadmour now takes a look at his financial situation—his net worth statement and the details of his income and expenses. Making sure that he takes inflation, taxes and savings into account, he then asks himself, "Can I in fact afford all these things over the next five years, or should I delay some purchases? Is Mai more set on a fine college education or a used car—or can I manage both by making my money work more efficiently? Which of these things do I want *most,* which do we want *now?*" Hadmour is seeking *financial perspective,* for it is perspective that gives him control.

Hadmour also asks himself, as you will, practical questions. If we do have to move soon, will painting the house be a good idea? Probably, but Hadmour can delay that until he knows for certain about his transfer. His thinking goes beyond money. This transfer business has upset the whole family; perhaps they *need* an exciting family vacation more than anything else. When Hadmour asks his family, he finds that Mary would be just as happy going to Europe this summer as buying that time-share mountain cabin. Hadmour makes the cabin a more distant goal, with Mary's blessing.

Perhaps Mai can help out, too. Would she prefer a car now or Europe now and a car later? Or both now and two years at a state school before finishing up at a private college? Or could Hadmour get the car, take the family to Europe and pay Mai's private school tuition, *if* she's willing to take a dining-hall job at college? Can *all* these goals be achieved by placing them in the proper order and planning for each individually? Hadmour is sorry he has to make these choices, forcing

his family to compromise, but that's the result of his late start on
financial planning.

Your situation, of course, will be different from Hadmour's, but
your analysis will be similar. Each of your goals will likewise entail a
different kind of planning, and that's one reason why the most important aspect of a financial plan is its balance. No ready-made or cookie-
cutter plan can achieve the balance you personally require: What you
want is a plan that reflects *your* needs and resources over a period of
time. For that reason it must also be able to evolve; it must be *flexible*.

A balanced, flexible financial plan allows you to accumulate wealth
for tomorrow without sacrificing the money you need today. You
must be patient, however, in accumulating that wealth; as the old
saying goes, "Success is one percent inspiration and ninety-nine percent perspiration." The same is true of financial success. It is achieved
in increments. Through patience, and by investing wisely, you'll eventually get to the point where you don't have to delay needed purchases
in order to assure your future. In fact, you may well find that once you
know your financial abilities and limitations, you'll only want those
things that lie within your extended grasp. You'll soon be living up to
your greatest financial potential.

In the meantime, be a little unrealistic. Go ahead and dream about
Ferraris. You should even put it down on your "wish list." But don't
confuse dreams with reality; if you suddenly did get that kind of
money, would you be better off buying a car immediately or investing
the money while you thought more about the purchase? An expensive
sports car will put you in the fast lane, no doubt about that. But
remember the story of the tortoise and the hare? Once you've thought
about it, you might prefer a Volkswagen tortoise to a Ferrari hare (after
all, your tortoise could be a Rabbit). The money you spent on investments instead of on toys will soon provide you with money (perhaps
even Ferrari money) for all your life goals. No matter what you decide,
you'll have made a conscious choice.

As your personal financial plan evolves, you will develop a balanced
portfolio of assets. You will have sufficient cash for emergencies, unexpected opportunities and investments targeted for your future and
that of your children. You'll have the flexibility, too, to respond to
changes in the economic climate, and you will no longer have to worry
whether the economy or the income tax rules are going to zig or zag.
Come hyper-inflation, dis-inflation, recession or depression, you'll be
prepared because your various investments provide income, growth
and hedges against disaster.

An impossible dream? Not after your financial plan is in place. Once you finally understand your asset and income picture, and are powered with goals, you'll have broken through the anxiety barrier. You will indeed be taking control. Just keep in mind that your *goals* are more important than your money. And that *you* are more important than your goals.

Chapter 2

Last Things First—Down-to-Earth Estate Planning

If Ponce de León had found the fabled Fountain of Youth instead of the Bahamas and Florida, we might have little reason to think about growing old or dying. Given the realities of life, however, it is a good idea to ponder the possibility of death and plan accordingly.

Dwelling on such a subject may seem a bit morose, but as a practical matter, all future financial planning is worthless unless estate planning is included. Without it you will dissipate much of the legacy that most of us spend a lifetime trying to accumulate. The lack of estate planning can be likened to letting your mother and your mother-in-law or an officious civil servant decide how the furniture in your living room should be arranged. The first two will fight over everything and wind up putting it all in the wrong places (not to mention throwing out your beloved armchair). And the civil servant will probably rope it off and not allow people to use it. You may believe life goes more smoothly when you ignore the inevitable. But I don't, and that is why I am addressing the issue of estate planning very early in the book. It *needs* to be noticed. If I buried the subject (pun intended) deep in the book, you might ignore the significance of estate planning.

You need to plan early for the orderly handling, disposition and administration of your estate after you die. You need to do so *before* you think about planning for retirement because you don't know *when* you are going to die.

Your Will, Your Way

The basic foundation of estate planning is a will. And the most important point about a will is that, ideally, it makes sure your property goes to whom you want it to go in the most efficient and cost-effective manner possible. In other words, it guarantees the distribution of your property after your death according to your wishes. Therefore, anyone with property should have a will.

Estate planning has been called an "old trade with a new name." At one time it appeared to involve merely will-making, but today it is recognized that making a will is just one part of a more elaborate process that should begin early and last for most of your adult life.

Without estate planning you might lose much of your estate to taxes (now your heirs can watch your estate purchase more MX missiles); or such inaction as the lack of a will, for example, can lead to chaos and confusion for your family. When state laws and courts become involved in the process of dividing an estate, or when serious arguments develop over insignificant material possessions, the conclusion is not a happy one.

Imagine, if you will, a formerly close and loving relationship between brothers and sisters transformed years later into a distant, tense silence—or worse yet, open warfare—and all because of a fight over their parents' property since no will existed. It is a sad commentary on human nature, yet disputes over estates, if unnecessary, are common. And when such battles result in lawsuits, all parties wind up losing as the property and money go for attorney fees and court costs.

One man I knew, a bachelor who died intestate (i.e., without leaving a will) when he was about 55, presumably wanted most of his money to go to his elderly mother, whom he had supported, and the rest to his sister. He had been estranged from his father, who had abandoned the family for another woman. However, the law of the state where the bachelor lived mandated that his estate be divided among all his closest living relatives. That meant his mother got only two-sevenths of his estate, his sister one-seventh, and the four children from his father's second marriage, one-seventh each. It was hardly pleasant to explain to his mother that the law was going to give over half of her son's money to the children of the woman for whom her husband had left her.

Another true story—this one about a widow left with three children. Her husband died leaving a $200,000 estate. And because he had not bothered with a will, the state probate court decided that more than $130,000 was to go to his three children. However, since they were minors, their mother was appointed sole guardian. As guardian she had to get court approval for every major expense, and in this instance, even though they were her own children, also had the added expense of posting a performance bond (which is a surety bond underwritten by a surety company and given by one party to protect a second party against loss).

In at least one state, the surviving parent can't be the sole guardian of minor children; control of the family's money must be shared with someone else. And there are other situations where the court's control over children's money can translate into tremendous power over their upbringing. For example, only "necessary" expenditures can be paid out of the children's money. Getting court approval to spend those dollars on, say, private schooling can result in a lengthy and expensive court battle.

When there is a will, however, there's a way to avoid family fights, money flowing to the wrong people and your mate being forced to depend on a court for the financial welfare of your children. Preparing a simple will—the first and most important step in estate planning—can help you avoid all those disasters.

Despite the proven effectiveness of a will, fewer than 30 percent of Americans have written one. Why? It can't be the cost of hiring a lawyer, for a pair of relatively uncomplicated wills for a husband and wife may require only one consultation with an attorney and a total cost of $200 to $400. Time can't be the problem either, for the task in similar cases only takes about an hour. And I can't believe, as some people seem to think, that a will is silly, like some sort of legal science fiction.

Perhaps the true reason for such illogic is that no one likes to think about, talk about or prepare for death. Statements like John Maynard Keynes's "In the long run, we are *all* dead" make most people squirm. However, if you have property, and you don't want either the government or your crotchety Cousin Harold to get their hands on it, you *must* have a will.

Nevertheless, there are some people (the completely intransigent ones) who are still quick to declare, "I don't need a will," usually basing that statement on one or more of the following assumptions:

1. I don't have enough money or property to bother. Or I'm below the federal estate tax minimum—my estate won't owe a tax.

2. I am single and without dependents who need the money.
3. My spouse will automatically get everything.
4. All of my more substantial possessions are jointly owned and will automatically go to him or her when I die.

All four assumptions could easily be wrong.

Not enough assets to bother? Take another look at your financial net worth that you calculated in Chapter 1. Now add to it the estimated worth of personal possessions such as your car(s), boat(s), plane(s), recreational vehicle(s), collectibles, jewelry, antiques, furs and your home and/or vacation home, unless you are planning to sell them and use the proceeds as an investment asset. Once you add the proceeds from your life insurance policies (don't forget company-paid policies) and pension/retirement benefits to your estate, you will know the extent of your (after death) worth. Surprising, isn't it? No doubt you will leave more than you had ever thought. And it may be subject to the inheritance taxes of your state, even if it is below the federal minimum.

Single? That excuse is a cop-out. I'll bet you don't know for sure where *your* state says your assets must go if you don't specify your intent in a will. I'll also wager if you're living with someone, you don't really wish him or her left out. And have you any idea how long it can sometimes take for an estate without a will to be settled? Very often the time is measured in years. And what about the possibility that you may become unable to take care of yourself because of an accident, an illness or old age? You probably don't know that you can establish a living trust (which I will discuss later on in this chapter), which allows a caretaker of your choice to step in and take control of your funds without having you declared incompetent.

Your assumption that your spouse will automatically get everything may also be completely unfounded. When you die without a will, the rigid descent and distribution laws of your state completely take over, and a will would be drawn on your behalf. The following state-drawn will doesn't look like a real one, and it's not. But let me assure you that in most states, though the words will certainly be different, the result will be similar.

Being of sound mind and memory, I, Hadmour Gelt, do hereby publish this as my last will and testament:

First, I give my spouse one-third of my possessions, and I give my children the remaining two-thirds.

A. I appoint my spouse as guardian of my children, but require that she report to the probate court every year to account for her expenses in caring for them.
B. I direct my spouse to put up a $500,000 performance bond so the probate court will have a guarantee that she will exercise proper judgment in handling, investing and spending our children's money.
C. I give my children the right, as soon as they reach legal age, to spend their inheritance as they see fit, and to demand and receive a complete accounting from their mother of all her financial actions with their money.

Second, should my wife remarry, her husband shall be entitled upon her death to one-third of everything she possesses, including what she inherited from me. Her husband shall not be bound to share any of this portion with my children, regardless of their ages, should they need additional support.

Third, should my spouse predecease me or die while any of my children are minors, I do not wish to exercise my right to nominate their guardian. Should my relatives and friends be unable to select a guardian by mutual agreement, I direct the probate court to make the selection. If the court wishes, it may appoint a person completely unknown to me as guardian.

Fourth, since I prefer to have my money spent by the government rather than used for the benefit of my wife and children, I direct that no effort be made to lower the taxes incurred at my death.

Now you see how an assumption may be false.

If you don't leave a will designating an executor or administrator, who can elect to serve "without fee or bond," a court-appointed administrator frequently is faced with the need to secure (as mentioned earlier) a performance bond equal to or greater than the value of the estate. The bond and the step-by-step reporting mandates of the court all cost the estate money—considerably more money in all likelihood than the fee a lawyer would charge for preparing a will. In some states, the law requires that the money set aside for minor children must be put in trust until the children come of age. In the meantime, their mother may be desperately short of funds.

The fourth assumption, that joint ownership replaces the need for a will, also has its fallacies, especially if you have no understanding of the concept of "with rights of survivorship." Should a husband and wife die in an accident at the same time under circumstances that make it impossible to determine which one died first, even property held jointly can be distributed under intestacy laws. Again, the state takes over unless there is a will. If a childless couple dies in an accident, but the wife lives a few seconds longer than her husband, the couple's jointly held assets could end up in the hands of the wife's relatives, with nothing going to her husband's family. This could happen even though her nearest relative may be a wealthy and much despised cousin while his husband's parents are alive and in need of funds.

Maybe you need a will to put "brakes" on surviving beneficiaries so they cannot spend their inheritances like drunken sailors. Maybe you even need a will to deliver a final insult to one of your unloved ones. One of the more famous examples of this type reads:

> To my wife I leave her lover and the knowledge that I wasn't the fool she thought I was. To my son, I leave the pleasure of earning a living. For twenty years he thought the pleasure was mine. He was mistaken. To my daughter, I leave $100,000. She will need it. The only good piece of business her husband ever did was marry her. To my valet, I leave the clothes he has been stealing from me. To my partner, I leave the suggestion that he take some other clever man in with him at once if he expects to do any more business.

Indeed, there are as many advantages to writing a will as there are drawbacks to dying without one. But most important, having a will puts *you* in control. If you are one of those people who does not have a will and *honestly* knows it will take more than one week before a will can be drawn up by an attorney, then after you finish the next four paragraphs, please put this book down and follow these instructions.

There basically are three types of wills. The formal or attested will is the most popular and common form of will and the easiest to prove valid. This will is written, usually in consultation with an attorney, signed by the maker of the will and properly witnessed. The second type of will is the nuncupative will, which is an oral declaration made soon before death and in front of witnesses. It is later put in writing by someone other than the dying person, who is leaving the will. The third type of will, and the one I shall now emphasize, is the do-it-yourself will, called a holographic will. Not all states recognize holographic or nuncupative wills, or do so only under specific circumstances. Many holographic wills have been declared invalid by the courts for technical errors that seem silly. Should your lack of knowledge about the fine points of the law, or about whether your state recognizes holographic wills, stop you from writing one? Absolutely not. Anything is better than nothing. The important thing is to make a will—one hopes a thoughtful one.

Just take a plain piece of paper (yes, it can have lines) and, *entirely* in your own handwriting, state your desires clearly and succinctly. Though some states now permit "fill in the blank" wills, it is always better if your will is completely handwritten. If you make a mistake or want to change something, write the page over. Date and sign the will, and that's it. No witnesses are required. You do not have to have it notarized, and do not make a joint holographic will. It is valid only for the person who wrote and signed it. As a general rule, a holographic will, to be valid, must also be found among your valuable papers. If you wish to take a precautionary step, you can convert what would be a holographic will into a witnessed will by asking at least two people who are not beneficiaries to witness your signature. They should also sign your will as witnesses and should see you and each other sign it.

Here's an illustration of a very simple will, but nevertheless what could be legally binding, that might be used as a guide, again written completely in your own hand. Important, too, is that it is a "thoughtful" will, that covers all your property and to whom it should go upon your death. If you have minor children at the time you write the will, you might also wish to nominate a guardian if both you and your spouse die.

Date: _____

I _____ hereby make this my last will and testament.

I give my entire estate, whether real property, tangible or intangible, wherever situated, to my wife if she survives me.

If my wife does not survive me, I give my entire estate to my children in equal shares.

I name my wife executor of my estate and I request that bond be waived.

Signed: _____

Sure, there's more. But I'm not trying to practice law—far from it. I just want to get you started, and now you've taken an important first step. Though you are not legally required to have an attorney involved in this process, and though some attorneys have written books to help people write their own wills, I still recommend that the next (or first) step is to get yourself to a lawyer who can draw up a formal will for you.

Recently, I visited with a neighbor who has five young children. When he informed me that he and his wife had no will, I was compelled to jump up on my soapbox. Though they are warm and compassionate people, they were unintentionally and unknowingly being selfish in the extreme. It wasn't so much the money, but if something happened to both of them, just what *would* happen to their children? Who knows? The family might even have to be split up. I had them write a holographic will then and there. About three weeks later they were able to visit an attorney and have a will professionally prepared.

If you already have a will, you probably haven't looked at it in years. Most of my clients, upon reflection, realize their wills are a great deal older than they at first believed. Since 70 percent of the population doesn't have a will, it is entirely possible that a combination of those who do not have a will and those who do not have an up-to-date will comprise more than 80 percent of the population. An obsolete testament can create problems. It was once wise, for instance, to incorporate a marital trust in a will, in order to reduce or eliminate federal estate taxes incurred on the death of a spouse. But laws change over the years; for example, the Economic Recovery Tax Act of 1981 significantly limited the number of estates subject to estate taxes, making some marital trusts unnecessary or even counterproductive.

If your attorney has not contacted you about updating your will (or trust), then take the initiative yourself. In particular, you should recognize that your estate-planning documentation should be updated:

• when a child or grandchild is born (unless your will makes provisions for children born after the will was signed);
• when you marry, separate or divorce;
• when your net worth changes substantially;
• when a beneficiary dies before you;
• when tax laws change in a way that affects your estate or financial plan;
• when you acquire or lose major assets (for instance, your art collection is singed in a fire or you buy three classic Mercedes-Benzes);
• when you change your mind about division of your property;
• if you move to another state.

Now, how good do you feel about *your* "up-to-date" will or trust?

By the way—*don't* forget to prepare a detailed inventory of all your holdings. The most carefully drafted estate plan is worthless if your family and executor can't find your assets and outstanding debts or your employee benefits and how to collect them. "I finally got it all together," a popular poster reads, "then I forgot where I put it!" Don't let this happen to you. Your executor, in particular, must know where your bank accounts, joint accounts or real estate properties are. You might also consider writing an informal letter to your heirs telling them where your important documents (will, life insurance policies, etc.) are located. Even if your spouse knows, he or she might die before you do. Also include your wishes and desires on nonlegal matters, such as burial requests, whom to consult about major financial decisions, how to dispose of certain properties, what income or debts are still expected and even who gets which personal effects. Although such a "letter of intent" is not legally binding, clear instructions from you may help settle any disagreements—especially when Greedy Aunt Gertrude comes to claim your Picasso.

Trusts

Though wills have an advantage over trusts in that they are relatively inexpensive to draft and do not require you to change ownership of your property, trusts are another enormously important estate-planning tool. There are two primary trust forms. The first is called an *inter vivos* (or "living") trust because it goes into effect during the lifetime of the "trustor" (you). The second is called a "testamentary" trust because it is set up in your will and does not go into effect until after your death.

Living Trusts

There are two primary categories of living trusts: revocable and irrevocable. However, the most important to consider now is the revocable living trust, how it can help you during your lifetime and how it operates at your death. As an oversimplification, imagine a revocable living trust to be a vehicle that is designated to carry your assets throughout your lifetime. You operate the vehicle and have full control of it as long as you are capable. The trust vehicle may be amended, changed or revoked completely at any time. Assets may be added to the trust or removed from it at any time that you reach a point in life when you cannot continue to operate the trust.

Who needs one? You should have a living trust established if:

• you wish to avoid probate of some or all of your assets;
• you seek estate privacy;
• you plan to move often between the various states;

• you would like the opportunity to see it in action—to test it and perhaps to make certain changes;
• you want to establish a method to handle your affairs in the event of incapacity.

As its name implies, a revocable living trust takes effect now, while you are here, but can be dissolved or changed at any time during your lifetime. Furthermore, a living trust acts like a will, that is, it makes sure that the property in the trust is disposed of at your death in the manner that you desire. Though there are no income or estate tax benefits for assets in the revocable living trust, your property passes to your beneficiary without the necessity of an elaborate probate and usually without delay.

The probate procedure is a process of the law to prove the genuineness of a will, but probate procedures can vary greatly from state to state, and in some states they can be very costly. Each state has a schedule of commissions or compensation allowed for administrators and executors, although some statutes simply provide for "reasonable compensation" of the representative. The following is an estimated cost (about average among states) of estate administration in California. It combines probate, lawyer and executor fees. (That fee, however, is often waived if the executor is a family member.) These fees do *not* include taxes, appraiser fees, cost of the sale of assets, tax preparation and litigation. Check on the minimum costs in *your* state.

Assets	Probate and Administrative Expenses
$100,000	$6,300
$200,000	$10,300
$300,000	$14,300
$400,000	$18,300
$500,000	$22,300
$750,000	$32,300
$1,000,000	$42,300
$2,000,000	$62,300
$3,000,000	$82,300
$5,000,000	$122,300

In addition, both the attorney and the executor have the right to petition the court for "extraordinary" fees should they do any more than what the court interprets to be ordinary work in connection with the probate of the estate.

I once gave a speech and mentioned this statement as part of my presentation. A kindly, older gentleman came up to me afterward and explained he had recently retired from the bench as a California probate judge. He told me that in his twenty-seven years on the bench, never once had an attorney not asked him for extraordinary fees.

The probate procedure can be lengthy. Creditors have from four months to a year to make a claim. While the executor must file federal estate tax returns within nine months after death (an extension is possible for an additional six months), the Internal Revenue Service and state tax authorities may then take as long as three years to indicate their acceptance. Studies made in Wisconsin show that the average time spent in probate was twelve to fifteen months on estates averaging about $30,000. The average probate takes two years to complete in California. Because I often advise clients with inherited multimillion-dollar wealth, I have heard more than my share of horror probate delay stories. The worst by far was a more than fifty-year delay, but I have also heard of numerous fifteen- to twenty-five-year delays—with fees that were large enough for you and me to be able to retire on.

During the long drawn-out probate procedure, the court only allows a limited payment of support to a widow. In some states, children and other beneficiaries may not be so entitled. So the result is an interruption of income, which can work a hardship upon beneficiaries. In the case of a living trust, there should be no delay whatsoever. The transfer period is virtually immediate.

Often, another reason for probate delay is the contested will. Contested wills are an everyday occurrence, and estates do not always go to whom the deceased has named to receive them. Because of the probate process, there is in a number of states a legal requirement to advertise the fact that the will is in probate—drawing the interest and attention of those who may feel they have a legal basis for contesting the will. A living trust is distinguished by its privacy. Its terms are not disclosed to a probate court, and its assets and the identity of the persons to receive them are closely guarded secrets. The parties likely to protest may not even learn of the death of the creator of the trust until long afterward, when the transference of the property is made.

Have you ever wondered why Bing Crosby's or John Wayne's reported estate size seemed relatively modest compared to what you had thought these people were worth? The press and public were only able to ascertain information about those assets that were named in their respective wills, and no more. Their living trust assets were not a matter of public record, therefore untrackable. That can also be a benefit for the heirs of people with far more modest means.

Another benefit of the living trust is that sometimes you may select the laws of one of several states most beneficial to you when drafting the trust. Under a will, the laws of the state where you live prevail. But with a living trust, you can have it written under the laws of your state of residence, the state where property in the trust is located or the state where a beneficiary or trustee resides.

Speaking of trustees, every trust requires a trustee. You, another individual or a bank can act as trustee. Most people appoint themselves as trustee with the beneficiary also named as successor trustee, although there are some states, New York, for example, in which an individual cannot serve as sole trustee for himself. The instructions then read that upon the creator of the trust's death, the successor trustee is to turn the trust assets over to him or herself, then terminate the trust.

By setting up a trust during his or her lifetime with someone else as trustee, a person also has an opportunity to observe the efficiency of the individual or institution whom he has named as trustee. It has been described as an opportunity to see one's will in action. If you're unhappy with that trustee, a successor trustee can be "activated."

Another important use of the living trust is that it can provide a vehicle for property management if you become incapacitated. In the document, you designate a person (or persons) who will have the authority to care for your estate if you are someday unable to manage your affairs. In the event of such a disability, whoever was designated can quickly step in without unnecessary publicity, expense and delays.

Without such a designation, a friend or relative would have to petition the court to be appointed conservator of your person and of your estate while you remain incompetent to manage on your own. That could involve substantial expenditures of time and money, and you have no assurance that the court-appointed conservator would display any more wisdom or humanity than a parking violations department bureaucrat. For this reason alone, I often recommend the living trust for my "senior-years" single clients. It doesn't have to be Alzheimer's disease that creates the inability to personally handle your affairs; a stroke or an automobile accident could be just as debilitating. By the way, a will can't be used for this kind of contingency.

There are two primary disadvantages to a living trust. The first is that it is more expensive to prepare initially than a will; set-up fees usually range between $1,000 and $1,500, although I've seen estate attorneys charge as little as a "flat $300." The second is that it may require you to change the titles to homes, other property, investments, bank accounts, etc., into the name of the trust. Putting aside the emotional factor that the title to those assets won't be in your very own name, in practice this makes very little difference since you can still control those assets, unless a co-trustee is required.

As you can see from the above, I have a strong preference in favor of the living trust. But this does not mean the revocable living trust is a cure-all. Far from it. Though there are no probate fees, there still may be costs for administration, distribution and appraisals for tax purposes, tax preparation fees, etc. Living trusts can also be contested or there might be contradictions in its instructions that could place the estate into court—incurring similar contested-will nightmares. As for the incapacity feature of the living trust, that too can become complicated if, for example, the trustor doesn't agree with a co-trustee that he or she *is* incompetent. And in many states, beneficiaries of living trusts are not exempt from claims against the assets they have inherited, and certainly not taxes, so they may find themselves in court or forced to sell assets.

And there are indeed instances where probate can prove to be an advantage. For example, because probate is a legal proceeding, the court gives protection to the executor and the beneficiary. You might also say the court becomes a built-in watchdog over your desires by making sure they are carried out to the letter.

A Will vs. a Living Trust

Does this mean if you establish a living trust you no longer require a will? If everything goes as planned, and everything you leave is covered by a living trust, there will be nothing to probate and your family doesn't require a will. But that is not the real world. You still need a will for several reasons. It may not be possible to anticipate and retitle to your living trust every last asset that you might have at time of death. For instance, it may not be possible to transfer personal property items such as clothing, jewelry, paintings and so forth, or you may not wish to transfer some of these items through the trust. Without a will, you will have died "intestate" for those assets; the laws of the state in which you live will determine which of your relatives are entitled to that share of your wealth. Additionally, you need a will if you have minor children. While the living trust makes it unnecessary for the court to appoint a special guardian of the property of your child, there must also be a guardian for the child him- or herself, which a living trust generally doesn't deal with.

Testamentary Trusts

Another important tool in estate planning, and one of the most popular, is called a testamentary trust. This is a trust created under the provisions of your "last will and testament." It does not become an effective trust, therefore, until your will has passed through the probate process (with all the delay, expense and publicity). Since no trustee yet exists, you might, for example, direct the executor under your will to turn the net proceeds of your estate over to a local trust company, which will invest the money and distribute income and principal in accordance with the instructions contained in your will. Your executor may also act as trustee.

A testamentary trust serves a very useful purpose when heirs are inexperienced or likely to be imprudent in their handling of money they are to receive. A financially astute relative can be named to manage the inheritance of youthful or potentially spendthrift heirs. The testamentary trust is the traditional method of setting up a trust, whereas the living trust is a far more modern estate-planning tool. Once the testamentary trust becomes activated, the effect of the provisions can be exactly the same as those of living trusts, once you are deceased. Some of the reasons so many people use the testamentary trust are: because there is no change in property ownership; because it is in some cases, and some states, only around half to three-quarters as expensive as the living trust to establish; because many people have a strong emotional resistance to the creation of an operating trust intended to handle their "after death" affairs; and because of the idea of putting their property even slightly out of reach.

If any of these reactions or reasons apply, you may be happy with a testamentary trust that can be altered or revoked at any time during your lifetime simply by rewriting you will. An irrevocable trust, on the other hand, established during your lifetime, can never be canceled once it has been put into effect. But because of the complexities and tax and other consequences involved, this type of trust should only be considered after discussions with an experienced estate planner or attorney. It should, in any case, only concern those in possession of large estates.

Although you now know about the concept of trusts, I do not want you to think I am putting the cart before the horse. Since you probably don't have a will (even if you are an attorney yourself, because few lawyers do), don't feel you now have to jump to a higher level of estate planning. You don't. As a matter of fact, almost any type of a will is better than what you now have—nothing. If you are like most people, any plan to move directly to the living trust unfortunately remains that —a plan, but no action.

If, however, you already have or have just completed an up-to-date will, you are to be commended for having faced the issue of estate planning. Though it may not have been the high point of your week, you probably feel pretty good about it, too. The next step—that higher level of estate planning—might make you feel even better. But I'm not going to mislead you. You will *never* feel as good about your death plan as your life plan—maybe you can't take it with you, as they say, but you can certainly enjoy it while you're still here.

See an Estate Planner and/or Attorney, Please

I want to be sure you are aware that the best estate planning does require the services of a specialist, not only because the subject is complicated, but because, for example, it is also illegal for nonlawyers to give legal advice. That may sound unfair, but there is a reason for the restriction: Our legal system is complex, difficult to understand, differs substantially from state to state and is constantly evolving in very subtle ways. You need to sit down with a qualified estate planner and/ or an attorney who is an estate specialist to examine all the options available and to consider both the advantages and disadvantages of the various types of wills and living trusts. Then you can make the choices that best suit your wishes and needs.

You and Your Heirs

Something else needs to be placed into perspective. Simply put, a will and a living or testamentary trust merely distribute your property after your death. What must also be taken into account is the ability of your heirs to handle their newfound "wealth." One study indicated that one-half of all heirs have spent their *entire* bequests within seventeen months. Your choice. You can "heap" the assets on your beneficiaries, taking the attitude that "it'll be their problem," or you can attempt to address and correct the very real problems that can come with inheritance, problems caused by lack of experience with relatively large lump sums of money or assets, or lack of emotional experience, which creates self-doubt.

You may take pride in the way you manage your family's financial affairs, but you must also include your spouse in any financial plan in order for her or him to be able to cope should you die first. Let your spouse know whom to consult about major financial decisions, and have the two parties meet and develop a comfortable working relationship. Better yet, involve your spouse in every step of your financial and estate planning. Though your wife or husband may not be interested in the details, this information is enormously important if you intend your family to have any type of decent financial future. When working with a client, if married, I insist that the client's spouse be present at least part of the time; otherwise, I fire the client. I'm not being smug. I honestly believe I am employed by both clients and am doing them a disservice by not including both of them. We are no longer in the Dark Ages when it comes to informing others about personal money matters, and we should no longer behave as though we were.

Children can also be victims of inheritance. Even the act of giving as much as you can while you're alive to reduce your estate gradually and to provide your kids with the experience of having money isn't child's play. Coming into a windfall without having worked for it does not always result in a happier, more fulfilling and productive life. This is especially true when a major inheritance is involved. As a matter of fact, more than four out of five kids have serious difficulty learning to cope with the problems that accompany a major legacy—even if they can afford the best financial advice available.

The price many heirs pay, young or older, is guilt. They find it hard to accept unearned good fortune and may not be able to find ways to prove themselves worthy of it. When you haven't played much of a part in creating your favored place, it's hard not to keep wondering "Why me?" Also, such heirs may be constantly anxious, worried and often unreasonably tightfisted with their new money because they fear that should they lose it, they wouldn't know how to earn it back again. But most of all, heirs of wealth tend to be unable to value or admire themselves. And this kind of self-doubt is reinforced by the behavior of others who resent their good fortune. Haven't we all at least momentarily questioned someone's ability once we learn there was inherited money behind him?

If you are a parent and reading about how an inheritance (particularly a large one) isn't always wonderful, I hope you're going to think further about how you can help your children avoid becoming victims. An important starting point is to communicate to your children constructive attitudes toward money in general and specifically their inheritance. Parents can start by instilling a sense of family pride. All children, and especially those of the rich, benefit from a sense of heritage. As with the subject of sex, well-intentioned questions about the family assets and about their own prospects should be responded to directly whenever children bring them up.

I have often had clients bemoan the fact that their parents wouldn't talk to them about the family assets. The feeling was either that the numbers were none of the child's business, or if they knew how much money was involved, the child(ren) might be too anxious for mom or dad to die. Such attitudes commonly lead to financial disasters and dislocations. One such unfortunate incident involved a father who denied his daughter any family financial information. His attitude was a combination of "You're a girl, so you shouldn't be involved in such matters" and "Trust me." Dad died leaving all financial matters, including the decision-making, under her brother's control. You guessed it, big brother was not as benevolent. While also professing to watch out for his sister, he used her share of the estate to further his own interests and she found herself torn between love of family and self-preservation. Had her father considered this possible result of his earlier attitudes, I'm sure he would have taken the necessary steps to prevent it.

Another client of mine was a single woman who had both a doctorate in psychology and a legal degree. Though she inquired, her father refused to inform her about his vast holdings in the stock market. She then informed him she did not want the responsibility of those holdings and directed him to leave them to someone else. Sure enough, upon his death, he bequeathed the entire portfolio to her. She now very much resents what he did to her, for she literally stays up late every night worrying about each stock. Had he taken her into his confidence, she would have felt more comfortable and confident about her decision-making abilities.

Children should feel good about money. Even young people with "expectations" should have enough experience earning a living so that they are able to convince themselves and others that their worth is not dependent on their parents' or inherited wealth. That can also go a long way toward helping them understand "the value of a buck." It's essential, too, that parents who want their kids to be both responsible and self-confident when it comes to financial matters give them the necessary time, attention and information to help them avoid becoming victims.

Chapter 3

Of Course You Can Retire!—
Planning Is Half the Fun

It happens all the time. This one client reminds me of so many others. He was 63, earned $100,000 a year, had assets of $380,000 and wanted to know where he should now invest his money. It had to grow rapidly (without risk) because he intended to retire in two years.

He didn't need a financial planner, he needed a miracle worker. My first observation was that he spent almost everything he made, since most of that $380,000 came from an inheritance. Unless he and his wife dramatically lowered their life-style, they would easily outlast his retirement funds. When I pointed out the financial problems they would be facing, he didn't believe me and two years later he retired anyway.

Alas, their lives seem to be working out just fine, and while they have had to lower their expenses, they figured out a way not to lower their standard of living. As a matter of fact, they have a larger home in retirement than when he was employed. All they had to do was move from San Francisco to Peoria.

Sooner or later retirement planning becomes an important part of everyone's financial concern. Yet planning does not mean you must actually plan to retire. It is simply a method that not only ensures that the money you don't need right now will be available to you in your later years, but if invested wisely should also enable you to maintain your standard and quality of living when and if you ever do retire. Say, for example, that prior to retirement, you are living nicely on $50,000 a year. You will usually need to come up with 75 to 80 percent of your preretirement income (the higher the income, the smaller the percentage needed), not including inflation, to provide a foundation for that standard of living in retirement.

If you earn:

- $200,000 a year you will usually need 65 percent or $130,000
- $150,000 @ 70% or $105,000
- $100,000 @ 75% or $75,000
- $50,000 @ 80% or $40,000
- $25,000 @ 90% or $22,500

Unfortunately, 98 out of every 100 people retire on a creaky foundation. They have been unable (*I* say unwilling) to set aside enough money. And with more and more people retiring before 65 (the average retirement age is now 61½ years)—nearly 60 percent of private-sector employees, according to a U.S. Department of Labor study—a greater percentage of the elderly population may be caught short of retirement funds. The length of retirement (and money required) today is greater than ever before. Just to retire early, say, by age 55 or so, you will probably have to save more than 20 percent of your gross pay annually for twenty to thirty years. That's four times what the average American saves.

So you might ask, "How can I possibly retire and maintain my previous standard of living? Where's the money to come from?" Since you will no longer be able to count on that regular paycheck, how can you have enough capital to pay your bills, have some fun and still feel confident that you will not outlive your cash?

Answer: Advance planning and the execution of that plan, which will provide the funds to help replace the money you won't be earning if you want to slow down or retire. That strategy can even supply the means you need to change jobs or careers.

Unfortunately, most people haven't heard that message. Otherwise, why do statistics show that more than 70 percent (60 million people who are 50 or older) of the population approaches retirement without any preparation? It gets worse. More than 90 percent of Americans reaching age 65 find their standard and the quality of living actually decline when they retire. Social Security data indicate that out of 100 Americans age 65 or older, an astonishing 62 percent have an annual income of less than $6,000. Seventy-nine percent have assets less than $35,000 and only 8 percent have incomes over $15,000 per year, *including* their Social Security benefits.

You could be among those statistics, even if you are relatively well-off today. A recent study on consumer financial behavior from SRI International (formerly Stanford Research Institute) revealed that the working person between ages 50 and 65 who made more than $40,000 per year had median (half had more and half had less) investment assets of only $131,000. Scary, isn't it? Can you imagine attempting full retirement on the income generated by that sum?

One Million Kinds of Retirement Plans

Fortunately, our government recognizes the need for adequate retirement planning. It also recognizes that Social Security (yes, I believe there will be a Social Security fund in the future) will not come close to taking care of all our needs during our later years. So it provides tax incentives for you, your company, or both, to encourage us to set aside money today that will someday augment our Social INsecurity check. There must today be a million different kinds of company retirement plans and two million additional ways to achieve your retirement goals. In later chapters I will discuss appropriate investment strategies that will enable you to achieve those goals, and how you can or should invest money that is in some of the types of retirement plans. In most of these plans, though you may not have specific investment choices, you can, however, choose a category of investments, such as income, growth, balanced and so forth.

So why not take advantage of *all* of the investment opportunities and tax incentives that are available to you? Though your annual contributions to all your retirement plans—plus the money your employer adds and your own after-tax contributions—will count toward the $30,000 ceiling (increased with the cost of living), if you are a middle-income taxpayer, these ceilings are rather high. And if you're a high-income taxpayer, don't scoff, it adds up very quickly.

As usual, however, "to know and not to do, is not to know." We still have to take the initiative. If you have done nothing toward building retirement assets and are thirty or forty—an age where retirement still seems very far away—you probably have lack of perspective, but at least you still have the advantage of time. The sooner you get started, no matter how small you start, the easier it will be. However, if you can only count the number of years to retirement or prospective retirement on both hands, perspective isn't your problem—time is. You had better *immediately* employ all tools possible to the maximum of your financial ability. But remember, whatever your age, it makes good sense first to consider those opportunities that are government encouraged, because they are usually also "tax smart." It's like climbing a ladder: the lowest rung is not only the safest, but it also provides you with the surest footing to get you to the top. Understanding this reality, and putting a disciplined, periodic investment program into action, is *the* most important key to successful retirement planning.

Do-It-Yourself Retirement Funding

Individual Retirement Accounts (IRAs)

You have probably read or heard that the 1986 tax law made major changes in the IRA area. Despite these changes, for most of you, your IRA will *continue* to be an important tax shelter and retirement asset for years to come. All the press hoopla about how so many people now won't be able to contribute to an IRA and receive a tax deduction is just that—hoopla. Of the 25-plus million IRA owners, just one out of four are affected adversely by the change made in the tax laws. For three out of four who operate under the rules put into effect by the new law, it's business as usual.

What is an IRA? It is an arrangement by which you make annual contributions to your own retirement fund, an account held by a bank, mutual fund, insurance company or any other institution that qualifies as a trustee. Under the old law, such contributions were fully deductible. They still are—with certain restrictions. If neither you nor your spouse is covered by a qualified pension or profit-sharing plan or a tax-sheltered annuity, you may continue to contribute and deduct up to $2,000 per earner to an IRA, or $2,250 to a spousal IRA if only one spouse is employed. If you are covered by a company retirement plan (or a tax-sheltered annuity) and you are married, you can still fund and deduct your IRA contributions as long as your family income is under $40,000 a year. If you are single, your income must be under $25,000 a year. If, however, either you or, if married, you and your spouse are covered by a qualified retirement plan, and your income exceeds these amounts, your annual IRA deduction is determined by your level of adjusted gross income, depending on your filing status.

For couples filing jointly with incomes between $40,000 and $50,000, and $25,000 and $35,000 for unmarried individuals, as a rule of thumb, the deduction is reduced one dollar for every five dollars of income in excess of $40,000 on a joint return and in excess of $25,000 on an individual's return. For example, an individual with an income of $30,000 could claim a maximum deduction of $1,000.

I used to tell clients, "Put $2,000 in an IRA and you'll save $1,000 in taxes." Almost all my clients could appreciate that. Now with tax reform lowering top tax rates to 28 percent, when I say, "Put $2,000 into an IRA and save $560 in taxes," it just doesn't have the same ring to it. An IRA contribution nonetheless can remain an important ingredient in achieving financial security in your later years, even with its diminished impact on tax savings.

Currently, the most common IRA question is "If I'm not eligible to receive a tax deduction on my IRA, should I still put money in the nondeductible IRA?"

Answer: IRA's central advantage has always been its tax-free buildup of funds (see Chapter 9) rather than the initial deduction. And although tax reform has limited up-front deductions, all Americans are still eligible to contribute up to $2,000 a year ($2,250 for one-income couples, and a combined $4,000 for two-earner couples) to an IRA and reap its more long-term tax advantages. (If you have an IRA already, you have to establish a new account to distinguish deductible from nondeductible contributions.) So deductibility should not be the major determining factor. Even when everyone had full IRA deductibility, only 35 percent of all eligible Americans bothered to contribute. Furthermore, a recent survey commissioned by the Heritage Foundation, a conservative Washington think tank, discovered that one-fourth of those who set up IRAs didn't use them to augment their savings but instead shifted money away from other savings accounts.

Now whether or not you should make a nondeductible contribution is pretty straightforward. It depends primarily upon your willingness to tie up the money in a long-term investment that you can't get into without paying tax as well as a substantial (10 percent) penalty for early withdrawal. Thus, it's not a smart idea if there is any chance you are going to have to pull the money out early. For a taxpayer in the 28 percent tax bracket, after taking the 10 percent early withdrawal penalty into account, it would take nineteen years to break even with what would have been earned in an 8 percent account.

Therefore, before making a nondeductible IRA contribution, compare returns from other tax-deferred or tax-free investments. For instance, a 7 percent return on a tax-free municipal bond will leave you with more than a 7 percent return on a nondeductible IRA, because you will be taxed on IRA earnings when you make withdrawals. If you can get a higher return on an IRA investment, however, the municipal bond's advantage may disappear.

What most people have lost sight of—or never understood—is that an IRA provides only one of many methods of building assets for the future. Many bank and mutual fund company ads have made an IRA sound like the only passport to financial security, if you started contributing early enough—with their firm, of course. Those claims were misleading. While an IRA can certainly provide an important part of your future financial requirements, it will pay only a portion of your total retirement expenses—even if you start making contributions while you are still quite young. Example: You place $2,000 per year into an IRA with a 10 percent rate of return, and inflation runs at an average rate of 8 percent. Though the gross value of your account will have grown to $216,364, your IRA savings will be taxable when you withdraw them. If you are in the 28 percent tax bracket, after twenty-five years the after-tax value of your fund will be only $155,782. Then, after adjusting for an 8 percent average inflation rate, your IRA will be worth only $23,367 in terms of today's dollars. Though you may earn more or less than 10 percent, and inflation may or may not average 8 percent, you still cannot expect to live like a millionaire on the income produced by one retirement plan—unless you are lucky enough to win the lottery or inherit Aunt Hattie's Coca-Cola stock.

Thus, you must contribute to a variety of retirement plans. If investing for you comes more easily in small doses than all at once, IRAs are an excellent device to promote financial self-discipline. If you are worried about locking your money up where you can't grab it without paying stiff penalties, you may prefer other strategies—municipal bonds or U.S. savings bonds instead of IRAs. But an IRA can be a very flexible investment over which you can exercise a great deal of control—control not available in other tax-deferred investments. For example, you could also purchase a deferred fixed- or variable-rate annuity, which allows a tax-deferred buildup of income, but the investment alternatives are usually limited to a specified family of mutual funds. Believe it or not, with an IRA you can select almost any investment you desire.

WHERE TO PUT YOUR IRA CASH
I have often found that confusion reigns supreme when people learn there are a variety of ways IRA funds can be invested. Though most IRA money lies in banks and savings and loan associations in certificates of deposit, CDs, money market accounts and mutual funds simply are not the only possibilities. The law also allows you to put your IRA funds in stocks, bonds, insurance contracts, real estate investment trusts (REITs) or partnerships in real estate, oil and gas, equipment leasing and venture capital. Now, recently minted U.S. gold and silver

coins have been added to the list. (Although coins may appreciate significantly in value, they produce no taxable income until they are sold at a profit. In my opinion, holding them in an IRA creates no tax advantage.)

Today, as the high-interest-rate CDs you bought a few years ago mature and you look in vain for similar yields for your IRA, I recommend you consider purchasing high-quality growth mutual funds, debt-free investments in real estate and even income-oriented venture capital deals that provide some opportunity for exceptional growth for a portion of your money. Previously, I advised clients to keep pure growth investment opportunities (which could be taxed at a maximum rate of 20 percent) outside their IRAs. But no longer. Tax reform essentially eliminated any distinction between capital gains and ordinary income. I still firmly believe you are safest with an income-oriented investment for your IRA, and least safe purchasing individual shares of common stock. I recommend, for most of you, that an IRA should include 75 percent income-oriented investments, with the remaining portion a mixture of some of the above recommendations.

If you require safety and predictability, then the above formula will work. Usually, if you are 55 or older, you will want to (and should) select almost exclusively safe income-producing investments (see Chapter 8), for you must have predictable results. If you are 35 to 55 years old, growth opportunities should also be your investment target. Here I recommend 75 percent income with 25 percent growth. And if you are less than 35 years old, I recommend 50 percent income with the other half growth, since you have time on your side.

Which IRA Is Which?

An IRA is an IRA, but not all are equal. Like different kinds of hammers, the various types are suitable for different tasks and temperaments. So many government-encouraged retirement tools now exist that with your own private investing and Social Security it's hard to see how you can fail. But it's like building a house: the only way you can do it is one board at a time. First, however, you have to learn how to use the right hammer for the right job.

SELF-DIRECTED IRAS
Self-directed IRAs allow you to control day-to-day investment decisions through the custodian of the account. For example, you can set

up a self-directed IRA with a brokerage or a trust company, and buy and sell stocks in your IRA account just as you would in an ordinary investment portfolio. Under current law, most corporate, U.S. government securities and many limited partnerships may be held in a self-directed IRA.

This IRA is subject to the same rules, such as early withdrawal penalties, the types of investments that can be placed in an IRA, the $2,000 maximum investment, and so on, as garden-variety IRAs. However, I believe that it makes sense only after your account has built up beyond a certain level—say, $10,000. Self-directed IRAs make less sense for smaller amounts, since fees and brokerage commissions eat up too great a proportion of your principal. Through a self-directed IRA, you can purchase individual stocks, which I don't favor. But also through a self-directed IRA you can purchase income-oriented equipment-leasing or income-oriented venture capital partnerships, which I do like for a small portion of your IRA money.

THE SIMPLIFIED EMPLOYEE PENSION PLAN (SEP)

Owners of very small businesses have lousy reputations when it comes to helping their employees plan for retirement. In businesses with twenty-five employees or less, only one in seven workers is covered by a company-sponsored pension plan. By contrast, four out of five employees of larger firms are covered.

Congress tried to remedy the problem by creating the Simplified Employee Pension (SEP) plan. The aim: to give small companies a way to establish retirement plans without the complexities and costs that normally go along with them. SEPs are nothing more than IRAs that permit employees to voluntarily contribute part of their pretax salaries to the SEP as if they were contributing to a 401(k) plan. Under a SEP, each employer sets up a retirement plan, gets each employee (at least half must do so) to open an IRA account at a bank, brokerage house or through a mutual fund. The limitation is $7,000 a year for the employee, rather than $2,000 under a regular IRA. But the employer can also contribute to your SEP (the amount is also excluded from gross income) as long as more than $7,000 in total—or 25 percent of compensation—is contributed.

So far, SEPs have not been very popular, for few companies are using them. Yet a SEP is probably the easiest of any qualified retirement plan to establish. Administrative hassles are few in number for an employer, because employees manage their own SEP–IRAs. No lawyers are needed to set up a pension trust fund nor accountants to perform an annual audit.

Thanks to changes in the 1986 tax law, SEPs may finally live up to their promise because some of the other more popular types of retirement plans, such as 401(k) and Keogh plans (see below), are now more restrictive. For example, a 401(k) can only distribute money at retirement, death, disability, separation from service, financial hardship or after the participant reaches age 59½—the same as an IRA.

Although SEPs are designed only for small employers, it is estimated that approximately 15 million employees could be eligible to participate. A novel idea: If you are a small business owner, you might want to set up a pension plan to reduce your own tax burden. A SEP allows you to shelter some of the salary you pay *yourself* as an employee of your company.

THE IRA ROLLOVER OR TRANSFER

You can receive retirement plan earnings (called "distributions" in accountantese) when you retire, change jobs, become disabled or if your employer terminates your job for any reason. If you die before receiving the distribution, the plan will also pay your heirs. Such distributions can come from all qualified retirement plans, whether the plans are corporate-sponsored or self-employed workers' Keoghs. Other varieties (which now all have similar withdrawal rules) include money-purchase pension plans, profit-sharing plans, 401(k) plans, defined-benefit plans, 403(b) nonprofit corporation plans and, as described above, SEPs.

You basically have three possible distribution situations or choices with all these retirement plans. The direct shift of your account from one qualified plan to another is called a transfer. The money goes from the old plan's trustee to the new one, so you never actually possess the money. No IRS reporting is required, and transfers from trustee to trustee can be done as often as you want, thus assuring continued tax deferral.

The two other distribution options are either to take the money (and run) as a lump-sum distribution and pay an income tax based on the five-year forward-averaging method, or to continue to defer the tax by rolling over (or transferring) all or part of the proceeds into a special IRA rollover account until time of withdrawal.

If you qualify to take the money as a lump sum, the tax is calculated as if the money were to be paid out over the next five years, and is paid separately from that due on any other income. The lump sum is not added to gross income, and the principal balance is never taxed again. Whether you earn $10,000 or $250,000 a year, the income tax you pay on the distribution is the same under the averaging system.

With the elimination of ten-year forward averaging for most people, it is estimated that a very high percentage of the $4 billion to $5 billion of distributions received each year from retirement plans will now be rolled over into IRAs for the tax-deferral opportunities. The five-year averaging method is not as desirable as its predecessor, because not only will you get less of a tax break as a result of the lower tax brackets, but also the current law restricts the number of taxpayers who would be eligible to use the five-year forward averaging method.

BEST METHOD

Whether you should take a lump-sum distribution or roll your funds over into an IRA will primarily depend on your own tax circumstances and your personal financial planning needs. But I have found in most instances the rollover was clearly the best decision.

One method to figure out which way is best for you is to calculate what you would get if you paid taxes now and invested the remainder in tax-exempt bonds. Then compare the result with what you would get if you rolled the entire sum into an IRA, received a higher yield from normally taxable investments and paid taxes on the withdrawals. If you wish to use a rollover IRA, be aware that most of the time you may not touch the money before you reach age 59½, without penalty for early withdrawal. However, if immediate money is your need, and you meet minimum age requirements, a penalty-free partial IRA roll-over is permitted. Regardless of age, you can receive a distribution in your name and actually use the money for sixty days (no more) before reinvesting the money in a rollover IRA. But pin a large note on the wall reminding yourself of the deadline. The IRS does not accept an "I forgot" excuse.

It must also be kept in mind that this will, for most of you, be by far the largest chunk of cash you will ever receive. Unless you have previously thought out a game plan for where the funds should be reinvested, you may spend many a sleepless night. Solution: If you choose to roll over your funds, but can't or haven't decided where and how you should reposition these funds, you can always place that money in a bank or mutual fund money market rollover IRA account while you're determining what to do. This will give you all the time you need to investigate fully your options. Once you decide, you then have the ability to make an IRA transfer to another qualified custodian, and to invest your funds as you would in any IRA account.

The worst mistake you can make is to feel pressured to make immediate investment decisions. Remember, one day, one week or one month of a little extra interest or a missed opportunity simply is not going to alter your life-style on a long-term basis. You'll never even notice the difference if you miss a few extra dollars, but you certainly would if you lose too many of your original dollars by making a hasty decision.

Keogh Plans

If you are self-employed or are in a partnership or have a sideline business, you can set up a Keogh plan. A Keogh allows you to deduct your full contribution and, like all other retirement plans, the money in the plan is allowed to grow and compound tax-free until withdrawn.

As a self-employed person, you can set up an individual Keogh plan either as a money-purchase pension plan, a defined benefit plan or a profit-sharing plan. With the money-purchase pension Keogh, you can make a tax-deductible contribution each year of up to 20 percent of your earned income from self-employment, or $30,000, whichever is the lesser amount. The drawback is that you must agree to contribute the same percentage of your income to the plan every year, unless your business shows a loss. If you fail to make a contribution, you could face an IRS penalty of up to 100 percent of the shortfall.

With the more complicated defined-benefit Keogh, you contribute an amount that is necessary to fund an eventual payout based on actuarial tables for your life expectancy. The annual benefit can't exceed the smaller of $90,000 or 100 percent of your average salary for your highest-paid three years. The closer the business owner is to retirement age, the more income he or she can defer in such a plan. Under a profit-sharing plan, you can contribute up to 13.043 percent of earned income or $30,000, whichever is less. The great advantage is flexibility. As owner (or with your partners, if it is a partnership) you can decide how much to contribute, but you can change your contribution from year to year or not contribute at all. However, any covered employees must receive contributions at the same base rate.

If you earn less than $15,000 a year from all sources of income, there is still another Keogh program. You are allowed to contribute 100 percent of your self-employment income or $750, whichever is less, to a Keogh plan. For example, if you earn $750 from your own sideline business and make less than $14,250 from a paid job, you can put the entire $750 in a Keogh.

Many self-employed individuals have not taken advantage of all the Keogh possibilities. I believe that if you have the opportunity to participate in a Keogh, do so to the fullest extent possible. If later you are not happy with your present decision, you'll be amazed that it's not the end of the world. You can freeze your Keogh and shift your emphasis to other retirement methods.

Employer Retirement Plans

Today most medium and large corporations provide attractive retirement plans for their employees. Such plans enable you to use funds you might otherwise spend for retirement purposes.

Will you contribute to the plan or does the company pay all the cost? Practice varies. When you contribute by payroll deduction, benefits may be larger. In any event, all the income the money earns during your working years is tax free until your retirement. Remember, the funds contributed to the retirement plan on your account are part of your compensation, just as much as your salary. So it's vital you understand the plan.

Qualified and Nonqualified Employee Benefit Plans

A qualified employee benefit plan includes pension, profit-sharing and stock bonus plans. They offer exceptional tax benefits to both shareholder employees and regular employees. If certain tax law requirements are met, the employer gets an immediate deduction for contributions under the plan, and the employee is not taxed on his or her share of the funds until amounts are distributed. Furthermore, qualifying lump-sum distributions and plan termination payments can be rolled over tax free to another plan or an IRA.

There are a large number of requirements that must be met before an employee benefit plan is considered qualified. For example, the plan must meet numerous nondiscrimination, eligibility and broad coverage tests. However, in general, the plan must be established by the employer for the exclusive benefit of the employees or their beneficiaries.

A nonqualified plan allows an employer to provide key employee benefits that are above the limitations for qualified plans. Nonqualified plans need not be currently funded by the employer; therefore, the deferred compensation arrangements are exempt from taxation until received. Of course, the employer will not be entitled to the deduction until the employee is taxed on the benefits. One of the advantages of the nonqualified plan is that it can be used to avoid many of the traditional antidiscrimination requirements. For example, a select group of management could defer receipt of earnings above a specified amount to later years, thus avoiding current taxation on those earnings. Not all employees have to be offered that opportunity.

Defined-Contribution and Defined-Benefit Plans

A defined-contribution plan obligates a company to contribute a certain amount (either a dollar amount or a percentage) each year to a separate account for each employee.

A defined-benefit plan is a single account for the whole company, and the contribution is determined by how large a retirement benefit each worker will eventually receive (usually a percentage of the employee's final salary, times the number of years he or she worked for the company).

There's a limit on the amount an employee can contribute each year to a defined contribution plan ($30,000 or 25 percent of the employee's salary, whichever is smaller) and a limit on the total amount of defined benefit a plan can provide ($90,000 or 100 percent of the employee's average salary for his or her three consecutive highest-paid years).

Pension or Profit-Sharing Plans

Sometimes the term "pension plan" is used to include profit-sharing plans as well. As stated earlier, under the Keogh plans, technically the difference is that an employer (once a pension plan is established) must make contributions to the plan every year, no matter how inconvenient this may be. A profit-sharing plan (as the name suggests) involves sharing of profits only; the employer, therefore, doesn't contribute in years in which the company shows a loss.

A Deferred Plan—401(k)

The 401(k) plan, also known as CODA (cash or deferred arrangement), is another employer-sponsored plan that allows employees to set aside pretax chunks of money, which accumulate tax-deferred and are paid out at retirement or upon termination of employment. Employees pay a tax on this money only when they draw it out, usually at retirement. However, a 10 percent excise tax (penalty) also generally applies if you withdraw the money before death, disability or age 59½. Thus, the money you're putting in is hardly liquid—it must be considered a long-term investment. (By the way, all qualified plans also have in common the fact that withdrawals must commence by age 70½.)

A 401(k) behaves much like a profit-sharing plan. It can be set up anew or added to an existing profit-sharing, thrift or stock bonus plan. Whatever the design, the 401(k) plan offers financial flexibility. Employees may decide whether to contribute, and if so, how much. The employer may also contribute to the employees' plan. On an average, companies surveyed a few years ago matched 50 percent of the amount deferred by employees.

More than 50 percent of the Fortune 500 companies, and many smaller companies, have adopted 401(k) plans. And they remain as popular as pretzels in a bar despite the fact that, in 1987, employee contribution limits have been reduced to the smaller of 25 percent of salary or $7,000, rather than $30,000. Employee benefits specialists believed that interest in this particular plan would evaporate with this lower limit. However, they forgot that more than 98 percent of all 401(k) contributions have always been below today's $7,000 limit (indexed for inflation), and that there is far more money in 401(k)s than in IRAs. If you think about it, $7,000 is extremely generous, except for the person making well over $150,000 a year. Common sense says that the vast majority of employees covered by the increasingly popular 401(k) plan have never had any intention of deferring more than $7,000 a year, even if they could.

The 401(k) allows a full range of investment options, including common stock funds, fixed-income funds, money market funds, guaranteed interest contracts and aggressive growth funds. A 401(k) plan may also include employer stock and participant-directed accounts similar to SEPs. It's good for participants to have the opportunity to control the investment of their retirement funds, but most of the available investment vehicles are not insured, so the participant could lose money if he or she makes bad choices.

If a 401(k) is available, go for it! But don't worry if you haven't heard of the 401(k) plan. It is still relatively new. You cannot nor should you try to keep up with all of the retirement plans—let alone the latest. What is of prime importance is your awareness of what your company is providing you in the way of retirement benefits. You should be familiar with all of your options and choices—as well as the actual dollar amounts involved. Contact your personnel or benefits department, or ask management. Don't always expect them to call or inform you first. The responsibility for your future financial security ultimately rests with you. You will find, if you haven't already, that others will never be as concerned about your money as you are—even if it's their job to do so.

Company-Sponsored Thrift Plans

Your employer may offer a qualified plan usually known as a thrift plan; however, often it is called a savings plan or savings incentive plan. Whatever its title, it invites you to contribute an after-tax portion of your salary, which your employer may agree to match. For example, a customary match may be up to 50 percent. Many plans also allow you to contribute unmatched dollars, once you exceed the employer's maximum matching level.

As with all qualified plans, money that you and your employer contribute grows tax-free until you withdraw it. But if you are under age 59½, you will still have to pay a 10 percent penalty on early withdrawals unless: you die and your beneficiaries receive the money; you become disabled; you leave the company and take your cash as an annuity payable over the rest of your life; you are at least 55 and take early retirement; or you need the money to pay medical bills that exceed 7½ percent of your adjusted gross income. Furthermore, annual contributions that you and your employer make to all qualified plans combined still cannot exceed $30,000, despite the fact you are contributing after-tax dollars.

As a result of the more restrictive 1986 Tax Reform Act and because of the popularity of the 401(k), thrift plans have been reduced to a supplemental position. But they can still be an important part of funding for your retirement. Remember, you make an automatic "profit" if your employer chips in.

Tax-Sheltered Annuity Plan—403(b)

Employees of public schools, an exempt educational or charitable organization, hospitals and certain other tax-exempt organizations have the option to contribute to a tax-sheltered annuity, or 403(b) plan, to fund their retirement. Through this plan, which imposes the qualified plan coverage, the employee can purchase annuities or contribute to a custodial account invested in mutual funds. The money can come from two sources: additions to salary contributed by the employer and salary deferrals elected by the employee (in a fashion similar to conventional corporate cash or deferred arrangements). Employees can pay in up to $9,500 annually. However, employers can put in the difference, up to 25 percent of the employee's pay. As is the case with all qualified plans, total contribution to this and to other plans cannot exceed $30,000 annually—a sum that is indexed for inflation. The $9,500 limit on 403(b)s won't go up until the consumer price index has risen 37.7 percent, or enough to hoist the $7,000 limit on 401(k)s to $9,500. As a bonus, the IRS allows higher "catch up" contributions for some employees who made low contributions in earlier years.

Lump-sum distributions or transfers from plans of exempt organizations or public schools are also eligible for tax-free rollovers into IRAs or other employer plans.

Other Retirement Plans

To make a complicated picture even more complicated, there are also qualified plans for employees of state and local governments and major corporate retirement plans of all types. And additionally, there are a host of nonqualified plans. As previously mentioned, these are not boilerplate pension plans preapproved by the IRS, but plans specially designed to put more retirement money in the pockets of a select group of employees—assistant vice-presidents, for example. Such plans are only available to firms that have a fair amount of latitude in determining who will receive benefits. The IRS attempts to discourage companies from showering excessive benefits on owners and officers. However, since some nonqualified plans can be very attractive under the new code, you should further be aware of them and their benefits. As an employer you might choose to utilize one or more of these plans yourself. As an employee, can it hurt to ask?

Split-dollar life insurance is a nonqualified benefit plan. The company pays for the investment or cash value portion of the premium on an ordinary life insurance policy, and the employee pays for the risk portion—namely, the amount to be invested. Also available are REEPs, real estate executive compensation plans. Under this plan, the company buys a primary residence, vacation or office condominium, and each year turns over a fixed portion of the ownership to the employee.

I could go on, but by now you certainly must get the idea. There are many prudent retirement-plan avenues down which you can travel to achieve financial security for your future years. And need I restate the obvious? The path you take is your responsibility. The sooner you get started the better.

Though taking full advantage of the retirement plans available to you is a necessary part of every comprehensive financial plan, it is not the only part. There are also other choices to be made and opportunities to be considered in accumulating and investing your assets at every stage along your path to a financially secure future. This will be the subject of later chapters. But what if the future is now? . . .

Chapter 4

"Gone Fishin' "— A Financially Secure Retirement Is the Other Half

I have a little strategy to emphasize the importance of retirement planning for my clients. I simply ask, "How would you be fixed financially if you retired tomorrow?" Among my younger clients, the question is hypothetical, but it usually results in a sincere effort to plan for retirement when that time comes. Among my clients at or near retirement age, that question is real. In fact, many of them have come to me specifically because they *are* considering retirement (or may have already retired), and quite apart from the psychological consequences of that decision, they are concerned about the financial consequences as well. Even if they have been conscientious about planning for that fateful day, there are still decisions that must be made and strategies that can be followed to ensure that the days, and years, that follow will be financially secure.

"Retired" does not mean "to be tired twice." But regardless of how you get there, or when, once you do retire, your goal is to enjoy a *comfortable* retirement. So you must calculate now just how much money you will need to maintain your current standard of living for the rest of your life; you need prudent cash flow strategies for a decent return on, and sometimes of, your capital. Once accomplished, however, retirement doing can be both a busy time of your life and a golden one.

Taking an Early Retirement

If you work at a corporation of any size at all, there's a good chance your company will present you with an early retirement option. In the

current environment of mergers, acquisitions, corporate restructur-
ings, foreign competition or stagnant profits, hundreds of firms are
looking for ways to cut their staffs. Increasingly, companies are design-
ing incentives to induce workers of all ages to leave, with gambits such
as accelerated pensions, cash bonuses and continued insurance benefits.

Most people have great difficulty deciding whether or not to accept
an early retirement offer. Not only do they suffer tremendous emotional confusion at the prospect of losing their jobs and status, but they
become paralyzed with indecision. Why? The fact is that most such
early retirement packages are so complex that it becomes almost impossible to distinguish a terrific offer from a lousy one. Yet employees
are under pressure to decide quickly—usually within two to three
months. Furthermore, the packages are offered on a take-it-or-leave-it
basis, no haggling allowed.

Unfortunately, many people come to grief by listening to their co-
workers. One of my clients, who was then 57 years old, wasn't ready
to retire, but let others tell him how a man of his talent, experience and
vigor should spend his retirement years. So he retired, then taught,
and then consulted, but was miserable for eighteen months. He didn't
snap out of his melancholy until I advised him to write a book about
his experiences. He has written one (about retirement) and is now
struggling cheerfully to write another.

If you believe the chances are good that you will be made a serious
early retirement offer within the next few years, then you should calculate *now* what kind of package you will need. The question your
figuring should answer is this: Can you afford to live on the benefits
being offered, plus what you have saved, after accounting for inflation?
No matter how attractive the offer, if you can't afford to accept it, then
you should try to avoid taking it. Of course, if you run a strong risk
of becoming the victim of a layoff later, you may not have any choice.

What kinds of offers can you expect? Incentive packages tailored for
employees in their forties or younger generally provide a one-time cash
bonus pegged to their years of service with the company. The best
bonus you can probably anticipate is one year's salary. If you are in
your fifties, however, the best packages will include a bonus, and a
sweetener for your pension program. Compare the offer with the pension you would have received by staying on until you reach the age at
which you expected to retire. Your benefits department can give you a
figure based on your present salary. The incentive package should
match that at the very least. The closer you come to the company's

normal early retirement age, the more likely you will profit by accepting the offer.

Let's say you receive an offer that gives you a choice between the present cash value of your pension or a lifetime income. I usually recommend taking the lump-sum payment, then systematically withdrawing money after rolling that lump-sum amount over into an IRA. Most annuities—that's what the company will buy to provide you with lifetime income—usually pay only a 7 to 8 percent interest rate (sometimes less). With a lump-sum payment, you have the opportunity to invest that money for a higher return.

While considering the alternatives, don't overlook the value of any fringe benefits you may keep. They are money in the bank. An incentive package may let you retain your medical and life insurance, often scaled-down versions of what you were getting before. If you can, either negotiate for those benefits or for fatter packages. If you don't, rising insurance premiums will cost many of your hard-unearned dollars. Unfortunately, if you do not yet qualify for early retirement, you probably will get health coverage for no more than 18 months, and company-provided life and dental insurance are apt to stop.

Fortunately, many people will escape the early retirement dilemma. However, if you have at least given the eventuality some thought, it will be less traumatic if and when it occurs. Follow my guidelines, but also seek the advice of either a benefits consultant, accountant or financial planner at the time. Then your decisions will be more considered. Also, please, never, never blindly follow an early retirement decision made by one or more of your fellow workers. I've seen it happen more than I care to admit—usually with unhappy results.

How Much Capital *Do* You Need?

Whether retirement is a number of years off, in the near future or already at hand, I again suggest that you assume you are presently at the retirement point of your life. Though you may never intend to retire completely, assume such is the case, for this is the best way to answer the question "How'm I doing?" as New York City's Mayor Ed Koch is constantly asking voters.

Let's fantasize together. You've done well for yourself; you've carefully controlled your spending, put aside money and invested it wisely. Now you have investments in amounts you never thought possible.

And you have anticipated the rainy days—or have you? My retired clients frequently worry about whether they have enough investment capital for the rest of their lives. They also ask me, "What if I have extraordinary medical bills?" or "Will I have enough if I have to live in a convalescent home with full-time nursing care?" or "Can I keep up my present standard of living?"

Even individuals who have relatively large amounts of money share many of those same anxieties. Not long ago a new client entered our offices, questioning his ability to retire. Even with a securities portfolio value in excess of $3 million, he was concerned that he might run out of money if he continued to spend $50,000 a year. I took his concern seriously. It's not that he was not intelligent—quite the contrary. He knew $3 million could readily produce $50,000 a year. What he was really asking was whether he had enough money to handle his *unknown* future needs.

I confronted his anxieties and fears by openly discussing the most catastrophic events he could imagine and how much money he felt he would need for each. Ultimately, I redesigned a portfolio that provided an additional level of comfort, for his insecurity was also tied into the volatility of the stock market. His primary problem, however, was that he had earlier refused to face the problem realistically; in his mind he had exaggerated his financial needs for the future.

Obviously, you cannot precisely predict just how much you will need in your retirement years. Nuclear war, hyper-inflation, world-wide economic collapse, anarchy, catastrophic illness are all risks every individual faces. Insurance and investment diversification can hedge such risks, but not completely.

Does that mean you should now concern yourself over these risks? Certainly not. For one thing, many of them are only remote possibilities. Second, if you place too much emphasis on such contingencies and sink your money into bomb shelters and survival gear, you will have lost sight of your primary goal: to be able to enjoy your retirement in comfort and style. Finally, if you stint on all spending to maintain a larger estate "just in case," you will inadvertently create a tremendous tax bill for your heirs after your death. Then neither you nor your children will enjoy the money because government bureaucrats will be spending it on $90 nails and $600 toilet seats.

Your goal must be twofold: to have enough capital to provide for yourself and your mate, along with reserves for possible medical or convalescent care costs not reimbursed by insurance. Therefore, I feel a reasonable starting point is first to determine your life expectancy. Of course, you can't predict your exit with any certainty, so financial wisdom dictates that you prepare for a very long life so that you and the money come out even in the end. Therefore, assume that you will live to an age well beyond what actuarial charts indicate. Somewhere between ninety and ninety-five is what I choose for my clients. If you're already there, congratulations! Your prize is to add another ten years.

Then, continuing on my conservative bent, you must calculate your current "standard of living" expenses, assuming they will neither increase nor decrease during retirement. Your budget will change, of course, during your old age. However, as I pointed out before, you will probably need about 70 to 75 percent of your preretirement income. As an individual ages, his or her living expenses do tend to decrease, because there is usually—alas—a loss of *oomph* that translates into less travel, less shopping, less entertaining and fewer hobby costs. Conversely, there will also be some offsetting and increased expenses —medical bills, for example. If you assume your living expenses will remain at their current levels, your analysis of future needs will be quite conservative.

Next, multiply that figure by the total number of years that represent the rest of your life (remember, you are currently at retirement age). Ah, but we can't forget a thing called inflation. So you must multiply the resulting figure by an inflation factor. And I recommend you use an inflation factor of 4.3 percent. That number is the equivalent of 5 percent inflation for thirty years. If your real current age is 70, then twenty-five years is your magic figure and you should multiply it by 3.4. If you're seventy-five years of age, multiply by 2.6. If you're eighty, then multiply by 2.1. By the way, don't be overly concerned if you fear that my inflation rate might be inaccurate. It probably is. But it's a starting point, and by revising your figures every few years, your predictions will come close enough.

You may have fainted after determining how much retirement is going to "cost." Now for the smelling salts—your assets. You probably have many more than you first thought. For example, your Social Security benefits are an asset. Pretend you are 65 or older and not already receiving monthly Social Security checks. Call your local Social Security office to determine the current monthly payments that would be made for both you and (if applicable) your spouse. Then multiply the total monthly benefits by 12. Since this benefit will increase, but not necessarily with the rate of inflation, multiply that figure by one-half the aforementioned inflation factor that is appropriate for your age.

You have pension benefits, which are another asset. Once again, you may already be receiving these benefits. If not, ask your employer to compute pension benefits, and add that figure into your calculations. Ask whether there's a built-in inflation factor. Now add the inflated annual income from Social Security to that of the total annual pension benefits figure. Then multiply that figure by the total number of years I have "planned" for you to remain on earth.

At this point, before you take a look at your investment assets, I ask you to assume that your residence would never be sold; i.e., only "investments" are available for living expenses. Again, this is a most conservative assumption since many people who retire, or who are close to retiring, do in fact sell their homes, purchase something less expensive or move to a retirement home, thus creating additional investment capital.

Finally, determine the value of your investment assets (see Chapter 1) excluding "personal assets" such as your home, cars, clothing and jewelry. Then multiply that figure by the same inflation factor you used above and add the result to your combined pension and Social Security assets.

To be certain you can follow my directions, read the example on the opposite page.

Result: The Plans need $3,870,000 and their assets total $3,941,000 —slightly more than their target.

Ideally, of course, there should be some excess. That means you will have more than enough assets to take care of yourself for the rest of your life. If your forecast is perfectly accurate, on the sixth month, second week, sixth day at 9:15 P.M. after your 95th birthday, you should have consumed all your assets.

Did you come up short? Don't worry unnecessarily, because the numbers are very soft. However, if the two sets of numbers in your calculations are very, very far apart—if you lack as much as 20 to 30 percent (or more)—chances are you'll still be secure, because even small positive changes in today's financial picture could have a very major positive impact on your future. Further, a small change today has a magnified affect in the future. For example, if you're firing a rifle (today's money) at a target a mile away (the future), a one-inch movement could cause you to either hit or miss the target by dozens of feet in either direction.

MR. AND MRS. STAN PLAN
(Current Ages: 65 Each)

Expenses:

Cost of living during retirement (75 percent of preretirement cost of living)	$30,000 annually
Remaining years on earth	30
Total expenses during retirement	$900,000
Times 4.3 inflation factor	$3,870,000

Assets:

Combination of Social Security benefits	$1,200 monthly
Times 12 months	$1,440
Times a 2.2 inflation factor	$17,280
Monthly pension benefits	$1,750
Times 12 months	$21,000
$17,200 plus $21,000	$38,200
Times 30 years	$1,146,000
Value of investment assets	$650,000
Times 4.3 inflation factor	$2,795,000
$1,146,000 plus $2,795,000	$3,941,000

There are countless variables. For example, your portfolio value could grow at a faster (or slower) rate than projected; you could work beyond age 65 either full or part time; your expenses could be considerably lower just by having paid off your mortgage; and you have not even figured in the positive effects of compounding on your long-term investments (see Chapter 9).

Many years ago I told a 72-year old pediatrician he would never be able to retire. He was used to a high income and had spending habits not too different from the Pentagon's. Thus, he had saved relatively little. In spite of the numbers, he retired anyway. His major asset was his home. He and his wife found a new condominium development and picked out a unit (a large one on San Francisco Bay) before the project was built. At that time, the California real estate market had just started to explode. The couple was able to sell their home, purchase their new condominium and still have a good deal of money left over. To his friends, it all seemed like a stroke of genius but, in fact, it was just plain good luck—one of the more important variables around.

You cannot count on good luck to pull you through. If your assets appear to fall uncomfortably short of your future needs, you *can* make reasonable fixes to assure a better outcome. You can plan to work beyond age 65; or if you are already retired, plan to work part time.

You can also begin to reduce some of your larger expenses now. Or you can attempt to achieve higher returns on your investment assets, though you should not take undue risk (traveling ninety miles per hour because you are late to the party is not very wise). You could even step up your spending program—on investments.

It might not hurt to seek professional advice, particularly if your retirement is still several years away. A good financial advisor will not only be able to determine how much you should invest each year, but he will also be able to counsel you on the rate of return you should aim for as well as help you determine how much capital you need and how to maintain it. Most of you believe that if you have, say, $750,000 in long-term Treasury bonds paying 8 percent in interest, you need not bother with this mathematical exercise because your principal will always remain intact. Unfortunately, this belief does not hold true in the "real world"; inflation can drastically erode the buying power of that money. If inflation averages 5 percent a year over the next twenty-five years, you would need more than $200,000 annually to maintain your present purchasing power. Meanwhile, your $750,000 in bonds would be worth only about $208,000 when adjusted for inflation. Even putting aside the future value of the bonds, in order to maintain today's "standard of living" each year you will have to withdraw an ever-increasing amount of money, causing an invasion of principal. Since interest rates generally fall behind the rate of inflation, you will also be invading capital at an ever-increasing rate. Working with a good financial advisor, you can experiment with the numbers at various levels of spending so you can view the impact on your investment capital. If your conclusion is that your net worth will continue to increase at a faster rate than you can spend it, you will be in good shape. If not, then it's time to make changes in your portfolio.

For those of you who want to experiment with the numbers for yourself, you can use "The Magic Triangle" (opposite).

For example, if you owned a mutual fund that was growing at an average annual rate of 9 percent (find the "9" in the column on the right side of the triangle), but were withdrawing money from your fund at the rate of 12 percent (find the "12" in the column on the left side of the triangle), your money would last sixteen years. This figure can be found by following each of these columns to the square where they intersect. An investment that is growing at an annual rate of 7 percent, but from which you are withdrawing funds at an annual rate of 15 percent, will disappear in ten years.

The Magic Triangle

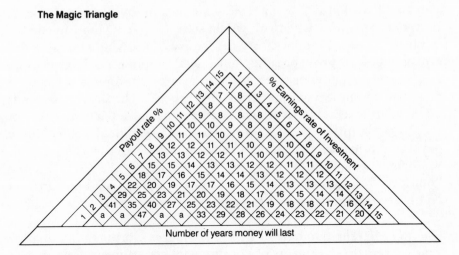

Years represent an approximation: In reality your payment would expire at different times during the year

a > 50 years

Earnings rate compounded monthly

Investment Strategies for a Return *on* and *of* Investment Capital

If, in planning for your retirement (or during your retirement), it is important to have your assets remain whole or grow, then you will have to combine your fixed-income and growth investments or reinvest a portion of the income. Studies indicate that "real" after-tax yields of fixed-income investments (savings and bonds) have not kept pace with inflation, while growth investments (such as real estate and common stocks) generate yields that exceed the inflation rate by a few points. Together, their overall return will track inflation fairly closely. That assumption is reasonable, though it contradicts the claims of many investment promoters who tout investment returns that exceed inflation indefinitely. I have found no evidence that any one investment can indefinitely and consistently provide an after-tax return substantially in excess of inflation. Business cycles and shifts in supply and demand tend to even out such returns over time.

If *only* fixed-income investments will allow you to sleep at night, to be safe in the early years of your retirement you could take out less than your investments are earning and reinvest the rest. In later years you could then afford to increase your income by 5 percent a year, postponing the time when you would start to deplete your capital.

But what if you cannot afford the luxury of allowing your assets to remain whole or grow because your capital simply is not large enough and time is not on your side? Would it ever be appropriate to suggest that you consume your principal on purpose? The answer depends upon your other objectives, your temperament and whether or not you have the privilege of choice. Though few retired people enjoy devouring principal, that strategy can be quite effective in keeping your "earning years" from turning into "yearning years." Here are some "quick fix" options to consider, with further background information on each of these investments to be found elsewhere in the book.

Quick Fix 1: The purchase of a fixed annuity is worth considering for very conservative segments of your capital. The payments are partly a taxable return of interest and partly tax-free principal. The total payment agreed upon at the time of purchase is often not competitive with other fixed long-term rates, nor is it indexed to the inflation rate. However, the payments are guaranteed by the insurance company, and you cannot outlive them. If death occurs earlier than mortality tables suggest, and the agreement contains no special ten- or twenty-year provisions (where the money must be paid for this amount of time), payments stop and the remaining principal is a windfall to the greedy insurance company. If you are long-lived, the insurance company loses. While I'm not overjoyed with a frozen rate of income that will not keep up with higher future costs of living, this source of never-ending income, when deployed with other chunks of capital that do fluctuate in payout, can indeed make sense.

Quick Fix 2: Ginnie Mae securities (see Chapter 10), like immediate annuities, pay returns on principal that is usually quite a bit greater than money market funds. But because the value of the investment is more volatile, they also provide a higher return than annuities. For the reason that they are reverse images of your home mortgage, the payments you receive, therefore, include both true income and principal. Investing in Ginnie Mae trusts or mutual funds has the added benefit of allowing for automatic reinvesting of part or all of the return on principal if and when it is not needed.

Quick Fix 3: One of my favorite alternatives is the mutual fund withdrawal plan. If you conservatively estimate a growth fund's long-term appreciation rate of 9 percent, and that is not enough, a withdrawal plan of 10 to 12 percent of the principal may be perfectly satisfactory. If a municipal bond fund is paying 9 percent, and that is also not enough, perhaps invading principal to the tune of an additional 1 or 2 percent would help. Suppose, for instance, you have a life expectancy of fifteen more years, your $100,000 segment of capital is earning 7 percent tax free, but you need it to produce at least $10,000 a year. Turning to the Magic Triangle, you will learn that your investment can pay out $10,000 a year for eighteen years before the investment is totally depleted. On the other hand, utilizing a systematic withdrawal plan in conjunction with a growth mutual fund offers the possibility that you may never outlive your capital. Most mutual funds would be happy to provide you with a historic record documenting the result had you withdrawn any amount of income over any period of time you chose. There are a number of funds where you could have withdrawn 10 to 12 percent per year for, say, the last fifteen years and still have a remaining dollar value greater than your initial investment.

A word of caution, however. If you choose to employ this alternative, you should monitor the situation closely over time. You could run into big trouble if you are systematically withdrawing a consistent dollar amount while the fund is simultaneously declining in value. You could quickly deplete all your capital. That is one of the reasons I strongly recommend you only withdraw money as a percentage of assets, such as 10 percent of $100,000 rather than a flat $10,000, whatever the value of the assets. Though the dollar figure you'll be receiving will fluctuate along with the fund's value, you will never have any nasty surprises, either. You must also keep watch on the fund's performance. If performance is off, then you should either switch to another fund or even move to another mutual fund company.

There are other alternatives—the charitable remainder trust, the private annuity, use of call options against securities, planned gradual liquidations of shares of individual securities, oil and gas royalty trusts and more. There are many ways to maintain your present "standard of living" without dramatically increasing risk. But don't pay so much attention to return *on* investment that you forget about return *of* investment. Better to eat up your own principal than lose it altogether. Remember, too, what Bob Hope once quipped: Leaving heirs with less than they expected makes them remember us longer.

Continuing Work

The fact that you might not be able to afford to retire may not be that terrible. If you really like to work, you may not want to retire anyway. Indeed, that may provide the explanation for your lack of savings: you secretly didn't want to retire. The need many of you have for continued productivity well past retirement can be a powerful advantage in financial planning for later years. If you are unable to continue in your present job, explore ways you can use your work experience and skills when you retire. You could consider consulting, part-time work or self-employment.

The simple "need" to work can often force you to find new ways to pursue goals. A great example: One of my clients "retired" at age 40 with a net worth of $1 million. He had worked very hard for that money. Now twenty-five years later, he has a net worth of more than $30 million. He simply devoted his time and energy to purchasing and handling his investments.

A new or second career may also fit your "retirement" goal. But you should be planning this career change while you are still in your present job. Many of us fear retirement because we don't really know what we're going to do. Look around to see what activities and training programs will allow you the greatest range of opportunities.

Now That You Are Retired

Only you can personalize what the word "retirement" means to you. But I have learned through my clients' experience that full retirement is usually traumatic at first. Of course, there's a big adjustment in how you spend your time, but you must also get used to living off your assets or income drawn from retirement plans. At first you feel vulnerable, perhaps even paranoid, afraid that you may run out of money. Most people in retirement tend or will tend to become very, very conservative.

No matter how vulnerable you feel at first, you will adjust. After a relatively short period of time, you begin to feel better. Loosening up enough to enjoy the fruits of your labor is probably the biggest problem you'll face at first, but it is important that you do so. Why else have you been working so hard for all those years? Retirement can, and should, be a happy time, a time filled with activities you were never able to do before, a time without all the problems and worries that were so much a part of your workaday life. If you constantly defer your own comfort and pleasure in favor of nonspecific goals or other people's needs, psychologists tell me you'll build up a store of resentment in yourself or engender it in family members. Instead, save, then spend joyously. You deserve it.

The clients who most often have to reschedule their appointments with me are those who are retired. They laughingly say they can't believe how completely their time is filled and how enormously happy they are. If you have planned carefully for your own retirement, that's exactly the way it will be for you, too—on both counts.

Chapter 5

The Great Risk Reducer— Insurance Strategies

If I were to ask you for a list of synonyms for the word "disaster," you would probably come up with misfortune, mishap, calamity, catastrophe, tragedy—any or all of which can be pretty terrible, especially when they happen to you. Other words can also mean personal disaster: death, an accident, a lawsuit, a permanent disability, a major robbery or the destruction of your house by fire, flood, earthquake or tornado. In a variety of different ways, disasters disrupt our lives as well as the lives of others, despite what we do to offset their impact. And unfortunately the odds favor that one of these awful events will happen, at some point, to each and every one of us—as sure as the shortest person in a group will be the last to learn it's raining. The choice we have to make is the *degree* of disaster we will tolerate, how much disruption we will allow. To believe "It won't happen to me" is naïve at best, and usually negligent.

One of the reasons I began this book with death and wills, depressing as those subjects may be, is that I believe in reality. And death, as I've said before, is the only "sure thing" in life. However, there are other events over which we haven't any control, but which can be measured and dealt with—especially those events that could have a major financial impact on your life, ruin today's peace of mind and seriously impair, if not destroy, your future.

How can the impact of disaster be softened? Insurance. How can we hedge our bets against life's unhappy exigencies? Again, insurance. What else is new? But there are lots of different kinds of insurance— and a lot of slick insurance salesmen. That is why you must understand the likelihood of one or more untimely events occurring in your life, and the insurance steps you can take to prepare for the bad stuff. Furthermore, after implementing the insurance plan that is right for you, you will sense a greater freedom to be able to invest for the future without that nagging feeling that you are financially vulnerable if a disaster happened.

Look back at your financial plan. An accident, sickness or disability could render it useless by forcing you to spend savings or redirect your income. I often make that point by saying, "What good is a financial plan for the future when you forget to insure your home—and it burns down?" Today I can give a very real example: One of my clients, a world-class architect, really did forget to insure his million-dollar home. His policy had lapsed, and since he had no debt, there was no "system" to remind him to renew it. Fortunately, nothing happened to his home, or one of his most valuable assets could have gone up in smoke—literally. You can bet that he mended his ways and is now prepared for the unpredictable by establishing a backup reminder system.

Since we can't safeguard ourselves against every conceivable disaster, the next best thing is to determine whether we are covered for the most obvious possibilities as well as the most financially devastating. Risks that *should* be covered and *can* be covered at a reasonable cost are: loss of earning power through death or disability, health expenses (particularly catastrophic illness), casualty losses (damage to your car or home) and liability for injury or damage to others.

Life Insurance

Certainly the most necessary precautions you should take are those against the economic problems caused by your own death. It can be, and very often is, an enormous financial disruption for all those who have depended on you for their support. And the only way to avoid this problem is to use insurance—either to cover yourself or someone else.

Regardless of the type of life insurance you choose, the object is the same: to help your family maintain the same standard of living it would have enjoyed were you around to bring home the bacon. A family with young children will need enough money to provide for the surviving spouse, the children and their education. If you die while there is a gap between what your family has and what it needs, that gap, without insurance, will remain unfilled. On the other hand, do not overinsure yourself; a better use of that extra money would be to invest it. Your death need not be a financial windfall for someone else. After all, "'Tis greater fun to be more loved in life than in death."

Life insurance is your second "estate," intended to replace the one that you—because of your death—did not have time to build. Simply put, life insurance is either the purchase of time or liquidity (quick cash without significant loss). If you are single and have no dependents, there isn't much point to purchasing time or cash—you don't need any more life insurance than it costs to bury yourself. The same is true for a newly married couple, each with a career, as long as they are childless. However, if this couple happens to receive group term insurance through their employers, there is no reason to spurn it, since it costs them nothing.

Now for the really big question, which everyone asks: "Just how much insurance do I need?" Don't feel guilty if you are "everyone." A chief financial officer of a major company came to my office just as perplexed as you probably are. We all know that if we ask that question of most insurance agents we will often get a confusing pitch not designed to inform but to peddle a product—in short, a fiendish plot to "insure" his or her own future financial security and not yours.

The really big answer: There are numerous sophisticated methods to determine how much life insurance you need. If you wish a quick, reasonable answer, all you have to do is determine what annual after-tax (because that is what you spend) income will disappear due to death, and multiply that by the number of years you estimate the need will continue. Don't forget to include possible extraordinary expenses, such as education costs or burial or related expenses. But you do not need to factor in inflation, for with any level of inflation, amounts of money that were adequate at the start of the period will be woefully small in twenty or thirty years. Increases in Social Security and investment value will, however, provide some protection. Subtract any income derived from your spouse's annual take-home pay, from investments and other assets, as well as Social Security payments to the kids that will continue after your death. That total number is the one you multiply by the number of years you estimate the need will continue.

The resulting figure might, for some of you, still seem astoundingly big. That is, it could be so large you would never be able to afford the insurance premiums. However, please don't feel guilty if you must purchase a smaller amount of insurance. If an extraordinary premium payment would cause you to cut into current expenses drastically, then the long-term trade-off isn't worth it.

Example:

$50,000	annual after-tax income
× 20	multiplied by number of years is will be needed (until the children finish school or for your spouse's expected life) equals
$1,000,000	gross dollar need for 20 years
− 520,000	minus annual income from investments, other assets and Social Security payments multiplied by 20 years
$480,000	equals amount of insurance needed

Remember, for most of you, your need for life insurance really is "stopgap." It should fill in that period of time between low income from assets with high family dependence and high-asset income with fewer family responsibilities. Ideally, at some point you will be "self-insured" by your own assets. You can then recalculate your insurance requirements by reexamining your family's continuing need for money, then from that figure subtract your investment assets. If there is a shortfall, that should be the size of your insurance policy.

The next most popular question involves what type of insurance I recommend. Your best bet is temporary, or term, insurance. Despite all the fancy new kinds of insurance products available, annual-renewal term insurance remains the lowest-cost life insurance. It offers protection on a year-to-year basis for a stated period of time, with premiums based on your age. As you grow older and the insurance premium rises, hopefully your assets are also growing. That's when you systematically decrease the amount of your coverage.

There can be further reasons for purchasing life insurance. It might be the only way to create an estate for your survivor(s) if you have not been able to accumulate much money during your lifetime. But what if you are 68 years old, are not in good health and may have trouble getting or affording term insurance? Is there a better type of insurance to seek out? I would still try term first. You must keep in mind that usually during the first ten or so years, the total premium paid for term insurance will often be lower than the total dollars spent on any other type of insurance, whatever your age or health when you take out the policy. But if you are in post-retirement years, come from a family where everyone lived to 105 years old, then seriously consider ordinary life (also called permanent life, whole life or straight life) insurance, for which you pay a set annual premium that does not rise as you grow older. However, this form of insurance traditionally offers a low return on the policy holder's investment.

A third reason to buy life insurance is to create investment money— liquidity—that can offset federal and, in some cases, state inheritance taxes that come due on a person's death. Heirs won't have to liquidate a large chunk of your assets in order to pay these taxes. However, recent changes in tax law have made the bite less severe; for example, you can now leave $600,000 to your heirs without their paying any federal estate tax. So the higher the value of your life insurance policy, the higher the value of your estate. As you increase your estate over $600,000, due to an insurance settlement, the larger the government "take" will be. Thus, the decision you face is how large an estate you wish to leave your heirs and how much money you are willing to pay (perhaps indefinitely) for insurance premiums that would increase your beneficiaries' inheritance. A policy worth $600,000 for the death of one parent and $1,200,000 for the death of both is usually sufficient to assure your minor children's financial security. Even if your estate exceeds those amounts, your children can at least receive these insurance benefits tax free. Under these circumstances, I have difficulty seeing any *economic* reason for most of us to maintain additional amounts of life insurance.

If a large illiquid asset—such as the family farm—might have to be sold to pay estate taxes, however, there would be a strong financial rationale for maintaining insurance coverage sufficient to do that. And in such cases, permanent life insurance could be appropriate.

If your family or holdings are so large that more sophisticated estate planning is required, I recommend seeking the advice of an attorney who specializes in estate planning. It would also be to your benefit to consult with a financial planner or an insurance agent with a financial planning background to make sure your estate plan dovetails with the rest of your financial plan. (How to seek competent advisors is discussed in Chapter 16.) Such advisors, as well as your attorney, will discuss irrevocable life insurance trusts, "gifting" methods, recapitalization techniques and more. All these techniques can help you reduce your estate tax bill. Always keep your priorities in mind, however; don't make lowering the amount of your IRS bill your only goal.

Granted, there are a bewildering variety of insurance packages available today—another reason why you might want to consult an attorney or an estate planner rather than rely solely on the advice of an insurance agent, who may have his own axe to grind. For example, in addition to term insurance and permanent or whole life insurance, universal life insurance appeared on the scene in 1978. The policy combines insurance with a cash reserve, which is really a savings account. The earnings on these savings are competitive with bond market rates of interest and are tax-deferred. With the best policies, you can withdraw your savings whenever you want and you can also adjust the size of your premium to vary the amount you put into your cash reserve. Last year, about 30 percent of all life plans sold were universal life insurance policies. But unless these policies exceed $50,000 of insurance, a smaller policy usually does not make sense due to burdensome fees.

Variable life insurance is another relatively new insurance product. This is where the policyholder bears the risk of securities investments that are made with the cash value of the policy, while the insurance company guarantees a minimum death benefit unaffected by any portfolio losses. During the last decade, still other new forms of life insurance have evolved: direct recognition life, vanishing premium life, second generation universal life, current assumption whole life, flexible-premium variable life, variable/universal life, and single-premium whole life.

Although most insurance products have traditionally been sold for their death benefits alone, many, such as single-premium whole life and variable life, are now providing benefits during one's lifetime as well, satisfying multiple needs in terms of risk protection and investment returns. What you have to determine is your greatest need. Is it a large amount of insurance protection for the dollar, or is it investment return? If it is protection, then, as stated earlier, term or maybe even whole life insurance might be the answer. With these products, particularly term, you obtain the greatest amount of insurance with the least number of dollars.

If you are seeking an investment (a cash value fund with a higher rate of return), then the other insurance alternatives should be considered. Now, that should simplify things for you. And because I consider most of these other products investments first, though they also possess some insurance features, I will discuss them more fully in Chapter 15.

The bottom line here: Be as fully informed as possible of the options available, and choose the one that is right for *you*.

Accidental Death Policies

Looking for a bargain? Try accidental death insurance, such as flight insurance. And it is a bargain, at least to insurance companies, because it pays them very well. Why? Because death by accident is a highly infrequent event (a reassuring thought when you're flying at 40,000 feet). Many such policies are often supplied as part of employer-provided group insurance or in connection with various travel associations and credit cards, like American Express, so there's no point to getting rid of them because they cost you nothing. However, buying specialized policies for air travel, hang gliding or bobsledding makes no sense. Not only are you unlikely to die while doing such things, face it—you don't even *do* them that often. Further, there are usually a lot of strings attached to these policies—for example, your heirs will only get their money when you die in an air disaster if you bought your ticket with a certain credit card. I believe this kind of coverage is a waste of money. The amount of life insurance you carry should depend upon your dependents' *needs* (paying for estate taxes, for example) and not on the particular cause of death—whether it comes by skydiving or accidentally choking on your linguini and clam sauce.

Group Term Life Insurance

Many of you probably have employer-paid group term life insurance. For many years the first $50,000 of such coverage has been a tax-free employee benefit (although the government will likely lower the figure at some point). You may have not realized it, but the premium cost of any insurance coverage *above* $50,000 is included in your taxable income.

As illogical as it may seem, you might actually save money by obtaining your own coverage and declining the company's coverage above $50,000—assuming that is allowed. But in order to do so, you have to be the kind of person who (1) enjoys bargains; (2) does not want to be dependent on your employer's benefit program; (3) loves taking physical exams and filling out insurance forms.

In the final analysis, the few dollars you save probably aren't important. Only 3 percent of you—that is, only 3 percent of policyholders' heirs—will collect on group term anyway. Remember, it self-destructs either when you retire or at ages 65 or 70, and that's usually before you do. Besides, it's unlikely that you will even need much coverage at that point. Yes, chalk up another win for the insurance companies!

Living Insurance

Finally, I can now stop talking about death and cover living events for which people usually need insurance, those unexpected things we cheerfully face throughout our lives—fires, tornadoes, car accidents. Insurance companies would have you believe that calamity lurks everywhere. I believe, however, that calm will prevail if you focus primarily on the areas of your life that carry the greatest risks.

Chances are high you haven't covered some of the *basic* risks in your life. Although you have intended to take care of them, you have been much too busy. Isn't it strange how after a disaster-type of event has taken place, you suddenly have the "time" that before never existed? A few extra moments *now* will provide you with a great deal more time to be "busy" once again in the future.

Risks, as I've said before, are part of living. Ideally you should be able to shift all your risks to insurers, but in many cases that is unfeasible or prohibitively expensive. To manage risk, you must strive for a certain comfort level and minimize actual losses. If you can't rest easy unless you have the maximum amount of insurance coverage possible, then fine. However, you must recognize that your peace of mind will come at a high price. The funds you sink into insurance will not be building and accumulating to help you reach your other goals—retiring comfortably, for example. While you cover some risks, you may be losing some opportunities by not having enough savings. So, no matter how fearful you are, you will have to strike a balance.

Disability Income

Your most valuable asset is *you*—and your ability to earn an income (which I'll be further discussing in Chapter 9). While most of you have some form of life insurance, chances are you have overlooked insuring your earning power. In fact, only 6 percent of all American adults have purchased individual, long-term disability insurance policies, despite the fact that statistics show that 3 of every 10 people between the ages of 35 and 60 will be disabled for more than 90 days. Disability insurance, consequently, should be at the top of your insurance list—especially since your chance of suffering serious disability is greater than the chance of dying prematurely. Just locate your age in the chart below, and play the odds.

CHANCES OF DISABILITY *VS.* DEATH

If you are age . . .		the chances of disability of 90 days or longer are . . .		times greater than the chances that you will die within a year.
	22		7½	
	32		6½	
	37		5½	
	42		4	
	47		3½	
	52		2½	
	62		2	

CHANCES YOU WILL BECOME DISABLED BEFORE AGE 65

Current age	Disabled at least 6 months	Disabled at least 1 year	Disabled at least 2 years	Disabled at least 5 years
22	34%	27%	22%	15%
30	33%	26%	22%	15%
35	33%	26%	21%	15%
40	32%	25%	21%	15%
45	30%	24%	20%	14%
50	28%	23%	19%	14%

With statistics such as these, why is disability insurance so unpopular? The reason: People expect that Social Security and group plan benefits will take care of this need. Wrong!

An insight: Most of you do not know that Social Security pays benefits *only* when a disability is expected to last for a least one year or result in death. Even then, there is a six-month waiting period, and you must be unable to perform *any* kind of work. And group disability insurance coverage usually offers only very short-term protection. Clearly there is a gap in coverage.

Adequate disability protection is vital in every financial plan. A good rule of thumb is to purchase enough insurance to provide 75 percent of your current after-tax income, however long the disability. But in contrast to life insurance, there is a limit to how much (disability) coverage you can collect. Generally, individual policies limit you to benefits equal to 60 to 70 percent of monthly income. Coordination of benefits between group or other individual policies can provide the necessary coverage. However, since insurance companies tell each other everything, there is little chance coverage can be more than 100 percent of your take-home pay. If you have a group policy, it is critical to check its limits on total coverage. You want to make sure you have the right amount.

You also want to make sure you have the right type of policy, so I will further point out four of the primary questions you must ask when analyzing and comparing disability policies.

Question 1: How does the policy define "disability"? If you become disabled and are unable to do much more than eat and watch television, almost any disability policy will pay off. But what if you are able to work at *some* job, even if it's not the one for which you are specially suited or trained? As a rule of thumb, the more specialized your occupation is, the greater the need for a longer period of "own occupation" definition. Under this definition, you can collect disability payments if you can't perform your primary duties, even if you are able to do some work.

Question 2: How long will benefits be paid? Many disability policies will not pay benefits beyond the age of 65, although some will pay benefits for life for disabilities caused by illness (but not by accident). If you will need total coverage beyond the age of 65, look for a policy that pays until the age of 70, even though such policies are more expensive.

Question 3: What is the elimination period? The elimination period is simply the waiting period after you are disabled and before benefits begin. It's possible to have first-day coverage or to select a waiting period of 180 days or more.

Naturally, the shorter the elimination period, the more costly the premium. A policy with a 90-day elimination period costs about 20 percent less than one with a 30-day period. Go out to 180 days, and save about another 15 percent. In my opinion the ideal is a 90-day elimination period, for you should be able to cover that three-month waiting period with your savings.

You should check to see when the elimination period begins. Is it from the date of disability or from the date of diagnosis? Date of disability is the most common, but in my opinion date of diagnosis is preferable. For example, if your bad back was diagnosed three years ago but you are only now losing income because of the condition, benefit payments could start immediately under a date of diagnosis policy.

Question 4: Is the policy noncancelable and guaranteed renewable? If it is, the policy can never be canceled—no matter how bad your health, and the premium rate remains the same for the life of the policy. While policies with such safeguards are more expensive than those in which the insurer reserves the right to refuse renewal, this extra cost is generally worth it.

Many of you will find that you're already covered—often more than once—by workmen's compensation, a group plan, an individual supplemental plan or even an auto or liability policy. Others, however, may find disability insurance hard to come by or terribly expensive—government workers and entertainers, for example. If that's true for you, it is very important to examine your disability income needs immediately and seriously consider purchasing a policy (unless you have enough savings and investments to see you through a disaster). And if you don't have the time or inclination, consult an insurance agent or a financial planner, because you'll also discover that there's an array of unique new disability insurance products available.

One is the universal disability policy. This new product mirrors the features of universal life policies. Premium options include the choice of annual renewable term insurance, a vanishing premium structure, a level-premium arrangement or a single-premium contract. With this policy you may make unscheduled payments and may, under some circumstances, skip premium payments without having the policy lapse. It even has a surrender cash value.

Who should buy a universal disability policy? Professionals, entrepreneurs or others whose income fluctuates from year to year. They can prepay premiums in a good year and skip payments in a bad year. In fact, if the policy holder stops paying the premium, the policy continues in force as long as the surrender value is sufficient to cover the costs of insurance charges. Innovations such as this make financial planning both very exciting and very rewarding.

Individual Health Insurance Policies

As with every type of insurance, you must plan for peril protection *before* the peril strikes. I'm sure you've heard the cliché "What is money when you haven't got your health?" Well, I have an expression of my own: "Where does your money go when you haven't got your health insurance?" Even though you may rarely be sick, health insurance is a must.

Medical expenses for severe or catastrophic illness obviously strain savings, especially those designated for retirement. Multimillionaires presumably can afford not to have health insurance. Poor people are covered by Medicaid, but everyone in between must have health insurance. The cost of treating a major, long-term illness can easily run over a hundred thousand dollars. And more people than ever before are surviving long enough to enter old age when catastrophic illnesses become more commonplace.

Health insurance is not something you can forget about just because you're covered by an employee health plan. Those programs may not cover all family members, all illnesses or all individual needs, and you may want to consider buying additional coverage for medical, hospital and surgical expenses. You'll want to shop for health insurance in the same way you would life and disability insurance—with caution. The most important eventualities to insure for are major health illnesses, not the routine expenses of physical checkups and dental examinations, which can be met from current income.

Alternative Health Plans

How do you know *which* health plan will protect you from financial disaster if you're ill or have an accident? For that matter, do you even know what they all are? In the beginning there were nice little private insurance policies and Blue Cross/Blue Shield. Maternity coverage was your greatest concern. But today the numbers and types of health plans have grown to the point where you could end up in a hospital with an anxiety attack. (Sorry, not covered.)

With policy costs at stratospheric levels, usually the first question you want answered is "What is the least expensive route?" The answer is via your job, where one of the benefits will probably be a group health policy. A good group plan will cover at least 80 percent of the cost of doctor visits, as well as full coverage for a semiprivate hospital room, fair compensation for surgical procedures and emergency room care, and maternity benefits.

Many large companies offer their employees a choice of plans (most of which are also available to individual subscribers). They include health maintenance organizations (HMOs), which are medical supermarkets offering every conceivable type of medical service for one flat annual membership fee. The drawback is that you must choose a doctor who is on the HMO staff and you may see a different one each time you visit. The attraction is that you pay not a penny above the cost of membership, no matter how complicated an illness nor how long its duration with only a few exclusions—usually for mental illness.

Preferred provider organizations (PPOs) are group medical practices that allow you to select a physician from their list of members and a hospital affiliated with their doctor. They will pay all reasonable charges. Should you choose to go to a doctor or a hospital not on the list, the PPO will still reimburse you, but not for the full cost.

You could also choose a private health insurance plan. If you are not insured on the job and prefer not to be locked into an HMO or feel that PPO coverage is not to your advantage, then you'll want to investigate the earlier mentioned private plans that are offered by many major-name insurance companies.

Major Medical Plans

Most Americans, about 160 million, have coverage for catastrophic illness in so-called "major medical plans." This type of insurance covers expenditures on nearly all types of medical care and equipment. But rather than having a schedule of limits for each expense, major medical plans cover a fixed percentage of all expenses. It is a form of protection against large medical bills not covered by the usual type of hospital and surgical plans. But in order to evaluate properly the quality of a major medical plan, you need to examine a few key areas: co-insurance provisions, deductibles, lifetime payouts or annual reimbursement limits and the schedule of benefits and premiums.

Don't become obsessed with getting a small deductible or a very low stop-loss (which limits your liability to a certain amount each year). You will be out of pocket no more than this predictable amount, but it represents a relatively small expense. Keep your priorities in order. You need insurance for the really *big* hospital bill that can spell financial R-U-I-N: You don't need a policy that covers hangnails.

A money-saving idea: Because most medical expenses are covered up to the policy's limits, I strongly recommend that you take higher deductibles, a high stop-loss, and insure for medical costs totaling at least $500,000.

Again, there are a bewildering variety of medical plans available: basic medical, comprehensive medical, hospital indemnity, and so on. Leave it to the insurance companies to create complicated plans and names that seemingly cover everything. I am convinced that these products are part of a conspiracy to stir up financial anxiety. Try to determine what the policy is really meant to do. Then your individual situation will give you a perfectly adequate sense of what plan is good, or best, for you. If you are planning to have children soon, for instance, make sure you have maternity benefits and don't waste your time worrying about the bubonic plague.

Much of the information about medical plans is difficult to decode, and thus something you are not likely to understand all by yourself. So once again, you should talk to an expert—and be sure to communicate your worst fears. I might add, too, that a good way to uncover typical medical insurance problems is to visit a hospital and ask a benefits person what he or she sees as the most common areas of deficiency. *Then* you can come to an informed final decision.

Nursing-Home Indemnity Insurance

Nearly one out of two people will require professional long-term care in a convalescent home after age 65. Twenty-three percent of those over 85 years of age will utilize some form of long-term nursing care. When coupled with today's longer life spans—meaning, essentially, more years over which to spread retirement assets—it becomes apparent that nobody can ignore nursing-home expenses in their financial planning. Currently, few health insurance policies fully cover this gargantuan expense.

Many senior citizens are under the impression that Medicare pays for nursing-home and other long-term care costs; unfortunately, Medicare pays less than 2 percent of the bill on average. If you are over 65 or otherwise eligible, Medicare will pay for just twenty days of nursing-home care following hospitalization. For days twenty-one through one hundred, Medicare imposes a rather hefty $61.50 deductible per day. After that, you must pay all charges until your liquid assets have been depleted to near-poverty level—not a happy thought. At that point, Medicaid picks up your entire bill. Thank you very much. This situation has appropriately been called "the hidden threat to family assets."

Because long-term care insurance is relatively new, and very different from additional Medicare insurance, it is difficult to generalize about policy features. There are, however, several common threads among the policies now on the market. First, they provide coverage for professional long-term care services for a term longer than a six-month period. Second, rehabilitative goals and service restraints imposed in the Medicare program are not used in defining utilization criteria. In addition, while the majority of policies currently being sold are individual policies, group products will be entering the market as well.

Which private companies offer nursing-home policies? Ætna, Mutual of Omaha, American International Group, Prudential and National Blue Cross. A typical annual premium is $200 for someone in his or her early seventies, but can rise to about $1,500 or $1,600 for someone in his or her eighties selecting about $80 per day of coverage. That's not too bad, for nursing-home charges range from $30 to $120 per day; $65 is the national average. Given time, I'm sure we'll see more of these long-term health-care policies on the market. There is also the possibility that the government will increase its participation in coverage for both catastrophic illness and long-term health care.

Dental Insurance

Dental insurance coverage is generally difficult or expensive to purchase on an individual basis. When it comes as part of an employee group package, the benefit can be very valuable. The plans pay up to certain dollar amounts for routine and preventive dentistry and dentures, crowns and orthodontia. If you are covered by such a plan, enjoy —as much as you can while you're sitting in the hot seat getting drilled. At least, you're not getting fleeced.

Property Insurance

Property insurance is such a large topic it's going to be difficult not to spew out all those details I promised you I would try to avoid. But we might as well get started, because I bet your insurance agent probably hasn't called you to explain them; in fact, he or she probably doesn't call you to explain much of anything.

Homeowners' policies cover two areas of loss: loss due to theft, or damage to the dwelling, other structures and contents; and loss due to liability—that is, injuries suffered by others on your property. Some tenants' policies also cover similar losses. The best kind of policy to have is an "all-risk" policy, which means (for a change) almost exactly what it says. Basically, an all-risk or HO-5 policy extends all-risk coverage to your personal property as well as your home and detached structures. I prefer this type of insurance because the coverage is inclusive rather than exclusive. With an all-risk policy, you won't have to panic when an accident befalls you, because most of the time you'll be covered. However, in return for this all-risk coverage, you may have to pay up to twice as much in premiums as you would for any other policy. In addition, I recommend that you obtain a replacement cost endorsement for the policy. This provision means that the insurer will pay for the full cost of replacing your home, even if the cost is more than the limits of the basic policy.

It's also a good idea to insure the contents of your home for their replacement cost. Most policies pay only actual cash value—the difference between an item's original cost and its depreciation. Your belongings turn to junk—in the opinion of insurance examiners—very quickly, and in the event of a major disaster loss, the difference between the insurance payment and what you *actually* pay to replace your personal property may be huge. A personal property "floater," i.e., coverage that supersedes your policy's lower dollar limits, generally adds 10 to 15 percent to the basic homeowner's premium, and it's well worth the additional change, if that is the charge and you can afford it.

Almost all insurers apply special limits to certain types of property. Coins and currency, for example, are covered only up to a given amount depending upon the policy, and that amount also includes loss of cash on hand. Other kinds of property subject to special limits are your diamonds, furs, gold and silverware, Rolex watches, Hasselblad cameras, precious gems or metals and the like. These specific items can also be covered by a special articles "floater" or endorsement; however, an appraiser has to place a value on the property. Update such an appraisal at least every five years so you won't lose appreciation or lose out to inflation in case of loss.

But here's a surprise. Since inflation rates have come down, a number of these items have actually *decreased* in value since your last appraisal. You may have insured your favorite teddy bear for $500, and have conscientiously paid premiums on that amount. But if Pooh can now be replaced for $300, that's what the insurance company will give you. So you should review all coverage of valuables to take current values into account.

A money-saving idea: Many insurance companies offer a discount, for example, if jewels are ordinarily kept in a safe-deposit box or vault rather than at home. It's called "vault" insurance and is at a very low cost—but what a nuisance to get your tiara out every time you go to the supermarket! Paintings or other works of art displayed at home will cost less to insure if your home has a burglar alarm system. The question I inevitably ask a client is "Are there valuables you possess that, if lost or stolen, you would immediately attempt to replace?" If not, why pay the extra expense of the extra insurance? You'll probably find that a review of your floater policy will reveal numerous items for which you've been needlessly paying premiums.

You should also make a photographic inventory of your home (see

Chapter 14). Take pictures room by room, and then individual snap-shots of high-priced items such as antiques, furs and jewelry. Store this inventory in a safe place away from home—at your office, or in a safe-deposit box with your tiara.

If you can save a meaningful sum in premiums by raising your deductibles to $500 or $1,000, then do so. As you've probably heard, the first dollars of protection are the most expensive; higher deductibles reduce premiums. Besides, the insurance company is likely to drop your account if you put in too many small claims, fearing—and cor-rectly so according to the statistics—that you may soon be due for a *big* claim.

The second purpose of a homeowner's policy is to provide compre-hensive personal liability coverage, which protects you from losses—property damage, bodily injury to others—you are legally obliged to pay because they occurred under certain circumstances at your home (or even away from home). Ask for high limits—$300,000 to $500,000; you never know how high your liability may be. These limits will in effect be increased substantially if they are integrated with the excess liability policy discussed below.

Another message from the "you probably didn't know" department: A homeowner's policy insures the person named, the resident spouse and anyone under age 21 in the care of any person already named. I recommend that both you and your significant other, or others, be identified by name, in order to avoid any ambiguity regarding the definition of "resident spouse."

If you don't own a condominium and never will, skip this para-graph. But if you do, or intend to, read on, for condos can have very confusing insurance terms. Under many condominium deeds—docu-ments more properly called "covenants, conditions and restrictions"—the individual owner owns only air space: the condo's inner walls, built-in appliances, carpeting and cabinetry are jointly owned. In other CC&Rs, however, the individual owns everything beyond the bare walls: paint, wallpaper, appliances and so on. To complicate the picture further, the master policy covering the condo building may insure some jointly owned property, or all of it, and some individual prop-erty. I could go on and on—from loss assessment coverage to deduct-ibles on the master policy—but my point is made; there are major differences between condo policies and homeowner or tenant policies. Ask your insurance agent about your policy's coverage and cross-check that information with your association board.

Automobile Insurance

Next to your home, the second most valuable property you own is probably your car—be it a Rabbit or a Rolls. Again, you want to protect against the really big loss. In most cases, seek the upper insurance limits and the highest deductible. The car owner should pay for the inevitable minor fender-benders and let the insurance company mop up the major messes.

Risk exposure is another issue to consider. In almost every family, in my opinion, very high exposure occurs whenever one of the boys drives the family car. The car's *owner* may have legal liability in the event of an accident, not just the driver. If someone in the other car is injured, he or she can be expected to sue the person with the most assets—and it won't be Junior.

There are two ways to reduce this risk, aside from making the car off-limits to your teen-agers (good luck with *that* one). The first is to raise your liability limits with an excess liability policy discussed below. The second is available only for legally adult children and involves giving the auto to the child, registering it in his or her name and then acquiring a separate insurance policy for the child. Obviously, this will decrease your insurance costs because a family policy with multiple-car discounts is less expensive than separate policies, but . . .

Excess Liability Insurance

This policy is designed to supplement conventional auto liability and homeowner's insurance. It provides additional protection if you are sued for dog bites, slander, bad driving and a raft of other mishaps and misdeeds.

Whether or not this extra coverage makes sense depends on how worried you are about being sued. Don't forget, either, that having a great amount of liability coverage can be an invitation to a lawsuit. I believe, nonetheless, that this type of policy is a "must." Your risk isn't measured by your assets but by the amount of the *potential* claims against you. With personal liability coverage, the insurance company pays the legal bills if you get sued, and the award as well if the plaintiff wins.

Coverage levels start at $1 million and require specific limits in your underlying auto and homeowner policies. If you are liable for damage, then an auto or homeowner's policy will usually pay first; after that, the umbrella policy takes over with coverage available up to $10 million. A $1 million umbrella policy usually runs about $100 to $140 per year, and that makes it probably the best insurance buy around. If you think there is the slightest chance of being involved in a lawsuit (auto liability is probably the biggest worry), don't pass up this kind of insurance. If you *are* sued, and you *aren't* covered, the plaintiff won't be the only one injured.

Recently I was asked by *USA Today* to name my number one investment recommendation for a major lottery winner. I recommended he purchase excess liability insurance. The reason: His first job is to protect the money he just won. He is now a target, and in this litigious society, there will be those who will try to take it away. Before he had money, if he bumped into someone, he might have heard a few heated words; but now the words would be written on a piece of paper called a legal complaint.

Economic Insurance

Personal loss or liability insurance is intended to help you out when you suffer from a well-defined problem—say, an accident or a robbery. But what can you do about a recession? About inflation? A declining dollar? We'll get to more specific advice later (Chapters 10 through 14). Here we're more concerned with theoretical strategies for dealing with economic crises—what I call "economic insurance." Although in most of your investments you'll be looking for potential profits—the accumulation of investment capital—when it comes to risk planning, you're still looking to preserve your capital.

If buying insurance is one of the best ways to prepare for *personal* hard times, diversification of your assets is one of the best ways to prepare for *national* or *global* hard times. The reason for diversification is obvious: You don't want to concentrate all your assets in one area. If you divide your investment assets equally, say, among seven different money instruments, you're not going to take a beating in all of them. Seven such investment groups are: U.S. Treasury bills, bonds, notes or a mutual fund invested in U.S. securities; a professionally managed portfolio or a mutual fund consisting of high-grade common stocks; individual high-grade, short-term or intermediate-term corporate or municipal bonds, or a mutual fund incorporating these investment vehicles; real estate; a tax-deferred annuity; natural resources; and precious metals. Each of these investments hedges against a particular problem, and all but one is high in liquidity—meaning you can get your money out fast, and respond quickly to changes in the economy.

Because life is a risky business, your financial plan should always take that into account. Better, as the old saying goes, to be safe than sorry.

PART TWO

Accumulating for the Present—And the Future

Chapter 6

The Roof Over Your Head— Getting the Most for Your Money

A t one time almost everyone believed that he or she would someday own a home. But despite today's relatively low interest
rates, homeownership has become so expensive that for many it is an
unattainable goal. First, there's the hefty down payment, then closing
costs, attorney fees, moving costs and other costs affiliated with the
purchase, mortgage payments, cost of periodic repairs, maintenance
and upkeep of your property, new furniture and other furnishings,
property taxes, additional insurance requirements—the list goes on and
on. For most people, however, owning their own home is still an
important part of their financial plans: a concrete, wood, stucco or
brick symbol of earning power. A house can be a measure of success,
a permanent, secure center in an everchanging world. And it's all yours
—if you don't count the mortgage or that generous loan from your
parents or in-laws.

Your Home As an Investment

Equally important to many people is the fact that a house can be a good
"investment." But in my view that should normally not be a significant reason for purchasing a home; remember, I called a home a personal asset rather than an investment asset back in Chapter 1. Unless
you *plan* to sell your home without repurchasing another (and perhaps
use the one-time credit against profit)—it is still a personal asset that
happens to have risen in value. And today in such communities as
Houston or Denver where there has been an economic downturn, the

loss of residence value has been just as dramatic. If you look upon your dwelling as just a place to live and nothing more, then it doesn't matter much whether its market value goes up or down. As long as it serves your family needs, what should you care about market values? However, as soon as you begin to regard that home as an investment, too —a nest egg for retirement—then it's time to reconsider, among other things, whether you can "afford" to live there any longer.

Perhaps you are asking why you should be concerned or change your plans, just because your home increases in value. The answer is that now we are talking investments rather than places to live. And since a home can plummet in value as well as appreciate sharply, there is a danger that a serious drop in real estate values would wipe out the bulk of your estate. How about taking out some of the equity in a home by borrowing against it and using the proceeds for other investments? That only extends your risk further. If the value of your home then collapsed, you might be stuck with new debt and an asset that would no longer cover it.

Though in some areas of the country it seems that the price of homes will continue to rise forever, homeownership is never a "sure thing" investment. Nonetheless, a wise home purchase can still be an excellent "noninvestment investment." You won't find many investments that are both utilitarian and relatively financially sound, and the combination of these elements continues to make home buying a very attractive proposition.

Your Home As a (Tax) Shelter

The interest paid on your mortgage and property tax payments are tax deductible. Big deal. A married couple might be able to deduct as much as 33 percent of those payments from their taxable income. But that doesn't lower their expenses; only 33 cents of each dollar is deductible, but 67 cents is *not*. And the deductible portion, of course, still must be paid up front. You'll have to come up with *all* the money every month.

One of the greatest fantasies I know is the belief that buying a house is a good tax shelter. A client of mine who fell for this ridiculous line had gotten in the soup so deep that when I met him he was considering a fifth mortgage just to "keep afloat." He had forgotten about the associated costs of owning a home, like decorating, gardening, furnishing and so on. Yes, he had plenty of tax write-offs, but at what price! A house is *not* a tax shelter, particularly when Uncle Sam is paying a lot less freight than you are. Homeownership does not give you much of a deduction, nor does it provide any depreciation or tax deferral. Consequently, the first things to think about when considering buying a house are *why* you want it and *whether* you can afford it—all of it.

Buying *vs.* Renting

Recently I was on a radio show where the caller asked if he should own or rent. After learning more about the caller's circumstances, my answer was that he should probably rent. Oops! The phone lines were suddenly jammed. I obviously had hit upon a very sensitive and controversial issue. But that was before tax reform.

Thanks to tax reform, homeownership has become more valuable than ever. In fact, federal tax reform widened the economic gap between Americans who rent and Americans who own their homes, for it created an unequal tax situation. Under the pre-reform tax code, an individual or a couple could expect to borrow money for their child's college education and receive a direct federal tax subsidy. The interest payment could be deducted every April 15. Now if that couple or single parent rents, tax reform has taken away most of that subsidy. If the child isn't ready for college for a few more years, all consumer-interest deductions for any purpose will be fully phased out.

Under the pre–tax-reform tax code, renters could also deduct all the interest on their revolving charge accounts—the ones that enabled them to buy many of their furnishings and appliances. Now a renter's 14 to 21 percent interest charge on so-called "consumer loans" is no longer fully deductible. Consumer-loan interest is not deductible for a homeowner either, but he *can* deduct the 8 to 10 percent interest he pays on a revolving home equity loan.

Let's compare two families in exactly the same economic circumstances except that one rents and the other purchased a home six years ago by obtaining a Federal Housing Authority low-down-payment loan. Under tax reform, the family with property ownership will now clearly be able to move ahead financially by refinancing their home. The interest payments on the loan are tax deductible and they can use the money to help with their child's college education costs, purchase a new car, pay their most recent medical expenses, purchase some new appliances, go on a Caribbean vacation and even pay for consultations with their financial advisor to find out how to do all this tax-deductible stuff. The family that rents is clearly behind the financial eight ball, for any money they borrow will be at a higher rate of interest and their consumer interest deductions are being phased out. Furthermore, because their landlord loses important tax benefits under the new law, they may see their rent increased. And it doesn't end there. The family with the personal residence can also sell and replace it with a more expensive home within two years either before or after sale, and not pay any income tax on profit. Rather, the tax is deferred until they eventually sell for the final time. But the best is yet to come. For if the homeowner couple is past their fifty-fifth birthday when their personal residence is sold, they can pocket, free of income tax, as much as $125,000 of their profit from the sale.

There's no question about it, homeownership has it all over renting, with one or two exceptions: Buying does take away liquidity because a house is sometimes hard to sell. Furthermore, there is certainly no assurance that if you needed to sell your home you would even get what you paid. My cousin recently moved from Los Angeles to Dallas, made a profit selling his home in Los Angeles, but now is being transferred from the Dallas area and has found he can't sell that home for anywhere near his purchase price. As a matter of fact, in the last six months, there has only been one looker.

Then there is the fact that nationally the annual appreciation for the median-priced house has only been at the 3 to 4 percent rate over the last several years. If a home fell into that category, one would also have to calculate the "opportunity cost." That is, if the home buyer had instead rented, how much more money could he or she now have if the down payment and mortgage expenses were invested in, say, a quality growth mutual fund during the same period of time? Over the last five or six years, a lot of opportunity would have been missed.

Renters also have the additional advantage of not having to pay for maintenance or upkeep, be their own janitor or hire an electrician or plumber if something goes wrong. Not to mention all the other expenses related to being a homeowner—from the down payment to the monthly bill for utilities. In short, if a person or couple wants to buy before they're financially ready, they could end up cash-poor and unable to afford those things once taken for granted.

The answer to whether you should buy or rent should really be determined by what you value, as well as by the economics of your situation. Don't let the marketplace, family or friends, or even the media decide for you. If your'e a salesperson frequently on the road, you may feel it's not worth investing in a house. It's O.K. If you expect to be transferred by your company every two or three years, it just may not make sense to buy and furnish a house—unless your employer will help you sell the house, move and buy a new house. If renting month to month, or even leasing by the year, makes you fearful of eviction or of becoming a wandering minstrel, you may want to start an investment program targeted toward a house down payment. If living in the "right" house in the "right" neighborhood is important to either your ego, career or both, that can be a legitimate consideration. Or if you just feel good about the idea of owning your own home, though you can't explain why, then that too is the right decision —for you. Do I own my home? Yes, I do.

Successful Refinancing

"Refinance your mortgage *now,* while interest rates are low!" The message is seductive, yet it has to make practical as well as economic sense to refinance your present mortgage, for there are other alternatives.

But first I don't want you to be confused between refinancing your present mortgage and a home equity loan. Refinancing a mortgage involves paying off the old mortgage early and taking out a new one. You can refinance with the original lender or go to a new one, but in most cases you will save a lot in closing costs by staying with your current lender. A home equity loan, on the other hand, is essentially a dressed-up second mortgage that taps into the equity in your home. Home equity loans are getting all the attention these days, but in my opinion, they can also be dangerous.

Why would you want to refinance? To get a lower interest rate on your mortgage is only one answer. Yes, a lower interest rate on the same loan amount for the same terms will lower your monthly payments. But many people who refinance choose different terms. They may refinance a greater amount of debt, thus also tapping equity. Or they may refinance with short-term loans that have monthly payments about equal to the old loan, but with a larger amount going to pay off the principal. With a short-term loan, it's not uncommon to build equity at ten times your old pace.

Are you looking for a low-interest loan? It's not just the rate that counts: you have to pay close attention to the points—up-front fees paid at the time of your loan closing. Each point is 1 percent of the loan. The lower the interest rate, the more points you're likely to be charged. When do points cancel the savings from a low interest rate?

Rule of thumb: If you plan to keep the mortgage eight years, each point costs the same as adding one-fourth of 1 percentage point to your loan rate. Example: 7.5 percent interest plus six points is equal to paying 9 percent over the life of the loan. That beats a 9.5 percent rate with two points, which translates into 10 percent. If you plan to hold the mortgage for thirty years, a point is about an added one-eighth of a percentage point.

Most lenders will say refinancing makes sense when you plan to keep your home for at least three or more years and the new rate is at least 2 percentage points lower than the rate you now have. Their formula to show a borrower how soon he or she can recapture the closing costs on a refinanced loan is to divide the total closing costs (including the points paid) by the monthly difference in payments. According to the formula, if your closing costs are, say, $4,000 and the new mortgage is $200 a month less than the old one, the new loan will pay for itself in twenty months.

But the formula doesn't account for such factors as the other fees lenders may charge, including possible penalties for prepayment of the loan, which can more than double costs. The length of time you plan to live in your home and your tax bracket must also be taken into consideration. I would suggest that the 2 percentage point rule of thumb be used to trigger your curiosity, but that's all. Do the arithmetic. In some instances, you will find those 2 percentage points are far more than are needed. If one percentage point would make economic sense, then two points demands a change. In other instances, far more than 2 percentage points would be required to make refinancing your mortgage an economic advantage.

In some scenarios, three-fourths of a percentage point difference can be enough to justify refinancing if you are going to live in the house five to ten years. This example assumes an owner is in the 28 percent tax bracket, plans to live in the house for at least another eight years and pays closing costs of 2½ percentage points, or 2½ percent of the face amount of a 30-year mortgage, plus a $200 application fee. If the length of stay is expected to be (and in fact is) in the fifteen-year range, and the same 2½ points were charged for a new mortgage, as little as 0.4 percent is all that is needed on your mortgage rate to justify your making a change. But before you become too excited, bear in mind that the average person in the United States moves every five years.

You should also keep in mind that refinancing a mortgage is, in most cases, like taking out an entirely new loan. You must go through the same time-consuming process and you're in for the same expenses, including: application fee, appraisal fee, credit report and title search fees, attorney's fee (yours and the bank's) and various recording, filing and document preparation fees. Although some of the fees can be avoided if you refinance your mortgage with the same lender, all must be considered when calculating the value of refinancing. I was able to show a couple an instance where the rule of thumb said the new mortgage would pay for itself in about twenty-eight months. But after including all the additional costs and taking into account the amount of time they might be keeping their home, the real break-even point for that couple (in the 28 percent tax bracket) was actually closer to forty-two months.

You cannot possibly appreciate the ecstasy of the value of refinancing unless you have also gone through the agony of refinancing. To avoid as much of that agony as possible (and this applies to the mortgage needed to purchase a new home, as well as to refinancing a mortgage), shop around for the best rate and terms. Theoretically at least, banks *want* your business and there are often differences in rates of interest, closing costs, points, application fees, prepayment penalties and the like. Whatever lender you choose, find out when the rate on your refinancing loan will be set. At application? At closing? Sometime in between? Or do you have a choice of the best rate between application and closing? Get a mortgage commitment—a promise of how long the lending institution will offer you the proposed rate—in writing. Also find out what circumstances, such as a dispute over the appraised value of the house, might allow the lender to back out.

Let the loan officer *know* you plan to keep track of your application as it is processed. Find out when the paperwork is due at the loan office, especially the appraisal and credit agency reports. Then call on the expected arrival dates to check the progress of the loan. Keep in mind that the "squeaky wheel gets oiled," but don't pester the lender with daily calls. The lending process, for reasons best known to the lenders, always takes time. So hang in there. And by the way, for an extra fee, some lending institutions will sell you rate "insurance"—you get the lowest rate even if it's gone up by the time your loan closes.

Successful Nonrefinancing

Although it's not generally known, there are other ways to cut total mortgage interest costs in half without incurring the heavy expense and the joy of the refinancing process. Unless you have a seriously out-of-date mortgage interest rate, such as one in the mid-teens, you may not wish to bother with refinancing, yet wonder about alternatives. Yes, there are some. By doubling up on the portion of your monthly mortgage payment that is applied to the loan's principal, you can retire the debt twice as fast and save thousands of dollars in interest charges in the process. Or you can achieve practically the same result by persuading your lender to recast your monthly payment schedule into one that coincides with your weekly or biweekly pay periods.

Both methods work on "accelerated amortization." In other words, you will be building equity at a faster rate than originally scheduled. This concept has made 15-year mortgages very attractive to many buyers of late. And for present homeowners, it's the same concept as if they had originally negotiated a 15-year loan. Because payments are based on a schedule that's twice as long, the debt is retired in half the time, and total payments will be lower.

Whatever the original length of your loan, with double payments to *principal* (as opposed to interest), you will be eliminating every other month's interest payment instead of paying the full rate each month—and that can amount to a huge savings. By making 52 or 26 mortgage payments a year instead of just 12, you will be increasing the compounding effect in your favor while reducing the loan balance more quickly.

Naturally you ask, "How can I afford to make twenty-six or fifty-two annual payments?" Answer: That's the beauty of the double payment method. I'm not suggesting you double up on your full payment, only the principal portion. On a 30-year mortgage, it often isn't until after your twentieth year that your payment to principal exceeds your interest charge. For most of you, the interest portion of your payment *greatly* exceeds the principal portion. But if along with your next payment, you also paid the amount due on the principal the following month, you would shorten your loan by one month, and eliminate that month's interest charge. In the process, the normal third monthly payment becomes the second monthly payment. And if you add the principal amount due in the fourth month, you will eliminate that month's interest payment.

Continuing the process for six months, you will have reduced the mortgage to the same balance you would have had with twelve regular payments. And you will save the interest payment due with every other payment that year. Applying this prepayment method over the thirty-year term of the mortgage, you will pay off your loan in fifteen years and will have saved a tremendous amount of interest expense.

Of course, any prepayment schedule will become more burdensome over time as the amount applied to principal increases. But you don't have to double up every month, as long as you don't skip a month's payment—prepaying a month's interest does not eliminate the need to make at least the normal payment next month. The month prepayment eliminates is at the end of the loan term. Since you cannot skip a monthly payment, you won't realize your savings, therefore, until the loan is paid off and you don't have to make any more payments. But for every month you prepay on the principal, you shorten the life of the loan by a month and save that month's interest charge.

Lump-Sum Pay Down, or Paying Off Your Existing Mortgage

I often get one of two pay-on-mortgage questions. One is "I have enough extra money to significantly reduce what I owe on my home. Should I pay down my mortgage?" The other question is "I have enough money in my money market fund to completely pay off my existing mortgage. Should I?"

For most people, the choice again hinges more on your individual cash needs, family plans and, as much as anything, your comfort level. If you just apply a lump sum to pay down your mortgage, all you do is reduce the outstanding balance. Though that can be very significant in the long term, you won't feel any immediate benefit, for your monthly payment will stay the same as before, unless your bank or lending institution will reamortize the new reduced mortgage balance so that your monthly payments will be lower than before. "Amortization" should not be offensive money lingo. It is only the reduction of debt by regular payments of interest and principal sufficient to pay off the loan by maturity.

If you used that lump-sum amount to pay down your mortgage balance, you would be building the equity in your home, but if you ever needed that money in a hurry, you would probably find that it is a lot easier putting money in your home than taking money out—and more expensive, too. It would be much easier and less expensive to liquidate, for example, a Treasury bond or maybe even a CD than to get and have to pay for a home equity loan. So under normal conditions, even if your mortgage rate of interest is somewhat higher than what you could receive from alternative interest sources, it might still be prudent not to pay down your mortgage. If, on the other hand, you have a mortgage rate that is lower than prevailing alternative interest rates (and I'm including municipal bonds as an alternative investment source), then I suggest you keep your money in the alternative investment. The extra interest income could then be used to reduce your principal payments and your lump-sum amount would still be intact for a profitable investment opportunity or an emergency.

But there are considerations other than money. A very major one is called the "sleep-tight" factor. Some years ago it was fashionable to have a "burn-the-mortgage" party, and because the Depression was fresh in the minds of so many people, a home that was free and clear from debt meant security. The bank could no longer take away your home for nonpayment, even if you were out of a job. More recently, due to high inflation, it became fashionable to take out the maximum mortgage when purchasing a home, a means of enhancing your return without increasing your investment. But inflation has subsided, and with it, people have again discovered the comfort of a paid-for home in such a volatile economic society. Knowing your home is free and clear of debt transcends financial considerations. When you're entering your retirement years, you probably don't want a house payment. You want simplicity and you want predictability—both very legitimate financial goals. So if you have enough money to pay off your mortgage and still have liquid assets available for emergencies, etc., then yes, yes and yes, I certainly recommend you pay off that loan. And when you do, I'll be happy to stop by to light the match.

Mortgages

If you need money to buy a house, or wish to refinance the loan you already have, welcome to the wonderful world of mortgages. Mortgage departments used to be austere, and borrowing money was a fairly predictable event. They had one product to sell, and it was a little like Henry Ford's Model T—it came in three colors, black, black and black. The bankers even attempted to speak in a language we all understood. Yes, you could walk into a bank, say you wanted a loan, prove you didn't need it and before too long you'd get one.

Now, however, things are completely different, except for the fact that you still have to prove you don't really need the money. Mortgage departments have myriad mortgage products from which to choose, bankers speak in a language known only to themselves and the once-standard or conventional home mortgage now comes in almost as many varieties as there are colors of automobile paint. Sorting through them is a superhuman task. Yet if you can grasp a basic understanding of the various mortgages, you'll be better able to ask questions. And the better the questions you ask, the better you'll be able to apply this important financing tool—to achieve *your* goals, not someone else's.

Home Equity Loans

As I earlier stated, a home equity loan is essentially a dressed-up second mortgage, but it should not be confused with the more conventional second mortgage in which a (relatively large) fixed amount of money is borrowed. Both types can be used to pay off debt, but realistically most people aren't going to use second mortgages because they don't want or need to borrow $100,000 or $150,000 for reasonably small purchases such as a car, vacations, furniture or other "big-ticket" items.

The home equity loan, on the other hand, can be quite appealing for those very reasons. Rather than a lump sum, it's a line of equity credit for you to use at your discretion. So instead of financing the car (and not being able to deduct the entire amount of interest you would pay on the loan), you borrow against the equity of your house and pay cash for the automobile. At tax time, you can deduct the interest you had to pay to the lender because the loan is secured by your home.

Unless Congress changes the law (again), the mortgage interest you paid on your primary and second home (if it is for your personal use) is still fully tax deductible. And Congress makes no distinction between the types of mortgages. Other financing methods, such as credit cards, are now only partially deductible; and even that partial deduction is due to be phased out. You can borrow no more than what your house first cost, plus the price of improvements you have made to it, but because of its lower use amounts and flexibility, using a home equity loan for consumer-type purchases can make a great deal of sense. In fact, Congress has gone so far as to say that if you require additional money for medical bills, educational expenses (see Chapter 7), more home improvements or even for your business, you can borrow more than your original home cost plus improvements.

Remember the great hoopla over the 18 to 21 percent credit-card interest rates and Congress's inability to lower those rates? Well, another advantage of the home equity loan is that the rate of interest you pay is well below what you would pay on other types of consumer debt. If you own your own home, the market place and tax reform did the job, in effect, of cutting interest rates to around 10 percent (typically from 1¼ to 2¾ percent over a bank's prime lending rate).

So just what *is* a home? According to the IRS, it can be, among others, a "mobile home, boat or similar property"—as long as it has sleeping space and toilet and cooking facilities. It can be a condo, apartment in a cooperative and more. One can only imagine what the definition of a home will do to nautical designs: a sleeping bag, a Bunsen burner and a kitty litter box in a rowboat?

But you could unwittingly place your home (or your rowboat) in danger if you don't know how to manage credit. An equity loan still means debt. And debt means obligation, with principal and interest that must be paid back on schedule. Will you have the resources to repay your home equity loan in the fifth or tenth year? What if your loan was tied to a rising variable interest rate (see below), creating payment difficulties? What if under "normal" circumstances your monthly cash flow isn't sufficient to cover fixed expenses and the additional outlays of the home equity loan? You may be in the poorhouse (or no house) before you know it.

DOLLAR$ AND NONENE®

"Whatever you do, keep up with your
mortgage payments."

Then there is the person who uses the credit line for small purchases, eventually building up a large, outstanding balance. He may run into trouble later with no credit left to cover the cost of college or to make a major purchase, such as a car or a home improvement. I also have fears that people will use home equity loans for debt consolidation and then turn around and run up additional debts that are more than they can repay.

I guess the problem with equity lines is that, like consumer credit cards, they may be too easy to establish and much too easy to use. Once established, all you have to do is write a check or use a credit card. The danger could be analogous to giving a youngster a $100 bill and sending him or her to a candy store. The result could be a giant-sized tummyache. With a typical mortgage, the lender requires the borrower to have a specific purpose in mind for the money, and the process of application and approval is arduous enough to remind the borrower of the importance of such a step. The ability to access your home equity with a checkbook or credit card makes it so easy to grant yourself a loan that a number of people are, unfortunately, going to find themselves in dire straits. A new self-help organization may even have to be created for those people, and I have the perfect name—Equiholics Anonymous.

Fixed Mortgage vs. *Adjustable-Rate Mortgage*

With the resurgence of home buying and refinancing due to relatively lower interest rates, homeowners and buyers now have primarily two mortgage choices: a traditional mortgage with a fixed payment (which until recently was chosen by more than 75 percent of today's borrowers) or one of the more controversial adjustable-rate loans.

Adjustable-rate mortgages, or ARMs, are probably the best known of the nonfixed types of mortgages, though there are several mutant ARMs, the latest of which are "convertible" home mortgages. I will cover only the most common. With the basic ARM, the interest rate you pay varies according to an accepted economic index, such as Treasury bill interest rates, money market rates, cost-of-fund rates, the Federal Home Loan Bank Board's average of mortgage rates, the FHLBB National Average Mortgage Contract Rate, or the FHLBB Monthly Median Cost of Funds Ratio.

Most banks link mortgage rates to the Treasury bill index, which is not to be confused with Treasury auction rates commonly reported in the financial pages of newspapers. The index is based on a statistical model devised by the government to estimate what those securities would sell for on a regular weekly basis. Thrifts, or home savings and loan institutions, on the other hand, link their mortgage rates to a "cost of funds," which is the weighted average cost of its deposits and borrowings. Historically, the latter group's cost of funds has been less volatile than Treasury bill indices, but that index is more sure to rise over the long term as savings and loans periodically raise the rate of interest paid to depositors.

Depending on how the ARM is set up, your monthly payments may change in many ways. They may move up and down in tandem with the index rate or remain the same, with the length of the loan increasing or decreasing. Lenders have a lot of latitude in floating-rate mortgages, compared to the fixed-rate mortgage, and that means potential ARM borrowers must be alert to the constantly changing terms of the loan. But the term that concerns most people is the main drawback to an adjustable-rate mortgage: the possibility of a future significant rise in monthly payments. Many lenders limit how much your rate can go up —a ceiling of 5 percentage points over the life of the loan is common —but there is still a potential for steep monthly payment increases.

Aside from a lifetime cap on interest-rate increases, many adjustable-rate mortgages also have limits on how much the rate can rise each year, although that could still mean sharp increases in your monthly payments. But lenders supposedly take this factor into consideration when determining whether or not you qualify for the loan. Since lenders base their loan decisions on whether a borrower can make the monthly payments, they often figure that no more than about 36 percent of a borrower's gross income should go for debt of all kinds, including mortgage payments. But a problem can arise because the initial interest rate on an ARM is lower than on a fixed-rate mortgage. Therefore, the beginning payments on a house with an ARM would be lower than on the same house with a fixed-rate loan, which means that borrowers might qualify if they took an ARM, but might not if they chose a fixed-rate loan. If the initial rate on an adjustable-rate mortgage sounds too good to be true, it probably is. The idea is to help new home buyers qualify for a loan they otherwise couldn't get. But that also poses a problem. What happens when the rate jumps after the introductory period is over? Will new homeowners be forced out because they can't make higher payments? These questions are still a matter of debate.

Then there are the "other" problems with some adjustables, which haven't been worked out. The ARM-servicing software is often so sophisticated for the institutions selling them that no one quite knows what is going to happen. Lenders have been known to calculate adjustments using the wrong index, the wrong index date, the wrong interest rate equation, unfair rate rounding and the wrong payment amount at the right rate. In some cases they've also failed to provide adequate notice of a forthcoming change. From all appearances, some lenders are paying the price for freewheeling experimentation with ARMs over the past several years, which means that you may be, too.

In weighing the advantages and disadvantages of fixed-rate *vs.* adjustable-rate loans, you might want to start with a little self-analysis. How comfortable are you with risk? If you break out into a cold sweat at the thought of putting a dollar into a slot machine, it is probably safe to assume you dislike risk. You might be more comfortable with a fixed-rate loan, where you have a known monthly payment and you can make your plans accordingly. Then there are the tangible considerations beyond what you feel. If your current financial status tells you that you do not have enough money as a down payment for a fixed-rate loan (lenders usually only ask for 10 percent down on an adjustable-rate rather than the 20 percent required on a fixed-rate), using an ARM could make the difference between buying a particular house or not. Another advantage of the ARMs is that they are assumable, while fixed-rate loans are not. That makes selling a home with a fixed-rate mortgage more difficult, particularly if interest rates change dramatically. Also, many homeowners plan on staying in their homes for only a few years before selling. If that takes place, even if the interest rate they pay for an ARM is lower for only one year, there is a high likelihood that the initial lower payments would be worth it.

As for future circumstances, if you work in a field where wages generally keep pace with inflation, you don't have to worry as much about potential rises in interest rates with an adjustable mortgage. On the other hand, if you're in middle management working for a large company and don't know what your future pay increases might be, then a fixed-rate mortgage might be best for you.

Making a choice involving trade-offs isn't easy, so I'll make it easier for you. If you are considering an ARM, bear in mind these four principles: the lower the maximum and minimum caps are the better; a cap on the interest rate (rather than on payments) will avoid the problem of negative amortization; the less frequently the interest rate is adjusted the better; and finally, the more stable the chosen index is, the less subject to fluctuations, the better.

If you're considering a fixed-rate mortgage, bear in mind your "need," whether real or psychological, to have a known *vs.* an unknown, how likely you are to move in the next several years and your present financial circumstances (what you can afford).

Though there is no magic answer, your choice, as usual, comes down to a variety of factors, all dealing with you—but that's the way it should be.

The 15-Year vs. the 30-Year Mortgage

The 15-year mortgage is proving to be the preferred form of indebtedness for many home buyers as well as people who are refinancing. Undoubtedly the idea of saving thousands of dollars in interest over the life of the loan has something to do with its appeal. But I also believe there are two other major contributing reasons. The first relates to what I have already mentioned: because of uncertainty about your job, uncertainty about the economy and uncertainty about alternative places to put your money, the 15-year mortgage seems to make sense —especially since your monthly payments are not much greater (perhaps 20 percent) than a 30-year mortgage payment. The second reason, which has not received much if any attention, is in my opinion the primary factor in the popularity of the 15-year mortgage. It is the idea of forced savings combined with a goal, where you can "see" the reward while you are still alive.

Since the idea of missing a mortgage payment is intolerable for most of us, the 15-year mortgage provides us both the method and the satisfaction that a check we would have to write anyway is in this instance creating a tangible asset that in only fifteen years will be all ours. Don't underestimate the importance of the fact that we can relate to a 15-year time period (see Chapter 9), whereas thirty years is too far away, too abstract. To have a home that will be paid for in thirty years, when you might be grandparents, even great-grandparents for some of us, provides very little light at the end of the tunnel. And to make payments on a 30-year loan, knowing that only some infinitesimal part of that first check went toward principal, makes you feel as though all you are doing is paying for the privilege of living in someone else's home. However, the knowledge that perhaps 20 percent of your first payment is actually going to pay down the debt, and that in *only* fifteen years your home will be fully paid for, provides great psychological comfort.

As for the forced savings idea, my experience has shown me that most people would prefer to have their money systematically "disappear." Provide them with a methodology to get their money out of their sight, otherwise it will be spent. Some of you may remember the "Christmas savings club" of a few years back. You were given numbered bank deposit slips that corresponded to the number of weeks until Christmas (one through fifty-two), and each week millions of people would deposit a set amount of money, typically $5, $10 or $25. Then shortly before Christmas the bank would send you a check for the amount you had religiously saved, plus a small amount of interest, to enable you to purchase Christmas presents without having to go into debt. Convenience, regularity and predictable results made the Christmas savings club and similar savings club accounts tremendously popular. Ironically, that popularity was also the cause of their demise —they created administrative nightmares for the banks. Each week there were so many people putting aside their small dollar amounts that it actually started to cost the banks money. Though the payments on a 15-year mortgage obviously require people systematically to put aside a great deal more than the Christmas savings club account, in the minds of the borrower the convenience and the satisfaction of setting aside value are much the same.

Though I strongly favor the 15-year mortgage (yes, I have one of those too), I want you to know, or at least be aware, that the 15-year mortgage isn't appropriate for everyone. If, for example, you wanted to sell your home prematurely, a 15-year mortgage might make the equity so high that it would be very difficult to find a buyer to assume the mortgage. Such a problem would compound itself during high inflationary periods where the house is increasing in value and interest rates are also rising. Also, if you had taken a 30-year mortgage and invested the payment difference between the two mortgages, in the event of a major investment opportunity or an emergency, you could (as earlier described) have easy access to your funds without additional expense.

Another argument in favor of the 30-year mortgage is that this may be a time when your children are in college, and expenses could be unusually high. The monthly difference in mortgage payments might be put to better immediate use offsetting those unusually high expenses. And finally there is always the tax-deduction argument. All the additional interest expense with the 30-year mortgage is deductible. But let me remind you again not to let the tax tail wag the dog.

Real Estate Mortgage Investment Conduits (REMICs)

Now that you're beginning to understand ARMs, up pops a new color of paint. This is a mortgage-backed security created by tax reform legislation that could help make even more money available to home buyers. REMIC is the acronym, and they're hot. Though you won't walk into your neighborhood bank or thrift and ask for a REMIC, you should be aware of their existence, for they will probably lower the interest rate you'll be paying on your mortgage. REMICs are a series of securities with varying maturities from a pool of mortgages. By providing more money for the loan institutions, REMICs may help ease the problem of declining homeownership opportunities for middle- and moderate-income families. In addition, thrifts and savings and loans will more likely be able to offer fixed mortgages, as REMICs can reduce their vulnerability to rising interest rates. So next time you hear about a REMIC, your smile will be one of knowledge. And as Francis Bacon once said, "Knowledge is power."

Reverse Mortgages

Among the more innovative lending programs, reverse mortgages presently exist in thirteen states. Under a typical agreement, a homeowner obtains a loan secured by the house. But instead of receiving a lump sum of money, the borrower receives it as a monthly amount for a set number of years, and the loan principal and interest are due at the end of the loan period, when it might make sense to sell the house. This arrangement is typically used for people who are retired and have little in the way of assets other than their home. By utilizing the reverse mortgage, they can remain in their home, yet have the funds to live as well. A somewhat similar plan offers the homeowner a sale, then a lease-back arrangement in exchange for a guaranteed lifetime income.

Balloon Mortgages

Among the most controversial of mortgages are the balloon mortgages, similar to the home loans popular in the 1920s, before the ascendance of the fixed-rate mortgage. Many experts say these loans were a primary cause of foreclosures during the Depression.

Monthly payments on a balloon mortgage are set almost exactly as they are for a traditional 25-year or 30-year fixed loan. Balloon mortgages, however, must actually be paid in a much shorter time, usually within three to five years. At the end of the term, the mortgage payment is inflated into an enormous "balloon" and the borrower must either pay off the loan in a lump sum or refinance. A few years ago in California, these loans became so popular that it was said that "half the state will be coming due in five years." As luck would have it, many properties did appreciate and interest rates were lower when the balloons came due. Most borrowers, therefore, were able to refinance their properties favorably.

If, however, a borrower was *not* able to refinance the loan and the loan officer insisted on full payment at the end of the term, he or she will unfortunately have popped your balloon. It's best to stay away from this sort of mortgage if you can help it. Financial planner Venita VanCaspel mentions in one of her books that mortgages with balloon payments have been referred to as "neutron loans" because they leave the building standing but kill the owner.

Balloon mortgages are fine if you can ensure refinancing or manage to sell the house before the lump sum is due. If you can't do that and can't make the final payment, you lose your equity and your house.

Mortgage Buy-Downs

In this arrangement, the builder of a newly constructed home "buys down" the mortgage interest rate for two or three years by paying part of the loan him or herself. After that, the interest rate returns to a predetermined level or to the going market rate. Although the buy-down is strictly short term, many builders and developers believe the device can make a home affordable to financially strapped potential buyers.

Assumable Mortgages

If you're not buying a newly constructed home, you may be able to find an assumable mortgage. You pay the seller the difference between the sales price and the current mortgage, then take over the mortgage payments from the seller. If the seller has owned the house for some time, the interest rate is likely to be quite low, but the equity he or she has built up in the house will be correspondingly high. In order to assume such a mortgage, the lending institution cannot have a prohibition against the assumption of an existing loan, and your down payment will have to match that built-up equity. Fixed-rate mortgages are generally not assumable; ARMs generally are.

If the equity is large, even if the mortgage is assumable, or if you are not happy with the terms of an ARM, you may wish to consider a new mortgage or arrange a loan directly with the former owner. For unless you are trying to pay off your mortgage quickly, it may not be the best use of such a large amount of capital.

When and if you start shopping in the mortgage market, you don't have to be indebted to me for presenting this vast array of mortgage opportunities. The lenders have done that. And it's up to you to choose a mortgage that you and your significant other are comfortable with, which also meets your objectives as closely as you can define them. It may be wise to meet with your financial advisor to consider the alternatives. A loan officer may not always be the best person from whom to seek council. That person may be objective but not be trained to take your entire financial and personal picture into account. Then, too, many such loan agents are on commission basis and volume is important to them. It certainly isn't to you.

Chapter 7

Spell College M-O-N-E-Y— Planning for Expensive Educations

If you have a child bound for college in two to twelve years, funding that education is a task that appears to most families to be a mission impossible. The prospect of having to shell out from $35,000 (for a state college) to $85,000 (for a "name" private college) per child over a period of four years is frightening and frequently threatens the family's financial stability. Today, with more than 60 percent of current high school graduates in college, the affected parents not only strongly concur with that statement, but also add, "There's no other major expense in our lifetime that brings about such anxiety!" Even couples with comfortable six-figure incomes are either currently having great difficulty funding the cost of higher education, or are very concerned about the after-tax cost and cash flow drain when it comes to paying for those college years, particularly when those years immediately follow private and prep school expenses.

Whether you consider yourself reasonably comfortable financially or not, the exorbitant cost of a college education can be a terrible burden. Yet, while most parents agree they have some responsibility for helping their child through college, only about half the respondents in a recent private survey even knew the cost of a college education, and none were saving regularly.

It has often been said that after warmth, love and a stable environment, the greatest thing parents can give their children is a quality education to prepare them for life on their own. And since each person is his or her own best investment asset (see Chapter 9), education is a very wise investment in that asset. To have to deny your children the opportunity of a college education because you can't afford it, or endure a lot of pressure to meet the ongoing expense, can and often does place you and your children at an unfair—and unnecessary—disadvantage.

You, of course, know that education expenses are imminent, and the time to start setting the money aside is *now!* However, it will no longer do to say, "I'll think about it," or "I'm sure I'll be able to handle it when the time comes." If your child is in high school now, do you *really* believe that by 1990 you'll have the necessary (after tax) $35,000 to $85,000 to pay for his or her college education? That time is practically here. If you want to go into deeper economic shock, add an average annual 6 to 10 percent increase (which is greater than the rate of inflation) to those figures, and the number of years before your children will be ready to go to college. A college education of the future may be available only to the very select and very wealthy.

How, then, can you cope? The advice I give to young parents, many of whom are now single parents, is the same advice given to our parents twenty or thirty years ago when four years of college totaled in cost from $5,200 to $9,000. And that was the same advice given to their grandparents thirty years before that, when the golden sheepskin cost $2,500. Start saving early—and early means as soon as your children are born. Through systematically placing money aside each year, you can save yourself the excruciating headache of paying for their college education.

Today's Required Annual Savings for Tomorrow's Cost of College

To update that age-old advice, I have prepared a table (opposite) that will help guide you in terms of how much in annual savings you will have to contribute to achieve your goal. I have assumed the cost of college will have risen by 6 percent per year, a net after-tax return of 7 percent on contributions made until the first year of college, and a 5 percent annual inflation rate. Even if a family can't reach these particular goals, every accumulated dollar will count when the time comes.

As you can see, the parents of a one-year-old future collegian will face higher total costs but have up to more than 6,000 days to set aside money than the parents of an older child. Therefore, worry less about treating each child equally and more about building up the oldest child's account first. Not shown on the table is the consideration that

	STATE UNIVERSITY			PRIVATE COLLEGE		
Child's present age	*Four-year cost*	*Annual amount required[1]*	*Graduated amounts required[2]*	*Four-year cost*	*Annual amount required[1]*	*Graduated amounts required[2]*
1	$92,177	$2,444	$1,708	$223,523	$ 5,928	$ 4,141
10	$54,559	$4,107	$3,426	$132,302	$ 9,959	$ 8,309
15	$40,771	$8,279	$7,715	$ 98,865	$20,077	$18,709
18	$34,232			$ 83,009		

1. At 7% after-tax rate. A level, set aside amount
2. Payments indexed to 5% inflation rate. Lower initial amounts are set aside but increased as income is expected to grow with career advancement or due to inflation.

even a small increase in the rate of investment return can make quite a difference. For example, an annual investment return of 8 percent reduces the annual level, set-aside amount for a one-year-old to $2,189 for a state university and $5,308 for a private college.

Without an understanding of just how much money must actually be set aside, some parents have created their own funding strategies, which may or may not be adequate. For example, they may give their child $100 on his or her first birthday, $200 on the second birthday, etc. Or they may match their child's earnings, which are placed aside for college, or pay their child so much for each A, so much for each B, etc., and place that money aside into a college fund. To determine the strategy that is appropriate for you, you should first determine your attitude about higher education costs. Do you intend to pay for everything yourself, or do you plan to have your son or daughter help out? Nearly 60 percent of the students at private colleges and universities, and about 30 percent of those at public colleges, receive some form of financial assistance. Are you going to count on that assistance, or pray that your child's grandparents will come to the rescue? They may have to.

College Funding Strategies

Perhaps you want, or have to, handle the whole thing yourself. The challenge of creating a college fund has never been easy. But now the challenge of also creating a cost-effective program is even tougher since the tax laws have been revised. In the past, there were at least two primary methods that made the task a little easier. In one, you could give up to $10,000 annually, free of gift tax implications, to each child in a custodial account under the Uniform Gift to Minors Act (UGMA). The asset was owned by the child outright and came under his or her control in most cases at age 18. The beauty of this strategy was the income-shifting technique, for the income from the account was taxed at the child's rate, rather than at your presumably higher rate. That made it easier for you to build an education fund at the expense of the government.

The second commonly used method was also an income-shifting technique. It was the Clifford Trust (also known as a short-term, ten-year or reversionary trust), in which assets were held in your child's name for ten years before reverting to you. During the ten years, the earnings from those assets were also taxed at the child's presumed lower tax rate.

Now, the Clifford Trust strategy is all but gone, for all income from a newly created trust is taxable to whomever sets up the trust. And while you can still put as much as $10,000 a year ($20,000 if you give jointly with your spouse) in an UGMA account for each child, only the first $1,000 of passive income from new and existing accounts will be taxed at your child's rate if he or she is under age 14. Investment income over $1,000 is taxable if received by the parents with whom the child lives, or the parent with the larger income if they file separately. If a parent has two or more children, their income is combined and the tax the parent would pay on all of it is figured as though apportioned among all the children. The source of invested funds doesn't matter, whether it's from the parents, grandparents or purchased with income the child earned from a job.

But don't be fooled by all the changes; the main idea is to remember your goal—to save and invest for your children's higher education costs. Therefore, don't let them stop you from saving for your child's future. You'll just have to be more careful now about how you invest the money. And while it appears that income-shifting is dead, the obituary has been written a little early. Income-shifting is indeed alive, though it won't be quite as beneficial and it will be more difficult. Remaining, however, are numerous strategies to transfer income from a parent to a child. Whenever the child is in a lower tax bracket than the parent, the family will still save on taxes and their assets will grow faster.

Gifting Income-Producing Assets to Children Under Age Fourteen

In setting up a custodial account for your child, you should, of course, first seek the $1,000 tax break (actually there could be up to $75 in taxes due) if your child is under age 14. At a rate of 7 percent interest, a custodial account of about $14,500 would earn $1,000 in a year. Held in the account could be income-producing stocks, bonds, mutual funds or any income-oriented investments such as money market funds or savings accounts. You can trade investments or simply attempt to increase the yield, but always try to keep a watch on the investments so that they produce taxable income of no more than $1,000. If they do, you then must file a tax return on behalf of your child. After the $1,000 deduction, the remaining income will be taxed at your tax bracket.

Because the custodial account remains the most common vehicle used to invest for college or other future expenses, it should be further understood. Under current law, a parent sets up a custodial account in a child's name. This can be accomplished under the earlier mentioned Uniform Gift to Minors Act (UGMA), a law adopted by most states, or the Uniform Transfers to Minors Act (UTMA), adopted by some states. A gift given to a minor is fully vested, legally his and recorded under his or her Social Security number. That's good for the child; what's good for the parent is that the underage child must have a custodian trustee to manage the gift until the child legally becomes an adult. Under UGMA, adult means 18 in some states and 21 in others. Under UTMA, adult means from 18 to age 25, depending upon the state. One pitfall to avoid is this: If you gave the gift, became the custodian and died while still the custodian, the gift account will be considered part of your estate and must go through probate. The same thing could happen in your spouse's case, if he or she is considered a joint donor of the gift (as may happen in a community property state). Therefore it's best to have someone other than a donor act as custodian. In their own names, minors can receive life insurance policies on their own lives, Series EE U.S. savings bonds and savings accounts.

I should add, and emphasize, a note of caution. Gifts to your children really *are* gifts. You can't attach legal strings to a gift as you can with a trust, so if your child wants to buy gold-plated skis instead of going to college when he or she legally becomes an adult, he can. Of course, you can usually exert "parental influence," but if you have reservations about stockpiling money over which you'll have no control when your child is an adult, you may want to stop using custodial accounts, particularly after income reaches $1,000.

The next strategy you should consider also involves using a custodial account once it has reached the $1,000 taxable income level. You guessed it, you go for growth. Invest in assets that do not currently generate taxable income for appreciation and whose value will not be taxed until the investment is sold. For example, take a look at growth stocks paying low or no dividends. Of all possible investment vehicles used on behalf of a child, growth stocks are the most common. Due to their very nature, if the child is young, you can equate the advantage of time for growth stocks to mature with a similar amount of time before those funds are required for college. In other words, your stocks and your kids will both grow together. Of course, the drawback to any stock is that if it takes a dive when you need the funds for tuition, you may have to sell at an inopportune time. And naturally you should avoid purchasing higher risk investments, such as stocks, with college only a few years away. You may not have enough time to recoup losses. As you will further learn in Chapter 12, stocks for a custodial account can be purchased individually or (preferably) through a growth mutual fund.

Another investment, or one that can have investment properties (see Chapter 14), also worth a look-see for a custodial account, is precious metals. Again, the idea is to seek investments that stand to appreciate in value without producing taxable income, and precious metals (which might be purchased as stocks) can also fit the bill. Still another investment alternative that might be used as part of a custodial account is collectibles or art, which appreciate in value and produce no taxable income until the asset is sold. Even raw land stands to appreciate substantially in value without producing taxable income. Or a family can make a joint purchase of investment real estate. If the child owns the land and the parents own the building, the income from the property is split, but the parents get all the depreciation and other tax benefits. Of course, liquidity and timing of the sale (if needed) of both collectibles and real estate could present serious drawbacks.

Series EE U.S. savings bonds are a supersafe, highly predictable, taxable, deferred interest investment for a custodial account. Tax on the bonds' interest is deferred until they are cashed, and interest is exempt from state and local income taxes. Along with low minimum investment requirement ($25), and a guaranteed minimum annual rate, which has been 7½ percent (later reduced to 6 percent if the bond is held five years), the rate of the bonds can float above that if interest rates rise. The tax-deferral aspect allows you to buy them for your child now, to come due after he or she turns 14. The bonds are issued at a discount (half of face value), and at maturity will be worth at least face value. They come in eight denominations, ranging from $50 to $10,000 (face value).

Then there is the nonleveraged equipment-leasing partnership, which you could also use as a possible investment tool to help fund your under-fourteen-year-old child's cost of college. If inflation takes off, used equipment prices also rise, thus the investment acts as an inflation hedge. In addition, the first income payouts from such a partnership may be a return of capital; no tax due. Since the taxable income is paid at a later date, if your timing is right, you could have that portion arrive when it would be taxed in your child's bracket, not yours.

Happy Fourteenth Birthday—
Your Child Is Now a Tax Adult

Under the law governing custodial accounts, once your child turns 14, all the account's earnings (actually, all unearned and earned income) is taxed at his or her rate. Happily, all earnings in the account for the year in which your child turns 14 will be taxed at the child's rate, *even* if he or she doesn't turn 14 until the last day of the year. For most kids, with minimal incomes, that would mean a minimum tax rate (after 1987) of 15 percent for the first $17,850 of income. Wouldn't it be clever of you to purchase one-year Treasury bills just after your child turns 13? All income earned during that next year would be transferred to your child's fourteenth birthday, for Treasury bills are sold at a discount, with no tax due on the income until maturity.

Whether it be in Treasury bills or any other taxable investment, at the rate of 7 percent interest, it would take a custodial account of about $250,000 in size to produce the maximum income before your child moves into the "big league" tax brackets. Obviously, with that amount of principal, the cost of higher education is no longer a serious concern. But the real story is that if you previously purchased an investment for growth, and now that your child is 14 it still does not pay a dividend, you could sell that investment and any gain will then be taxed at your child's current (low) rate. Because the tax burden will have been eased, this would be the ideal time to reinvest those proceeds into safer, high-yielding investments such as high-grade corporate bonds and risk-free Treasury bonds, carefully choosing the maturity dates to coincide with when funds are required. You will now have the assurance that the full value of the funds will be available, for at this point college is only a few years away and you don't want to take unnecessary risk. I have never heard a university accounting department say that it would wait while you recouped either some of your gains or your losses. They may be sympathetic that the market didn't perform at college time—but that's all.

The Best College Investments for You to Hold

There is still another alternative that can power your child's custodial account through the magic of compounding (see Chapters 9 and 10) at a fixed rate of interest exempt from federal taxes. This useful investment tool is a tax-exempt security, which has come to be called a zero coupon municipal bond, even though it is neither a bond, nor does it have a coupon. The security is a form of trust receipt evidencing partial ownership of a huge stack of municipal bonds held in escrow in a bank trust account. Rather than paying interest, it is sold at a deep discount from its face value or value at maturity. The beauty is that you can purchase zero coupon securities that come to maturity every six months starting as soon as one year. Assuming your child is destined to attend Stanford ten years from now, you could buy a $10,000 tax-free zero coupon bond today for between $5,000 to $5,500, and ten years from now, when the bond reaches maturity, have that $10,000 as a down payment on his or her tuition. Hypothetically, the $10,000 cost of your child's sophomore year would only cost you between $4,500 and $5,000 today, and so on.

In the past, "real" municipal zero coupon bonds had their drawbacks. They were usually very long-term bonds—25- to 35-year maturities—and had call dates (a minimum period of time, after which the bonds could be "called," or redeemed, before the scheduled maturity) in ten or fifteen years. Because both types of zero coupon municipal bonds are the most volatile of fixed-income securities, you should invest in them only if you are prepared to hold them to maturity. In the case of the "real" municipal zero coupon bonds, maturity often did not correspond with when you needed them—unless you purchased them before you had any thought of having children. If sold prior to maturity, and interest rates had in the meantime increased, the bonds could be worth considerably less than you paid. Though this risk remains with the new type of zero coupon municipal bond, you can now choose much shorter maturity dates.

Of course, you could also purchase nondiscounted municipal bonds either as individual bonds, through mutual funds or through unit trusts. Each methodology has its advantages and drawbacks. For example, individual bonds afford you the opportunity to choose a specific maturity date, but you have to be more concerned with call dates and the fact you have no method for automatic reinvestment. On the other hand, with mutual funds you have the ease of reinvestment and the advantages of a withdrawal program (see Chapter 12), the fact that a small minimum investment can be made, and you can switch within a family of funds if needed, or if opportunity calls. However, you cannot choose a specific maturity. With the unit trust, you have the advantage of reinvestment (into another unit trust) and of choosing a specific maturity period, but the ability systematically to withdraw both principal and interest does not exist.

I recommend, when using municipal bonds as a funding tool for the cost of college, that you invest in a combination of the new zero coupon municipal bonds and municipal bond mutual funds. You can then employ the advantage of zero coupon timing with the mutual fund advantages of being able to add smaller amounts of money continuously, to switch within the family of funds if needed, and the withdrawal feature. Of course the investment ratio depends upon the available dollars and other individual circumstances, but I believe an appropriate percentage would be that three-quarters of those dollars earmarked for tax-free bonds should go into the new municipal zeros and the remaining quarter into mutual funds. With the zeros you will have the assurance of available money, and the knowledge of the exact dollar amount you will have when needed. And by placing one-quarter of your money in mutual funds, in addition to the other advantages outlined, you will have the advantage of building your fund through the use of dollar-cost averaging. By virtue of the fact that smaller dollar amounts can be added, you could possibly increase the value of the fund to where it eventually becomes one-half of the money earmarked for municipal bonds.

An alternative tax-deferred investment is life insurance, an excellent way of producing income because the cash value buildup of the policy is exempt from federal income tax and, if properly structured, state income tax as well. The policy's cash value will increase over the years with no taxes due on the earnings until withdrawal. Eventually you could borrow at low rates from the policy to pay school bills without owing any tax bill at all. For example, at age 30, you might pay annual premiums of $5,000 for an ultimate $325,000 universal life policy that nets around 7 percent a year. If your child was born this year and that rate held for the next eighteen years, you would have up to $160,000 to borrow against at below prevailing bank rates. Universal life insurance also allows you to add more money to your policy, and the interest earned on your savings is tax deferred. If you find a specific policy with low commissions and fees, it may be worth investing in it even if your child is only five years away from college.

You might consider single-premium deferred annuities, which also shield income from taxes until money is paid out. However, with the numerous early withdrawal penalties levied by both the insurance companies and the federal government, a better choice would be the single-premium whole life and variable life insurance policies. The primary difference between the two is that the former policy pays a guaranteed return for a fixed period of time, similar to a tax-deferred certificate of deposit, and the latter presents a choice of tax-deferred investment vehicles. But they both offer the terrific advantage of being able to borrow the increase in value without any taxation whatsoever, and without any pay-back period. And if you needed to borrow the principal, there would only be a modest interest charge of perhaps 2 to 3 percent. Clearly, the use of single-premium whole life or variable life insurance policies should be seriously considered when constructing a portfolio for the purpose of paying for those college bills.

Other Strategies You Can Use

There are quite a few additional strategies that can help you build an education kitty. For example, though the tax benefits may be modest or nonexistent, you may wish to develop a line of credit at a bank to borrow for future college expenses. You may also be able to borrow up to $50,000 from your qualified pension plan if it doesn't exceed the lesser of $50,000 or 50 percent of your accrued benefit. And of course you can borrow against the equity portion of your home (see Chapter 6)—a very popular technique to obtain tax-deductible dollars.

Mortgage and equity loan interest on a first and second home remains deductible up to certain limits under the new tax laws. One of the exceptions to the certain limits is that you can borrow more than the original price of your home, plus improvements, and still deduct all the interest if the loan is used for educational expenses (tuition, books, etc.), including reasonable living expenses away from home for students from primary through graduate school. So if you've owned your home for a while, it should be fairly easy to find college money in your walls if you're willing to use the accumulated equity as collateral. However, if you haven't been dilligent about putting money aside for college, or even if you have and it's not enough, you may have no choice but to borrow against your home. In that event, it certainly makes more sense to pay interest that can be deducted than interest that cannot be. The additional benefit is that as you repay your home equity loan, you pay at a lower rate. But with all the benefits of borrowing against your home for the cost of college, there are also some words of warning—besides the obvious danger of overextending yourself and playing Russian roulette with your home. Because of all the publicity, as well as the easy availability of this money, will there be enough left for college later if borrowing power is used for loans that won't have been repaid by then?

Putting Your Child through "Working School"

And what about the good ol'-fashioned way of helping to fund a college education: put the kid to work! All wages and salaries and tips earned by children will be taxed in their own bracket, not their parents'. When a child has earned income, the standard deduction can be used to offset it. So a child is still able to earn up to $3,000 before any tax will kick in. A working child, however, can't claim the personal exemption if he or she is claimed on his parent's return.

If you're self-employed, there's an even grander tactic. Your kids can work at home or at your business, performing duties such as keeping your office clean, bookkeeping, filing, selling, envelope stuffing, word processing, programming and so forth. You pay their salaries, all or part of which can be set aside for the future and which you can claim as a tax-deductible business expense. In addition, if you are a sole proprietor of a business and your children (and/or your spouse) work in your operation, Social Security taxes are not due on wages paid, and you also don't have to pay the employer's share of the tax. Furthermore, if your children are bona fide employees, they will be eligible for the fringe benefits you provide your other workers, which could include paid vacations, company-paid educational benefits and even retirement contributions.

But you had better make certain that you hire your children to do something important in the business, and they receive reasonable compensation. You can't deduct $2,000 a month for bookkeeping performed by your four-year-old. It is, of course, plausible that a talented teen-ager could earn several thousand dollars a year for after-school or weekend office duties, errands or the above-mentioned tasks related to the business. You should, however, give your children regular paychecks, and be sure they deposit them in a separate custodial account. You want to establish that the money was indeed paid.

Look for All the Help You Can Get

Finally, there is the technique of prepaid tuition for a state school (as well as private schools). A parent deposits $3,000 to $4,500 (depending on the age of the child and the plan chosen) with the state, either in a lump sum or a payment plan. The state invests the money in order to cover undergraduate tuition. Even if the investments don't keep up with increased costs, the state tuition payment is guaranteed. And some programs also include room and board and other fees. But there are traps. Admission is not always guaranteed, and the school may not be the right school for the child. Furthermore, the IRS is not thrilled about the idea, so before you try this one out, be very sure you first check with your tax advisor. And while I'm on the subject of advisors, it would also be wise to seek the assistance of a lawyer, an accountant or a financial planner in weighing the various options and alternatives available to you, and in setting up, if necessary, the machinery of the more complicated college funding techniques.

Earlier in this chapter I mentioned that 60 percent of the students at private schools and 30 percent of those who attend public colleges receive some form of financial assistance. That includes everything from scholarships to grants, to guaranteed student loans where the government pays all the interest until six months after graduation. Though a student on a full scholarship, for example, has to list as income on his or her tax return an amount equivalent to the cost of room, board or incidental expenses at the institution, if he or she is seeking a degree, any scholarship or grant covering direct education costs is tax free, including the major items such as tuition, books and course-related fees. Clearly grants and scholarships remain a major source of funding for the cost of higher education. By some reports, many scholarships go begging for recipients each year, so your college funding plans should include a careful investigation of any assistance for which your child might qualify.

By the way, if you have a child who expects to apply for college financial aid, as a rule of thumb, a student who has a savings account in his or her name doesn't qualify for as much financial aid as he would if the savings were in a parent's name. That sort of places many of you between a rock and a hard place (or does it?). But if you consistently set aside the necessary amounts, make your principal deliver the best possible return, time your investments so the money is available when needed and shift income to children (at the appropriate time) to be taxed at their lower rate, you will ensure that your children are financially able to attend college. And isn't that an important part of your family's overall financial well-being, thus their ability to sleep at night?

Chapter 8

Filling the Half-Empty Glass— The Key to Accumulating Assets

I t makes no difference whether you are just starting to invest or have been investing for many years. It's all the same. You want to feel confident about your investment decisions even if you don't think you know a lot about investing. However, it can be a very intimidating experience. And to encourage that feeling, there are literally thousands of investments to choose from, and hundreds of *types* of investments, with as many as twenty new ones appearing on the scene each day.

Just when you've reached a decision to buy something that's offered by the government, you discover there are practically an infinite variety of government-guaranteed investments on the market—everything from zero coupon bonds to EE savings bonds, from the so-called "Ginnie Maes" to straight Treasury issues with short-term, to intermediate, to long-term maturities, from tax-free investment income to tax-deferred income, from bonds backed by the full faith and credit of the U.S. government to issues backed by the *expectation* that the government will act as guarantor. Should I go on? The extent of investment possibilities can be, and usually is, a great headache.

The major reason for investing is the hope of receiving a greater return in the future. The *key* to investing, and actually *achieving* that desired result, is—that's right—a good plan. If your financial plan is a road map, investment is the vehicle that gets you to your destination. And to take the analogy a little further, you need the right *kind* of vehicle—one that reflects your style, keeps you comfortable and is capable of giving everything you ask of it. You'd probably prefer to drive a four-wheel-drive station wagon than an open convertible over a snowy mountain pass. By the same token, when traveling coast to coast, you're likely to prefer a comfortable, smooth-riding car to a motorcycle. If you keep your destination in mind, and how long it will take to reach that goal, you'll have a pretty good idea both of what kind of vehicle you should buy and what kind will best suit your personality. And you should not, of course, limit yourself to one vehicle. In the investment world, you may buy different modes of transportation for each goal in your life!

Unfortunately, however, most of you don't have a financial road map, and therefore may be driving around in a pretty odd assortment of vehicles. I understand. Like it or not, you've had to make decisions relating to the interest rates you are receiving on your invested funds, the taxes you are paying, the amount of insurance coverage you should have and all the other details related to the financial facts of your life. But without an overall financial plan, you have probably ended up investing your money in whatever seems "reasonable," basing your choices not on your own goals, but on the persuasiveness of the salesman or the popularity of the product. "Reasonable" is not bad, but "right" is a whole lot better.

Getting the Right Fit

I hope Chapter 1 inspired you to do some serious thinking about your overall financial plan. Here and in the next few chapters I'll discuss and explain many of the investment vehicles you might consider to put that plan in motion—and headed in the right direction. Don't put on the blinders. And don't get caught up in the details, either. Look at the big picture to see which ideas seem generally applicable to your situation. Remember, one size does *not* fit all. In making investment decisions you have to take into account, for example, who you are, how you (and, if applicable, your significant other) feel about money in general and about a certain investment in particular, how much money you have to invest, what risks you are willing to take and the results you expect. You have to think, too, about your stage of life. At each stage there are both financial and emotional factors involved in every investment decision. And those factors can change when you move on to the next stage.

Let me give you some examples. If you're young and single—say, 23 to 35—your investment decisions may be oriented toward greater risks, with the possibility—but not the certainty—of greater rewards. You may not have the expense of raising children and probably aren't thinking much about retirement. At this stage of your life, most of your plans are for the present. If you lose money, you're not worried very much because you know you can earn it back fairly quickly. Time is on your side.

However, if you're married, in your late thirties to fifties, and have a couple of kids, you are probably concerned about how you are going to fund their future college expenses. You may even have started to think about retirement. Your assets will have grown by this time, and your impulse is to protect them so you can meet both your present and future responsibilities. Sensibly, your investment decisions now lean toward greater security, and the portion of your portfolio geared toward growth or risk may have declined from more than 50 percent of your young singlehood to less than 50 percent today.

Finally, if you're between 51 and 65, you may be spending a lot of money—traveling, helping out your grown children—and getting ready for retirement. You certainly want to keep what you have, but you're not sure you have enough. So risk or growth investments may now take up less than 35 percent of your portfolio, a ratio that will probably decrease even more when you retire. Income, not growth, is now of primary importance because of your awareness that your paycheck will have to be replaced.

I am aware that none of these examples may exactly reflect your own situation. I have clients in their twenties and thirties who have been banking every dollar they can toward their retirement years. I have clients in their seventies embarking upon a major construction project as a long-term investment. Look at George Burns—he has entertainment commitments past age 105. But you get the idea: though everyone has different goals, personal investment decisions have been and usually are dictated to a large extent by the investor's age. If you're like most of us, the first really serious pause for concern occurred (or will occur) on your fortieth birthday, for at that point you start(ed) thinking in terms of having lived, perhaps, one-half of your life.

After you've thought about your current stage of life, and related it to your overall financial goals, the next step in making the right investment decisions is to find out what's available in the marketplace. Remember the vehicle analogy? Ideally, you'll start looking at brand names only *after* you've determined what kind of transportation you want to get where you want to go, whether it's a truck, a station wagon, a sedan, a sports car, roller skates or a camel.

The specific, detailed information you need before you decide to buy any investment can be obtained from a good professional financial advisor (see Chapter 16). Specialized current books, various local radio and TV shows, as well as national shows such as CBS Radio's *Business Report,* or TV's *Business Morning* on CNN, or Eva Dorn's excellent *Consumer's Corner* show on Financial News Network or *Wall Street Week* on PBS are also excellent sources of continuing information. Financial advisory newsletters can also be a major help, as can a number of investment-related magazines. For example, in *Money, Sylvia Porter's Personal Finance, Fact, Forbes, Changing Times, Business Week* and *Fortune,* as well as in the "Money" section in *USA Today,* I have found a lot of high-quality, useful and specialized information. "Your Money Matters" column in *The Wall Street Journal,* the quarterly financial Sunday supplements in *The New York Times,* and even your local newspaper's business section are marvelous places to look for this sort of information. Additionally, *USA Today* columnist Dan Dorfman, *Barron's* Alan Abelson, *Newsweek*'s Jane Bryant Quinn and *Forbes'* editor William G. Flanagan's "Personal Finance" section are but four of the numerous columnists or editors who provide insightful information.

You'll note that while I have mentioned financial information sources by name, I refrained from mentioning any "brand name" investments. Why? Because it's more important to help you create a solid foundation of understanding on how to use your money or other financial resources, to make sure that what *you* value most is realized. If you better understand the principles of investing, something about different types of investments and how different investments can satisfy your needs, you will have no difficulty locating the brand names. There will be no shortage of people eager to take your investment dollars, but before you hand them over you should know whether an investment fits into your personal life values and your overall plan. You should also know what the practical effects of that investment will be so you won't expect more of an investment than it can deliver. In short, you should know whether that investment is "right" for you. If you don't know, at least you'll know the right questions to ask of someone who does.

The Benefits of Investing

There are four basic benefits available in an investment: tax savings or advantages; current yield or income; appreciation or growth of principal; and safety of principal. No investment contains all four—in fact, the more the investment contains of one element, the less it contains of

The "Orange Juice" Example *

| Tax savings | Current yield | Appreciation | Safety |

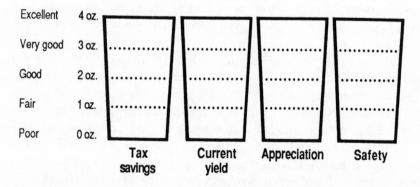

* Published in *Tax-Advantaged Investments* by Richard Wollack and Alan Parisse (Consolidated Capital Communications Group, 1982); and in "The Orange Juice Analogy," *The Digest of Financial Planning Ideas,* April 1985.

another. You can't have absolute safety of principal and a high potential for appreciation or growth at the same time. In short, trade-offs are unavoidable.

Many financial planners—including me—use a common analogy developed by Richard Wollack to illustrate the trade-offs between prospective investments. An investment is like an orange: There's only so much juice in it. If each of the four basic benefits above is represented by a 4-ounce glass, and each investment orange produces 8 ounces of economic "juice," you won't be able to fill up all four glasses. You can put 2 ounces in each glass, or 4 ounces in two glasses, or some combination in between, but you'll never get more than 8 ounces of juice from that orange.

Let's say that each glass represents four points, and that the best score an investment can achieve in each of the four benefit categories is also four points. Our orange juice grading scale would look like this:

4 points = Excellent (among the top 20 percent of all other investments in providing this benefit)

3 points = Very good (better than 60 to 80 percent of all other investments in providing this benefit)

2 points = Good (better than 40 to 60 percent of all other investments in providing this benefit)

1 point = Fair (better than 20 to 40 percent of all other investments in providing this benefit)

0 points = Poor (among the bottom 20 percent of all other investments in providing this benefit)

This rating scale assumes, and properly so, that every investment provides a finite amount of the four basic benefits: tax savings, current yield, appreciation and safety. In many investments, however, there will be *no* score in one or more benefit categories. The scale is intended to focus on objectives, not performance.

Now let's see how this rating system works with one particular investment—a high-quality municipal bond.

The completed diagram (on page 144) shows my rating of the bond as follows, with explanations:

Tax savings: While municipal bonds produce tax-exempt income, their tax advantages are not of the type as those produced by a high-write-off oil-drilling venture. (2 points)

Current yield or income: Presently, municipal bonds provide a relatively high amount of tax-free income. (3 points)

Appreciation: Municipal bonds are not meant to appreciate. Their value may even decline in the face of rising interest rates. (0 points)

Safety: A high-quality municipal bond is among the safer investments. (3 points)

Now it's your turn. Using the same rules and principles, you can rate a mutual fund or any other investment. Draw a blank diagram like the one we just looked at and rate the economic benefits from an existing or proposed investment. (If you don't know where to begin, read up on the particular investment you want to diagram or seek the help of a professional financial advisor.) Does the diagram for this investment (and similar diagrams for your other investments) match your financial profile? Are the benefits you're getting from your investment(s) appropriate to your stage of life and individual situation? If, for example, you are planning to send your two young children to college, you might place a great amount of value on long-term appreciation and invest accordingly. By making individual diagrams and scoring each of your investments, you'll know exactly where you stand with each of them. If, on the other hand, you are contemplating a new investment, I suggest you also consider how much money is involved, how long you are willing to leave the investment intact, and your expectations regarding the performance of the investment.

Investment Objectives Rating Model ®

High Quality Municipal Bond

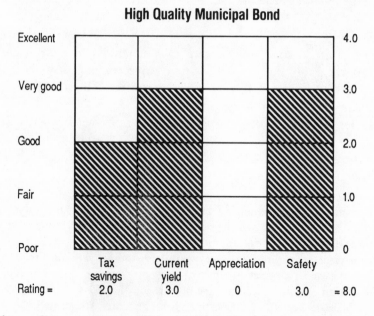

	Tax savings	Current yield	Appreciation	Safety	
Rating =	2.0	3.0	0	3.0	= 8.0

These diagrams, as well as the additional consideration above, should help you understand both the basic axioms of investing and the trade-offs involved in choosing the investments that best meet your needs. If you don't need current income, for example, why pick an interest-producing investment over one that potentially produces growth? And filling in these diagrams will also clearly demonstrate that you may have been expecting some of your oranges to produce twelve ounces of juice. It's your squeeze.

Hadmour Gelt Revisited

The types of investments I'll be talking about in later chapters are generally arranged from the safest to the least safe—from interest-bearing instruments (government, bank and bond investments) to income and/or growth vehicles (stocks and mutual funds); from precious metals and natural resources to tax-advantaged investments. This drive through the investment forest obviously is not a straight one, and that's because each investment type has unique strengths and weaknesses.

What you need is financial perspective, and that means deciding for yourself what you want from your money. Once you do, your portfolio of investments will no longer resemble a hodgepodge. You will be better able to determine what's really important in terms of your own investment goals. It will no longer suffice to say, "Well, I just want my investments to make a lot of money. I don't want to take any risks. And I don't like paying taxes." That, you will now know, is completely unrealistic—just as it is unrealistic to be influenced by what other people are doing with their finances. It's more important to know what *you're* doing with yours. And the sooner you do it, the better.

Remember Hadmour Gelt in Chapter 1? Hadmour, at 42, realized he had some major expenses ahead of him, expenses he hadn't really thought about until he defined his short-, intermediate- and long-term goals. If he's lucky, he'll be able to scrape up the money to pay for all of them; if he's not, he may have to delay his goals. But luck doesn't *have* to enter into such calculations. If Hadmour had begun to think about and plan for his goals ten years earlier, he might have peace of mind today. His immediate goals at the time, you may recall, were these:

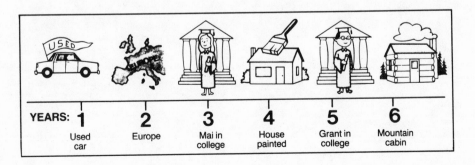

YEARS: 1	2	3	4	5	6
Used car	Europe	Main college	House painted	Grant in college	Mountain cabin

If we turn the clock back those ten years, Hadmour will at least have a sharper view of the future and much more time in which to accumulate assets to meet his goals.

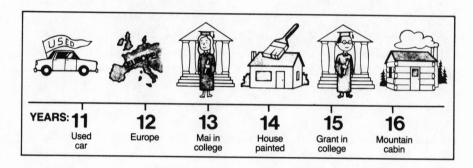

YEARS: 11 12 13 14 15 16
Used car   Europe   Mai in college   House painted   Grant in college   Mountain cabin

Naturally, Hadmour couldn't have been ready for everything—having another child earlier than he and Mary expected, for instance—but he could have budgeted enough so that his fixed expenses, and then some, were paid for. And meanwhile he could have chosen his investment wisely to earn the money for his nonfixed expenses down the line.

But once again, Hadmour is not you. So in the following chapters I'll discuss the many investment possibilities available that will suit your own life-style and financial goals.

PART THREE

Investing for the Present —And the Future

Chapter 9

Commonsense Investing—How to Make It Work for You

Just as we're getting to the exciting part—investing your money— I'm afraid I have to put on my black hat and be the bearer of bad news. Successful investing is not exciting, nor should it be. It is a long, oh-so-slow, boring process. It's about as exciting as paying bills. No wonder many people want someone else to do it for them! Money excitement explains why so many people go to Las Vegas, Atlantic City, the racetrack or poker parlors, or put a few bucks in football pools or state lotteries. The reason: They can cut out the middleman and the long wait to see how well they did. They move directly from the starting gate to the finish line without having to endure all those anxious steps in between.

Some love the thrill of competitive gambling and will always be ready to "bet the house, spouse and kids." And if they lose . . . well, they just start over. However, I know most of my clients don't like such high risks. Surprise—exciting as it may seem, "get rich quick" is a scheme that just doesn't work. Bernard Baruch said it best: "When hopes are soaring, I always repeat to myself, 'Two and two make four, and no one has ever invented a way of getting something for nothing.'" Despite a dramatic stock market rise and the boast of many speculators, the two best investments in the first half of this decade were corporate bonds and mortgage-backed securities. Each investment returned approximately 130 percent over the five-year period. And both are certainly considered conservative investments.

In all my years in dealing with people and their investments, I have yet to see anyone succeed quickly by design. Those who did succeed quickly did so by accident. They were careful, methodical and basically conservative people who understood that investing is a one-step-at-a-time process. Nothing more, nothing less. They never wager the house. They understand, instead, that when you're trying to burn a very large, very thick log, a single match is no match for it at all. As with investing, the first thing you need is a small flame—something to light some paper, which you then use to ignite small twigs, which in turn can fire up kindling, and then larger logs. Now you have a fire large enough and hot enough to burn a log of any size. A bolt of lightning can ignite a large log, but how many of you carry lightning bolts around in your pockets?

The Best Investment

The match that starts the fire, and the fuel that enables it to keep growing, all come from your earnings—from *you*. Before you worry about what to do with your money, remember J. Paul Getty's words: "Make your money first, then think about spending it." You must, therefore, always remember that you are your number one investment. No investment will *ever* be able to perform as well because only you can create an infinite increase in the value of your investment each year. On January 1 your "asset"—you—has no earnings, but by December 31 this asset has outperformed every investment ever made.

Your personal talent and professional value represent a virtually unlimited source of capital, just waiting to generate huge dividends for you. Let's say you earn an annual salary of $25,000. If you think of that amount as the income from an investment that pays a 10 percent return, you have an investment worth $250,000! And every time you increase your income by one dollar, you increase your equivalent investment value by ten dollars with no investment risk. Since your working hours represent an equivalent investment value (including benefits) of $2.80 a minute, if you could increase your income by, say, only 5 percent, you will have increased your investment value by $12,500, and the value of your working minute by 14 cents.

As you think of how you can improve your job or investment skills, remember it's the little things that count. Most people seem to want tremendous improvement instantly. But you'll probably find it's the little things you do that eventually add up to big results. For example, in professional baseball:

.250 hitters get 3 hits out of 12 at bat and may earn approximately $200,000 a year.

.333 hitters get 4 hits out of 12 at bat and may earn $600,000 or more a year.

Most 9-inning games give batters 4 opportunities to hit the ball.

To earn three times the income and be considered great, all the .333 hitters do is get *one* extra hit in *three* games.

Too old to invest in yourself? I again turn to the entertainment field for an illustration. The very finest athletes or world-renowned actors, singers, etc., continue to work with coaches. Why have *you* outgrown improvement? Learn to invest in yourself, and you'll discover the rewards will dwarf any outside investment you could make.

Somewhere in your present job exists the opportunity that will bring you everything you could possibly want, according to Earl Nightingale, a personal motivational expert. In his audio cassette album titled *Lead the Field,* he explains how you can find that opportunity and take advantage of it. The story that illustrates his message is called "Acres of Diamonds." It tells the tale of an African farmer who became so intoxicated with the news of other settlers discovering diamond mines that he sold his farm and hurried away to begin his own search for diamonds. Driven by a vision of glittering riches, the farmer wandered throughout Africa for the rest of his life. He never found a single diamond. Yet the man who purchased the farmer's land discovered diamonds right on that same patch of ground, which eventually became one of the world's largest diamond mines.

The point of the story is that you too can find the riches you seek, both financial and spiritual, by exploring and making the best use of the ground on which you now stand. There is another point: The farmer who sold his land tried to get rich quickly, but it was the man who simply purchased the land as a farm who became rich.

One result of investing in yourself will be increased earnings. Some of those additional earnings will go for deserved consumer frills. However, to ensure your future security, you must also save and invest those savings. Only new investments, and a continuous flow of new money into old investments, will provide the firepower needed to reach your goals. While it is important to achieve a high consistent rate of return on your present investment assets, you cannot safely command a high enough rate on, say, $150,000 without the addition of fresh capital to meet your long-term goals. Though the magic of compounding is wonderful (I will discuss it shortly), you'll need to achieve an uninterrupted after-tax annual return of something like 20 to 50 percent. Usually a 6 to 8 percent rate will be inadequate unless that rate consistently outperforms inflation, you live rather modestly and you have a large number of years before you require use of those assets. If you invest $150,000 in a savings account that pays an after-tax rate of 7 percent a year compounded annually, at the end of fifteen years your account will have $413,850. But if inflation also grew at 5 percent annually for those same fifteen years, your $150,000 would only be worth $252,200 in today's dollars. Would that sum provide you with financial security today? I doubt it.

Unfortunately, there are advisors who promote consistent 20 percent-plus rates of return. But talk is expensive—it can cost you money—and can cause its own problems by creating false expectations that influence our investment decisions. Wearing rose-colored glasses can only get you in trouble. So next time an investment claim seems too good to be true, you will be able to remove those glasses if you remember that an investment can lose at least as much value as it can gain. How would you feel if your investment was more than 20 percent behind? If that makes you feel uncomfortable, save yourself money. Don't make the investment.

The Second-Best Investment

You are your number one best investment, but the consistent addition of new capital to your portfolio—your ability to save—is your *second* best investment in terms of performance. Let's say you were able to place $5,000, which was excess cash from your earnings, into an investment. That would constitute an instant and riskless increase of your net worth by $5,000. But an existing $5,000 investment would take several years as well as greater risk to reproduce itself. Get my point? This is why professional financial advisors often say, "It's not what you make, but what you keep." And don't blame income taxes; they aren't the only culprit. Most of the time it's your spending habits. Example: I have a client who earned $50,000 but spent $60,000 last year; he maintains he always lives within his income, even if he has to borrow to do so.

In George Clason's *The Richest Man in Babylon,* my client would find a soul mate. One character says that "what each of us calls our 'necessary expenses' will always grow equal to our incomes, unless we protest to the contrary." And in Charles Dickens's *David Copperfield,* the impecunious Mr. Micawber says, "Annual income twenty pounds, annual expenditure nineteen nineteen six, result happiness. Annual income twenty pounds, annual expenditure twenty pounds ought and six, result misery."

Investment Performance

Even if you do add new capital to your investment from time to time, however, if you look at each investment in isolation, the numbers may lead you to believe that you are falling behind because you tend to focus on the losers. If your investment is losing money (or not living up to your expectations), and you are a reflex investor (reacting to each event), you sell. Instead, you should measure your "performance by objective"—in other words, how your portfolio as a whole is doing in relation to your goals. You should concentrate on your overall portfolio, not small changes in the value of individual investments. Almost any diversified portfolio will contain winners and losers. If you are caught up in tracking individual performance figures, you will find that you are examining the vein in each leaf, while failing to notice the growth of the tree.

Some investments may appear to be falling behind, or may even be causing a loss. Sell? Doubtful—if you reconsider the reason you bought the losing investment. If your objective in buying was to "hedge" or "insure" your portfolio, it may still be doing its job. If you purchased gold for that purpose, for example, your intention was to offset possible losses in other investments due to rising inflation. (Gold customarily rises in value when inflation climbs.) Just because those other investments are performing well, and gold might be dropping in value, that does not mean you should sell it. After all, do you sell the kitchen fire extinguisher after you've managed to cook one meal without burning down the house? If your home was now listed on the New York Stock Exchange and today you discovered the stock had fallen by 5 points, would you sell? The gold—like the fire extinguisher and your house—was purchased for a purpose and continues to serve that purpose despite current fluctuations in value. Remember, an unrealized loss is worth no less than an unrealized gain—you don't make or lose money until you sell the investment. So your holding should stay in place unless you alter your reasons for holding it.

Let's look at another example of performance by objective. If you invested money in a growth mutual fund and found it grew at "only"

10.4 percent last year, well under the 21.66 percent annual return of the previous five years, again that does not mean that you should sell. Unless you're aware of a problem unique to that particular fund, the investment should be viewed in context with your other investments. Ask yourself, "How are my investments performing overall, including the new capital I've put in, based on the goals I've set?"

Once you place your investments into perspective, then evaluating performance will no longer be like trying to follow a bouncing football down the field. You will also no longer be vulnerable to every hotshot scheme, system and proposal that comes your way.

Long-Term Investment Goals

If your goal is that intangible thing called "financial security twenty years from now," it's very difficult to gauge your progress because of the inflation factor. An example: If you presently live on $2,500 a month, twenty years from now it would cost you $7,295 a month to live the same way you do now, assuming an inflation rate of only 5½ percent. Think about it: Can you see yourself currently spending more than $7,000 a month? If you are already spending that much, can you picture yourself shelling out more than $25,000 a month?

If you are of a certain age, you may remember a 1930s insurance advertisement—once famous, now infamous—that read, "How I retired on $100 a month." Can you imagine your reaction if a person had turned to you at the time and suggested that within the next twenty or thirty years you would need $1,000, or $1,500, or more than $2,000 a month to maintain your financial security? Impossible!

Many of you will recall your reaction some years ago when forecasters suggested that you would someday spend more than $10,000 for a Ford or Chevrolet. You paid "only" $3,000 for one fifteen years ago, and a top-of-the-line Cadillac could be had for $6,500. Hard to relate to a five-digit car price, wasn't it? Today, most cars are in that range.

I have a copy of a 1969 U.S. News & World Report article that predicted what inflation might bring. Man's haircut—price now: $2; year 2000: $10. Food for four—price now: $40 per week; year 2000: $112. Having a baby—cost now: $200 for obstetrical care; year 2000: $640. It seems as though the year 2000 took place five years ago.

Such figures provide us a measure of changing times. And long-term goals perform the same function. Like a well-defined philosophy of life, long-term goals provide a standard by which to evaluate an investment decision—so that they aren't made in isolation. They help keep you from taking risks you can't afford, and from acting in ways that aren't in keeping with your nature. But they must be realistic so you will accept them subconsciously.

Short-Term Investment Goals

While long-range goals can give you a standard and general direction in making your investment decisions, it's your short-range goals that can be more accurately measured and give you hope that you can actually get somewhere. They can provide positive reinforcement ("I did it, and I can do it again!"), allow you to focus (laser vision), a sense of urgency (you can't procrastinate) and flexibility.

Short-range goals give your actions meaning. Your goal becomes a cause and your actions are the effect. If you are sailing and your home is halfway around the world, until it's directly in view, you must decide on various ports of call en route. At each port you must take your bearings and adjust your course, if necessary. As Henry David Thoreau once said, "In the long run men hit only what they aim at." So it is with charting your financial destination. Each port should be a specific and realistic step in the general direction of the longer-term goal: home.

You can drive comfortably and smoothly over the Rocky Mountains at Independence Pass, elevation 12,095 feet, and never exceed a 7 percent grade. You make steady, gradual progress. Likewise, you should experience steady, gradual progress in your financial life. Set goals and make every one. Once you've done that, you know you can do it again.

But you need to see the progress you're making to build a sense of accomplishment. So break your big, long-range goals down into small, short-range goals. Buying a new home in two years' time equals $X saved *this* month. Running the equivalent of around the world, 24,902 miles could be accomplished by running just 2.13 miles a day—for 11,688 days.

When viewing an investment program, I recommend a two-year benchmark or track. The two-year benchmark allows you to watch your investment net worth grow as you progress along the track toward achieving your financial goals. The two-year benchmark defines the investment net worth figure you want to reach every two years, and you can determine whether you are above your target, on target or below it.

Superb investments and above-average savings can result in "beating the track" and possibly achieving your long-range goals several years earlier than you expected. Poor investment performance, poorly disciplined savings patterns or a major emergency expense can result in a reduction of your investment net worth. Generally, if reductions in net worth occur with substantial time remaining before reaching your goals, your course can be adjusted. However, the closer you are in time to the necessity of making your goals, the more significant the changes in your tracking parameters will be. Some tracks will be so altered that the goals must be changed. For example, let's assume on a $10,000 investment, you lost $5,000 or 50 percent of your investment. From that point, just to break even and regain your loss, you must earn 100 percent on your money, twice the rate at which it was lost. This is not easy to do.

On the other hand, if your savings and investment program is forced "off track," you should not let unexpected aberrations deter you, nor should you overreact. Perhaps new investment decisions are necessary, and you will now need to take a more aggressive stance; but I usually recommend you simply continue to do the best you can within your comfort level. On the positive side, there are those unexpected windfalls, a future higher-than-expected rate of return on your investment portfolio, or a salary increase might occur. Any of the above could help make up for lost time without "forcing" you to take that extra risk. Throughout the entire process of investment net worth tracking, the two-year benchmark idea is designed to keep your savings and investment goals in clear view and allow you to make periodic adjustments when needed.

What kind of short-term performance should you strive for from your investments? It is a simple rule of thumb, but it works. Use the average of the rates of inflation for the last two years as a unit of measurement. If your investments as a whole, including the new capital you've put in, are at least meeting that figure (after current taxes have been paid), you'll have stayed even and maintained your purchasing power (usually measured in terms of inflation or deflation). Better yet, you should try to exceed the annual inflation rate by at least 1 to 2 percentage points. If inflation is at 13 percent, "all" you need do is to have your investments return an after-tax net average of 13 to 15 percent (not easily accomplished if a portion of your portfolio is in low-risk, and hence low-return, investments, such as a fund that in case of emergencies can become instantly liquid). If the inflation rate changes, as it has and will, you shouldn't feel overly pressured to maintain a high level of performance. Since the current inflation rate has dropped to below 4 percent, a 6 percent after-tax (or tax-deferred) return is a realistic goal. Forget the days of easy 13 to 15 percent rates of return. That's history. Today achieving those returns requires more risk than most of you are willing to take on. Since we live in the present we need to make adjustments based upon present inflation and current rates of return. If you are able to net 7 or 8 percent, so much the better. The excess can be "stored" for the years when keeping even may be difficult.

Another trap investors fall into is trying to predict the future inflation or interest rates. Don't try to predict the future. Predictions are entertaining, but they are also dangerous to your wealth. Nobody can predict the future accurately. Go ahead and make predictions if you want to, and read other people's predictions, but don't make an investment based upon those predictions until actual events begin to move in that direction. That explains my rationale for using the average of the last two years' rates of inflation. Year-by-year aberrations are not a dependable gauge of future trends.

Your long-term goal is financial security. If you continually add new capital, if your investment assets maintain an average net 2 percentage point margin (or greater) over the rate of inflation, and if you can reinvest your investment capital and its profits, the mathematics of compounding will transform your investments into a spectacular gain and a great assurance of attaining that financial security.

The Magic of Compounding

Compounding is not really magic; it's simple arithmetic. Though inflation compounds, too, today it is not difficult through compounding to achieve a net investment return that is at least double the rate of inflation. If you maintain even a net 2 percentage point margin over inflation in five years your investments and new capital would exceed the rate of inflation by 9.8 percent. That number would grow to 20.6 percent in ten years, 45.3 percent in twenty years, and a very handsome 59 percent in twenty-five years. On a year by year basis it may not sound like much, but that 2 percent compounded can indeed amount to a great deal over the long term.

If you add the rate of inflation to these figures, and add a bit more time, the total return can be astounding. The Dreyfus Fund, a large, conservative, growth-oriented mutual fund, proudly points to a gain of more than 3,800 percent since 1951. In the more than thirty years covered, the fund's average annual return was only 11.8 percent. Certainly respectable, but not what you'd expect to achieve a 3,800 percent increase. The secret? Compounding. Understanding how compounding works can help you calculate the return on your savings and investments. In fact, these calculations apply to almost any financial decision—from the reinvestment of dividends to the purchase of a zero coupon bond in a tax-deferred account.

Compounding is quite simply "interest paid on interest." The interest earned on an investment after a given period, a year, for example, is added to the principal amount and included in the next period's interest calculation. Here are a couple of dramatic examples of how compounding works. Early in the last century, an English astronomer, Francis Baily, figured that a British penny invested at an annual compound interest of 5 percent at the birth of Christ would have yielded enough gold by 1810 to fill 357 million Earths. And if you think the Indians made a mistake by selling Manhattan in 1626 for $24, think again. The Indians placed that money in a tax-deferred account and received a 6 percent per year compound rate of interest. Today Manhattan is supposedly worth some $27 billion, but that tax-deferred account, if liquidated, would yield more than $34 billion.

Fortunately, savers and investors don't have to live to age 100 or more to reap the benefits of compounding. Consider an investment with a current value of $10,000 earning an annual interest of 8 percent. After a year the investment grows to $10,800 (1.08 times $10,000). After the second year it's worth $11,664 (1.08 times $10,800). After five years, the investment has grown to $14,693. And so on. So don't forget to factor in the effects of compounding when you make new investment decisions or evaluate the performance of the investments you already have. Computers and calculators with built-in formulas make solving compound-interest questions relatively easy. But you can also use compound-interest tables available at your local library.

Your Basic Investment Choices

Now you're ready to invest, but you still have major decisions ahead. What kinds of investments should you choose? There are two basic choices: debt-based or lending assets—more commonly known as bonds; and equity-based assets—more commonly known as stocks. You can loan or you can own, and both types of investments have advantages as well as drawbacks. The type you choose will, of course, depend upon your personal financial goals.

Goal: Income

With a debt-based asset, a bond, you become a lender and you are usually investing for income. You have a contract that requires the borrower to pay interest regularly on your investment and to return the original sum at maturity. Usually, the longer the debt period, the higher the interest rate you receive. That's fair because inflation gradually lessens the value of the money you are lending. For example, let's say you commit $1,000 for five years at 8 percent interest, and inflation averages 4 percent. You're paid $80 a year—8 percent of $1,000—and at the end of five years you get your $1,000 back. But your $1,000 won't buy as many goods or services as it would have five years before inflation had raised prices.

In addition, there is an inverse relationship between bond prices and interest rates. If interest rates go up, the market value of your contract will go down, and vice versa. Say you invest $10,000 today in a bond paying 9 percent annually. Assume that interest rates rise during the next year and that one year from now new bonds similar to yours are being offered to investors at 10 percent. If you tried to sell your $10,000, 9-percent bond, another investor wouldn't pay full price if he or she could buy a similar bond paying 10 percent. Instead, the investor probably would offer about $9,000 for your bond. Reason: at that price, the $900 in annual interest (9 percent) would be equivalent to the prevailing 10 percent yield ($900 divided by $9,000 equals 10 percent). So if you had to sell your 9 percent bond, you would lose a bit more. The reverse also is true. If interest rates continue to fall, a 9 percent bond will be worth more on the open market than an 8 percent bond. That's why investors who bought long-term bonds in the early 1980s when interest rates ran as high as 14 percent are sitting on handsome gains.

If you purchase a long-term bond, when interest rates change, its market value can fluctuate as much as ten times more than a short-term bond. However, higher volatility may not concern you if you don't think you'll ever need to sell before maturity. A client of mine was once called by a newspaper reporter to "tell the world" how he felt about his $1 million municipal bond portfolio dropping more than 25 percent in value since interest rates were (then) so high. He responded, "That a fact! Well, I hadn't noticed. After all, they keep paying like clockwork."

For most clients, I recommend debt assets that mature in no more than three to ten years, called "intermediate term." A longer maturity may give you a small amount of additional income, but what if you're forced to sell the asset in those extra years when interest rates may rise, lowering the underlying value of your bond? The experts have enough trouble predicting interest rates in just six months' time, so how can you be sure that interest rates will be the same, or lower, twenty years from now?

The great speculator Jesse Livermore said it best: "I believe it is a safe bet that the money lost in [short-term] speculation is small compared with the gigantic sums lost by so called [long-term] investments. Don't get rooted in long-term investments." Betting on tomorrow is chancy enough; betting on a day in the distant future is crazy.

Goal: Profit

Money you invest for profit, by contrast with money you invest for income, has no guarantees at all. Investments for profit are risky. They are designed to grow over the long haul, even though they may decline in value at any time.

Most investments that have an opportunity to grow pay little or no yield (interest or dividends) and are considered equity assets. This simply means ownership in a venture. The most common of the ownership assets is stock in companies, but they also encompass real estate, precious metals, oil and other investments. Since no return is promised on these equity-based assets, their market value generally fluctuates over a much greater range than debt-based assets. Thus this sort of investment gives a much greater potential for appreciation or loss.

Factors to Consider When Establishing a Personal Investment Program

Each of you, of course, has your own goals that will influence your choice between debt and/or equity assets. While I cannot give you precise recommendations, since you have differing needs, desires and comfort levels, I can provide you with some commonsense considerations that should enter into every investment decision.

Age

How should you allocate your new and existing investments between equity and debt assets? Answer: That probably depends, first of all, on your age. The older you are, the less time you have to make up for investments that might reduce—forever—your overall return. At the very least, you hope to keep what you already have. So if you are only five years away from retirement, it is more than likely that most of your portfolio will be in conservative debt investments. You are probably now applying that old adage "Take little risk with big money and big risk with little money."

A few years ago I had the privilege of reviewing President Reagan's federal income tax return for *Money* magazine. I noted that the President is just like the rest of us: As we get older, we get "creeping conservatism." By that year, the President had sold all his investment real estate and taken back notes. The rest of his investment assets were made up of conservative stocks, bonds and Treasury bills. "It's classic!" I told the magazine.

On the other hand, if your lifework can still be measured in decades, and your chart of goals requires a legal-sized tablet, you should probably have the greatest concentration of your investments in assets that can grow. You'll discover that if you have time to establish your measurable goals, miracles will happen. Even unspectacular preparation will produce spectacular results. You will now instinctively put in place a comfortable and appropriate mix of debt and equity assets, depending upon your age and your individual comfort level. For some of you, that mix may be 50 percent equity and 50 percent debt; for others, 80 percent equity and 20 percent debt. At the risk of repeating myself, *you* decide what mix you need, based upon measurable goals and what allows you to sleep at night. If you do that, you cannot make a serious mistake.

There are four other factors you should consider besides your age when establishing your personal investment program: diversification, liquidity, taxes and risk. As a financial professional, I consider each of these elements to be enormously important, but I know in the real world it's difficult to achieve a proper balance among them. If you leave out one element, or have an otherwise unbalanced combination, you will probably incur a serious problem. That's not the end of the world, of course, but you have created an unnecessary roadblock to a secure financial future.

Diversification

Diversification is perhaps the most frequently ignored principle of investing. Too often, due to lack of time or knowledge, or because of overconfidence or paralyzing anxiety or fear of change, many people will keep a vast proportion of their money in only one asset: real estate, for example, or stocks or their own business. The result is that they are very vulnerable to the vicissitudes of one particular market.

Investment diversification solves that problem. A young couple whose major asset is a house, for example, should probably not buy additional real estate. Instead, they could consider an investment in the stock market. Executives who own a big block of stock in their company should probably steer clear of the stock market or assemble a portfolio of municipal bonds.

I've seen many times what a lack of diversification can do. A few years ago a man came to my office to discuss his situation, and it wasn't good. He was an officer of a publicly held Fortune 500 company and had been investing in the company's stock for thirty years. More than 80 percent of his net worth was tied to the fortunes of his employer, whom he obviously believed in, and he had refused to diversify though people had been telling him to do so for years. No change of course seemed necessary; the value of his stock continued to rise, as did the dividends.

By the time he came to see me, however, he had retired and his company was suffering a severe cash squeeze. It suspended its dividend, and the value of its stock dropped dramatically. This former officer was forced to sell shares to "enjoy" his retirement years. The lesson is clear: An investment may appear so attractive that it's hard to resist not sinking every dime you have in it. But if you decide to concentrate your funds in one place, you had better be willing to keep watch *very* closely, or brace yourself for potentially large losses.

If you have concentrated your holdings in so-called "safe" investments like an insured bank account or government bonds, you are also risking a loss. True, you will collect the interest and principal when due, but there's a greater risk today than in the past that the after-tax result will not keep pace with your needs for purchasing power. The interest paid by the government, banks or corporations typically lags behind the rate of inflation. Recent history demonstrates that every-thing from the rate of inflation to the rate of interest, and from invest-ment values to tax rates, are becoming more volatile and that the peaks and valleys are becoming more pronounced—the highs higher and lows lower. A sudden burst of inflation, and you will again find a wide gap between the net amount of interest you are receiving and the amount of income you need to stay even.

I believe a new notion of capital preservation is emerging, and its central credo is diversification. Its purpose is loss control. It is now far riskier not to diversify than to diversify. You will probably respond, "Sure, if I diversify, I'm less likely to be devastated by a factor beyond my control. But can I still make money while diversifying?" You bet. Diversification pays!

Here's a simple way to help you understand the importance of diver-sification and the value of accepting the risks of speculative invest-ments. If you have $10,000 to invest for twenty-five years, you could put the entire sum in, say, a zero coupon bond at 10 percent com-pounded annually. Therefore, $10,000 times 10 percent a year for twenty-five years equals $108,347. But suppose you put $1,000 into each of ten different investments and just one of those ten was a big winner and yielded 25 percent a year while the other nine produced nothing. The result would look like this: $1,000 times 25 percent a year, times twenty-five years, equals $264,698. So if only one of the ten investments yielded 25 percent, you would earn an extra $156,351.

A broad-based portfolio can also do well even without any overly speculative investments. Over the past two decades, a diversified in-vestment index has outpaced the U.S. stock market and the typical portfolio manager. The index consists of five equally weighted parts: U.S. stocks, foreign stocks, U.S. corporate and government bonds, real estate and Treasury bills. This index has grown at a 10.2 percent compound rate since 1965, compared with 9.4 percent for the Standard & Poors 500-stock index and 7.9 percent for the U.S. money manager of median performance who invested in both stocks and bonds.

Most of the extra gains came from foreign stocks, which today have grown even stronger, and real estate, which raced ahead of U.S. stocks for much of the 1970s and continues to keep up in the 1980s. Analysts differ on whether this performance will continue. But they agree that diversified portfolios can be less volatile than all-equity accounts, be-cause swings in different elements of a broad portfolio often offset one another.

But do not overdiversify. You must be careful not to put too many

things into your investment portfolio (too many categories of investments, too many specialized areas). You can't keep tabs on such a
portfolio, and you will end up diversifying yourself into bankruptcy.
The biggest danger of overdiversification is that you will lose your
sense of timing—your ability to make decisions about when to buy
and when to sell. Some of the most successful money management and
mutual funds operations in the world handle global portfolios that have
no more than twelve or fifteen stocks in them at any one time, and
they're doing so with a full-time staff. To further underscore my point,
a major money manager recently told me of a similar finding. His
computers determined that if his portfolio exceeded twenty securities,
the law of averages starts going against him.

In other words, don't go overboard. There's no sense in having your
money in forty different places or forty different investments in the
same place. It's better to pick five or six areas and maintain only one
or two investments in each. You need to keep your portfolio relatively
simple so you won't be distracted by every deal that comes along. If
you pretend you only have ninety days to live, it will clarify the picture
remarkably for you. You will know what to sell and what to buy.

Let me back up for a moment and give you some additional perspective about your need to diversify. In the last couple of decades, inflation
has jumped up and fallen back. During its upward movement, it
pushed up the value of the dollar, precious metals, real estate, oil and
other "hard" assets. In the last couple of years, however, we have seen
a quick drop in the rate of inflation and interest rates, a fall in the value
of precious metals, oil, farmland, many collectibles and real estate, but
a surge in the stock and bond markets. A rise in interest rates is great
for new bond issues, hard on old ones, and it hurts real estate and
business expansion. Unpredictable changes in the tax laws hurt everyone, and over the last decade we have had six very major alterations
and numerous minor ones, with more of both coming.

What does all this mean? By diversifying, you're almost sure to have
investments that benefit from different swings of the business cycle.
By diversifying, you need not worry about investments that have a
strong balance sheet, or earnings, or management team, etc., that
slump for short periods of time. Most of my clients had money committed to the stock market well before the Great Bull Market started
in the fall of 1982. The market had been weak, but rather than reacting
to that, we planned ahead and followed basic economic principles. In
September 1982, after the stock market had begun its dramatic rise, a

reporter called to ask me whether I was now directing clients toward the market. I proudly answered that we already had money there.

When creating your portfolio, what sort of diversification would I recommend today? I recommend three categories:

1. An inflation or deflation hedge portion, which will include either gold and silver coins or a precious metals mutual fund. Also consider having some of your cash holdings outside of the banking system—for example, a government-backed money market fund.
2. An investment portion, which will give you a combination of regular income, plus the reasonable expectation of appreciation.
3. A speculative portion, in which growth, not investment income, is the concern.

Liquidity

Your need for liquidity is also a factor that must be considered in your investment plans. Liquidity is the ability to quickly move your assets into cash without significant loss. A checking account at a bank is very liquid, since automatic teller machines can supply cash twenty-four hours a day. An apartment building, however, is usually illiquid, for it can take months to sell. To ensure at least minimum liquidity, I suggest you open (or maintain) a money market mutual fund or a money market insured deposit account, or a tax-free money market account if you are in at least the 28 percent tax bracket. Such accounts are easily accessible during emergencies, yet pay a market rate of interest. You can also consider as part of your liquid emergency funds your checking account, U.S. savings bonds, cash value on life insurance policies, cash that can be easily withdrawn from other insurance products, and stocks and bonds. To further ensure your liquidity, you could even open a line of credit at a bank, establish an equity line against your home (see Chapter 6), borrow money from your retirement plan, borrow against your securities, or include the cash available through your credit cards. Still, I suspect that most of you will feel the best place for funds that may be needed on short notice would be in some kind of money market fund.

Some financial advisors recommend that the amount an emergency fund should cover is three months' living expenses, perhaps six months if only one spouse is working. Each of my clients, however, is comfortable with a different level of liquidity—some at $250,000, others at

$1,000. Either level, or anything in between or above or below, is acceptable—whatever makes you feel comfortable is what you should keep in liquid assets, or have available.

Before determining your comfort level, however, you should examine your entire portfolio. How much of your assets can you readily liquidate if your goals change? If you get divorced? If one of your children needs money for a down payment on a home? Common sense should prevail. If you are not sure of your job security or are in a volatile profession like advertising, you should probably have extra reserves. One client in such an occupation told me that if it weren't for those extra funds, the between-jobs pressure she suffered would have been devastating. She would have been forced to take the first offer that came along, which would not have been in the best interests of her career. She was very thankful.

Risk

Many people, when they first consult with me, say they want to be in control of their financial future, but do not want to take any risk. But what exactly is risk? The dictionary defines it as "Hazard; peril; exposure to loss or injury." I tell those same people there is no way you can avoid risk when investing capital. There is market risk (shifts in investor attitudes that can cause your investment to decline in value); social risk (for example, the government changes its regulations, thus converting a good investment into a poor one, or war breaks out, or a strike occurs); tax risk (IRS or congressional changes in the tax code that affect you adversely by disallowing a current tax advantage or change the tax law again, again, again); finally, there's the risk that you can't sell your assets if and when you need cash quickly.

So, with the many advertised investment choices offering "safety," just where is the safest place to keep your money? Due to all the confusion, the proverbial mattress is coming back into style because it's simple and present inflation is relatively low. Simple, yes. But safe, no. Not safe from burglary, fire or a high rate of inflation. Purchasing power would still be lost even at a comparatively low rate of inflation. If we have only an average annual rate of inflation of 5.2 percent for the next twenty years, you will require almost three times as much cash (and a bigger mattress to hold it) to purchase the same things you are buying today.

Many people hoard their money by purchasing Treasuries—bills, notes and bonds. They're "safe" because they're backed by the full taxing power of the federal government. But investors in all fixed-income securities can still face loss, for they are exposed to market risk. If interest rates rise, the market value of their lower yielding bond will decline to make it competitive with newer issues.

I could go on, but I think you now recognize every investment involves some sort of risk. And there are only three things you can do with risk: avoid, transfer or retain it.

When investing capital there is no way you can *avoid* risk. And the *transfer* of risk usually involves an insurance company. Are you (and your family) able to accept the risk that you (if you are the primary wage earner) may face an untimely death while still young and have not accumulated much in the way of assets? Or do you wish to transfer that risk to an insurance company through life insurance and let the company take the risk? There are many different ways of doing that (see Chapter 5).

Investment risk can also be transferred, or partly transferred. Some individuals purchase zero coupon bonds, which mature in the same period that a second investment is supposed to mature. That way, if the second investment fails, they will still have the money from the zero coupon bonds. You can purchase insurance to guarantee timely interest and principal payments of municipal bonds. While this removes those risks, however, it does not protect you from interim interest-rate risk.

If you choose to *retain* risk, you first must decide what kind of investor you are—a risk-taker or a risk-averter—but do not forget the relationship between risk and return. If you desire to invest in what you perceive as low risk, you must place your money in projects that have relatively low rates of return. If you are willing to accept very high risk, you must expect and demand a very high potential rate of return to compensate for the risks you are assuming.

When measuring risk, you must consider the return that could be earned in alternative investments. I usually like to use tax-free bonds as my standard of measurement. "Since I can receive a tax-free 7 percent return without a great deal of risk, how does investment 'X' compare?" If you believe you wish to accept risk (whether high or low) you should do so only after careful study of the investment. You should also take into account your age, current income (as well as expected future income), tax bracket, net worth and family circumstances.

In assessing your willingness to assume risk, one other variable requires soul searching: time. How much time are you willing and able to devote to your investment program? High-risk investments require more attention than conservative ones because they involve more active trading and greater risk of loss due to simple neglect.

Then there's the consideration of how much risk you are psychologically equipped to take. Since most people have trouble assessing their taste for risk, ask yourself this question: "Would it disturb me more to lose an opportunity for significant gain or to experience a significant loss?" The answer will help provide direction for your investment decisions. Even so you may still make mistakes, so another critical consideration is how well you can accept and recover from a decision that didn't work out the way you planned. Regardless of your financial situation and your tolerance for risk, any time you've traded a known for an unknown and that decision caused you to lose sleep at night, then that investment should be avoided.

An "I can't stand taking big chances" attitude most probably should lead you to an investment portfolio of high-grade municipal or corporate bonds and government securities. You can reduce the interest rate risk by staggering the maturities (see Chapter 10). If, however, you are a person who wants desperately to achieve, and are motivated to accomplish the goals you set for yourself, you may wind up with a portfolio of stocks in emerging growth companies and similar speculative investments. But you should learn to balance your risks by diversifying your portfolio, for that is at the core of a sound investment philosophy. Then, if the risky investments don't pay off, the slow and steady ones will keep you from being totally wiped out.

What is the perfect investment for you? Simply stated, the perfect investment for you is when your personality and sound judgment are in sync. Chances are, that's when you'll also achieve the best results. As a professional, when discussing risk, I advise my clients never to invest more money in the most risky category than they have in the least risky.

Chapter 10

Sleep-at-Night Earnings (SANE) —How to Invest with Self- Confidence *and* Safety

Interest is interesting, but it can also be confusing. Even sophisticated investors sometimes confuse debt instruments that pay interest with certain types of equity investments that pay dividends. So I'll come to the rescue for all of you. A dividend is a distribution of earnings declared by a board of directors and paid quarterly, whereas interest is the cost of using money and is expressed as a rate per period of time, usually semiannually or annually. Dividends come from ownership, which can also produce growth; and interest comes from debt, which is not meant to grow, but to produce safety.

Interest-bearing investments are the most basic element of a financial plan because they are both secure and productive. What's more, most people seem to like an investment that pays income, whether from interest or dividends. A recent private study conducted by an investment firm revealed that the majority of people, regardless of their income or level of net worth, desire investments that produce income. This result was so surprising that the company recommissioned the survey because it thought an error had been committed. No error. That regular check not only somehow makes an asset feel like a real investment, but also produces a psychological safety net. Growth just doesn't have the same impact.

I think it is important to be aware of this phenomenon when making your investment decisions. If only nonincome-paying potential growth investments have been on your shopping list, you might be well advised to add an investment that pays interest (or a dividend) to your portfolio. Even if you don't require current income, that occasional check will possibly help you feel better about your investments. As a

169

matter of fact, high-yield, low-risk investments are the foundation of every well-designed investment strategy.

Let's look at some of the more common interest-bearing investment opportunities that offer both income and relative safety.

Passbook Money

Banks call it "dumb money" and they love it. Dumb money is a deposit that earns little or no interest, but which the bank and savings and loan institutions can lend for maximum profit. I call it cash and cash-equivalent money because it is safe, highly liquid and convenient. And I don't think it's that dumb at all. While there are alternatives that pay better interest, a passbook account still provides the sleep-at-night comfort few other cash equivalent alternatives can.

On March 31, 1986, the federal government ended the 5½ percent interest-rate ceiling on passbook and statement savings accounts, freeing banks and thrifts to pay any rate they wish on the almost *$300 billion* pool of funds. Since that time, while the interest rate has remained unchanged in some instances, there are a number of cases where it has been reduced. With lower passbook interest rates, has there been a mass exodus of accounts? Hardly. Despite concern about taxes and, secondarily, inflation, almost 70 percent of the population that saves money has regular passbook savings accounts. And there it shall probably remain.

Why? Most people are inert; they want to go through life unhassled. According to the bankers, passbook and statement savers generally are conservative, blue-collar, elderly and prefer liquidity and an actual passbook they can see and clutch. According to the Federal Reserve Board, about 90 percent of savings accounts have balances of $1,000 or more. It isn't unusual for new clients to walk into my office with $12,000 to $14,000 in these accounts, and I recall several new clients with a number of passbook accounts, each holding $100,000.

In addition to the liquidity and passbook features, people who leave substantial amounts of money in passbook accounts generally fit two profiles. The first, and the most common, is a person who was a product of the Depression. These were lean, often jobless years, in which frugality was a necessity, and when millions of people lost their life savings. The Depression was certainly enough reason to have made these people highly conservative forever. Security, more than additional income, is their primary concern. Even though the higher-paying money market accounts at banks and savings and loans are insured, these people are still skeptical. And this wariness about money is sometimes passed on to their children.

The second profile group is similar to the Depression-era individual. These people either grew up in families where a great deal of money was lost or have themselves experienced major fluctuations in income. For these people, too, absolute security is more important than an increase in income.

If you see yourself in either of these groups, take note of it. You need not change—chances are you couldn't in any significant way, even if you wanted to—but you should recognize why you do what you do. Once you've gotten that far, you may see the logic in earning more from your money with the same amount of convenience and risk, and may later feel more comfortable shifting money from a passbook account to an insured higher-paying money market account or even a certificate of deposit.

Bank Market-Rate and Super NOW Accounts

My favorite bank or savings and loan account is the market-rate or Super NOW (negotiable order of withdrawal) account because these accounts are liquid and have check-writing privileges. The market-rate account, as its name implies, pays market rates and is less flexible than the Super NOW because you are limited in the number of checks you can write each month. The Super NOW pays a slightly lower rate and offers greater flexibility and, like the market-rate account, is insured up to $100,000 per account by the Federal Deposit Insurance Corporation (FDIC). These are good accounts to have because they are even more convenient than passbook savings, offer higher yields, and are also more liquid than certificates of deposit.

Certificates of Deposit (CDs)

These are the familiar time-deposit accounts offered by banks, thrifts and now brokerage firms. I like them because CD yields are generally higher than those of Treasury bills, money market funds or money market accounts, and it takes only $500 to buy most CDs. However, you'll typically find $1,000 or $2,500 minimums, especially where higher rates or premiums are advertised. As with passbook accounts,

CDs are insured up to $100,000 by the FDIC. Since the recent Ohio and Maryland bank crises, you should be more careful than ever to purchase your CD only from institutions backed by federal insurance, especially since you lock up your money for a fixed amount of time. Though the six-month period is most popular, you can place money into a CD for up to five years or longer if you like. The longer the time period, the higher the rate of interest.

If you're considering the purchase of a CD, and there is a possibility you may need your cash before maturity, I certainly would not suggest buying one with a maturity of more than five years. This is because all CD penalty provisions are stiff if you have to sell prematurely; usually you'll have to sacrifice thirty or more days' interest. On the other hand, if interest rates rise enough, cashing in your CD and reinvesting the funds at a higher rate of interest might still be advantageous, even after the penalty. If you think you may need your CD principal before maturity, I recommend you stagger purchases of smaller CDs throughout the year; their expiration terms are usually three, six, nine or twelve months. By doing so, you are never far away from a maturing CD. If your funds are adequate, you could carry this idea even further by purchasing sequential CDs so that one comes due each year for five years. Then if you don't need the money from the maturing CD, you could purchase another with the longest maturity. By utilizing this system, you will have a higher (average) yield than you could receive by purchasing only one-year CDs, but still have flexibility as well as the knowledge that a CD will come due each year. Furthermore, if interest rates rise, by purchasing CDs with the longest maturities sequentially, you will not only be able to participate in the higher yield, but will also help increase your overall yield. All of this without locking up your money for five or more years.

Another choice whereby you can have CD liquidity is to buy a federally insured CD from a brokerage firm. Brokerage firms, unlike banks, maintain active secondary markets in CDs, so you can usually avoid the standard penalty for early withdrawal, but your sale price may be more or less than your principal plus interest, depending on whether rates are up or down.

And now there is also a new type of CD that is an earnings-based insured CD, combining the safety of government insurance with the up-side potential of a traditional investment in real estate. What it all comes down to is a possible 13 to 15 percent average annual return by the end of the certificate of deposit term.

Earnings-based CDs invested in real estate are usually a ten-year instrument for which the brokers (who sell them) will make a market for resale. You take a slightly lower guaranteed fixed rate of return than with a ten-year regular insured CD, but for accepting a below-market rate, you get something radically new: "contingent interest," which consists of interest income plus equity participation in a commercial mortgage pool that could add as much as 6 to 8 percent to the annual return.

Earnings-based CDs are not an investment in a real estate limited partnership. There are no tax deductions, and all interest income is taxed as passive income. They do, however, let you invest in real estate with the safety of an insured CD, since these CDs are also insured up to $100,000 by the FDIC or the Federal Savings and Loan Insurance Corporation (FSLIC). They are also an inflation hedge since you can benefit from a rise in interest rates, inflation and the value of real estate.

What are the CD drawbacks? First, nonbrokerage firm CDs are subject to early withdrawal penalties, as mentioned above, usually at least thirty days' interest. Also, unless the CD is part of an IRA, Keogh or other qualified retirement account or deferred plan, or unless you are in a relatively low tax bracket, you'll be fully taxed on the interest. There are, however, some CDs where the interest (and tax) can be deferred for a year.

Tip: Since interest rates vary from bank to bank, and there are many different methods of stating yields on CDs, it can be difficult to compare one with another. Shop around a bit and ask a financial institution representative exactly how much, in dollar terms, you get, and when you will receive it. That's the clearest way to compare rates and terms.

Wasn't life simple a few years back? Your choice in savings accounts amounted to two: passbooks or simplified CDs. Now if you ask, "What do you have?" be prepared for an avalanche of answers.

U.S. Treasury Issues

Backed by Uncle Sam, Treasury issues are among the safest investments you can make. And they are exempt from state and local taxes, too, but not federal.

Treasury Bills

Treasury bills, maturing in three, six or twelve months, are generally referred to as 13-week, 26-week and 52-week bills and are the shortest-term U.S. Treasury issues. They are sold in increments of $5,000, beginning with a $10,000 minimum purchase. They are issued in bearer form, not registered on the books of the issuer, and thus are payable to whoever possesses them; they should therefore be kept in a safe place. They are issued on a discount basis, which means they are sold below their face value—but that face amount is what you'll receive when the bill becomes due. The difference between what you paid for the bill and what you receive at maturity is, in effect, interest, and interest rates will vary with market conditions.

If you purchase a Treasury bill that matures in the following year, none of the interest will be taxed until the bill comes due. This feature can be an effective tax-planning tool when a lump sum of money has been received and you wish to transfer the income (and tax) into the next (lower tax bracket) year. As mentioned in Chapter 7, a new way to employ this tax-smart technique is to purchase one or more Treasury bills for your 13-year old child, to come due any time in the year when he or she is 14. Since 14 is now the age that for tax purposes a child becomes an adult, the Treasury bill income will then be taxed at a very low or nonexistent rate.

In addition to using Treasury bills for tax-planning purposes, they can also be effectively used when you have temporary uninvested funds, haven't yet decided what else to do with them and place safety above all. Treasury bills, and all other Treasury issues, can be purchased by individual investors from banks, brokers or from Federal Reserve Banks when first issued. You can also purchase them as part of U.S. government money market or securities funds, which I'll discuss later in this chapter.

Treasury Notes

Treasury notes are not discounted and so pay interest at fixed rates every six months. The rate, of course, depends on the time to maturity, which is from one to ten years. For Treasury notes of two, three and four years, the minimum purchase is $5,000 and increases in multiples of $1,000. For notes over four years, the minimum purchase is only $1,000, which means more people can afford them.

Treasury Bonds

Treasury bonds make up most of the federal debt because the government finances primarily for the long term. These instruments can be intermediate term—five to ten years—or long term—up to thirty years —and are available in units of $1,000 to $10,000 in both registered (with your name on it) and bearer form. Interest is paid semiannually, as with Treasury notes. In fact, Treasury notes and bonds are essentially the same, the primary difference being the length of maturity; the note's maturity is from one to ten years, while the $5,000 bond's minimum maturity is four years.

I believe both these notes and bonds can have a place in your portfolios for reasons similar to CDs. The bearer feature of Treasury bonds may be of special interest to some of you, but the extremely high safety feature should be of interest to all. If the FDIC had to step in to protect your CD, there might be some delay in payment and uneasiness on your part. That would not happen with Treasury issues.

Zero Coupon Bonds

Zero coupon bonds have fast become a staple of the small and large investor's portfolio. They are simple, inexpensive and particularly attractive as investment vehicles for IRAs, Keoghs, self-directed retirement plans and college education plans.

Zeros have an unusual way of getting to your portfolio. In effect, after buying Treasury bonds or notes, brokerage firms strip them of their interest coupons, rechristen them zero coupon bonds and resell them to investors at well below their face value. When the zero matures, all principal and interest is paid to the investor. Because a zero retains each interest payment and reinvests it at the same rate, it's the only investment that lets you reinvest interest payments and know exactly what you'll end up with at the time you make the investment.

To better understand zero coupons, a brief explanation of a normal bond is in order. Presume you have a $1,000 face-value bond, paying 10 percent annual interest, with payments semiannually and the principal to be returned in twenty years. You would pay $1,000, knowing the $1,000 will be repaid twenty years from now. For the use of that money, the bond issuer pays $100 a year ($50 each six months). The total payback, after twenty years, will be $2,000 in interest and $1,000 in principal.

What the normal bond does not provide is a guarantee that when you collect the interest, reinvestment interest rates will be the same. That is the beauty of zero coupons: They also guarantee the reinvestment rate. Instead of putting up $1,000 for a $1,000 bond, you can pay as little as $100, with interest accruing within the bond over time.

Though you forgo semiannual interest payments, you collect $1,000 when the bond matures. The same $1,000 used to purchase a normal $1,000 face-value bond, if used to purchase ten zero coupon bonds, could assure you of $10,000 at maturity.

The awful twist is that income from a zero is taxable *now*, even though you won't see a penny of it until the bond or note matures. That is why zeros are so appealing for qualified retirement plans, deferred income plans and for your children if they have an appropriately low tax bracket.

Corporations and municipalities also offer zero coupon bonds. But for maximum safety, U.S. Treasury zeros can't be beat. In fact, if you have limited cash, are in a low tax bracket and need to earn a specific amount for a future debt, zero coupon bonds may be one of the better ideas around.

EE Series U.S. Savings Bonds

U.S. savings bonds are another of the more popular government debt instruments. They involve no commission or fee, are totally secure, and there's no risk of principal loss. In addition, they provide the option to postpone federal tax liability until redemption, are free from state and local taxes, have a guaranteed minimum interest rate and a variable yield that is compounded semiannually. Minimum investment: $25. For more on this, one of my favorite investment vehicles, please see Chapter 13.

Though they almost sound like the zero coupon bonds, EEs have an advantage over zeros because they have a variable rate of interest. If inflation rises, usually interest rates follow. With an EE variable rate you will not be out of step with the times. The floating rate is reset every May and November at 85 percent of the average market yield on five-year Treasury notes and bonds sold during the previous six-month period. But as I stated earlier, the rate is guaranteed not to fall below a relatively high minimum, even if prevailing Treasury yields would indicate a lower figure. That's *especially* attractive if interest rates continue to drop. And there's no cap on how high the rate can go.

There are also series HH bonds, which are sold at face value and pay a fixed rate of interest twice a year. Their lowest denomination is $500. As with EE bonds, you must hold HH bonds at least six months after the issue date before redeeming them. But their primary advantage is that you can exchange EEs for HHs without incurring a tax liability. You would do so, presumably, because you now desire to receive a check and because continued safety is assured. HHs can be an excellent vehicle for some of your retirement funds.

Federal Agency Securities

Federal agency securities are similar to the government securities discussed above, but they usually produce a slightly higher rate of return. All kinds of federal agencies offer instruments, from Banks for Cooperatives to the Small Business Administration, from Federal International Credit Banks to the U.S. Postal Service. Federal agency securities come in so many shapes and sizes, you really need an expert —probably your broker—to help you determine which of these instruments, if any, would best suit your needs. With the exception of Ginnie Maes, my guess is that most of these securities will simply confuse you —unless you like staying up nights to study them.

Ginnie Mae Pass-Throughs (GNMAs)

GNMA pass-throughs, short for Government National Mortgage Association pass-throughs, a.k.a. Ginnie Maes, are the best known in this group. With those aliases, you might think that Ginnie Mae is a bit flighty, but she has always played it straight. She always has and I know she always will (like clockwork) make timely principal and interest payments. In fact, Uncle Sam believes in her so much that he unconditionally guarantees Ginnie Mae.

Ginnie Maes are created by grouping many Federal Housing Administration (FHA) and Veterans Administration (VA) mortgages into a mortgage pool. Following approval by the Government National Mortgage Association, certificates are issued against the pool and placed in the portfolios of investors like yourself. Interest and principal payments are collected from homeowners, and they are passed through to investors based on their degree of participation in the pool. All payments of principal and interest are guaranteed by GNMA to be on time and paid in full. Furthermore, "the full faith and credit" of the U.S. Treasury is pledged as part of this guarantee, and each certificate is imprinted with this pledge. That means Ginnie Maes have the same basic safety as U.S. Treasury bills, notes, bonds and EE savings bonds.

Because they have consistently paid more than Treasury bonds, Ginnie Maes are regarded as the highest yielding available investment opportunity provided by the "full faith and credit" guarantee of the U.S. Treasury. Specifically, Ginnie Maes usually yield between 0.5 percent and 1 percent more than long-term Treasury bonds. But Ginnie Maes differ from bonds because they retire part of the principal along with the interest payments. This can be either good or bad news: Bad news because, unless planned for, a holder will not get any money back when the Ginnie Mae matures, so unless the principal is being reinvested, there will be nothing at the end. The good news is that the self-liquidating feature could be used positively for retirees (see Chapter 4).

The maturity feature of Ginnie Maes is another investment quality that can be a two-edged sword. Though the maturity is typically thirty years, statistical studies show the average life is about twelve years, due to prepayments. I like that feature, since it places Ginnie Maes into the category of an intermediate-term bond. However, at present there is considerable uncertainty about the average maturity of mortgage pools. While GNMA funds are protected against default, they aren't guarded against prepayment or market fluctuations. Quicker repayments during these periods of falling mortgage rates have shortened the average life of a GNMA investment to as little as two years because many homeowners have been rushing to refinance. Sure, when interest rates rise, most homeowners will hold on to their mortgages, but at present that means that some of the mortgages backing up the Ginnie Mae certificates are being closed before all the interest payments have been made, which reduces the yield. Without understanding Ginnie Mae's sometimes unpredictable behavior, many investors are misled by the boldfaced type in Ginnie Mae ads, which suggest that the yield is constant when buying a Ginnie Mae mutual fund or unit trust. Of course, it is impossible to predict when prepayments will be made; therefore, a fund cannot reliably predict future yields, nor should you depend upon a rate as a fixed rate.

But Ginnie Maes are popular—and I like them. I like the fact that they are high-yielding, intermediate term and self-liquidating. I like the fact that they can and do still return a higher yield than competing similar-quality investments. You just have to understand Ginnie Maes, that's all. And if you invest in them through a mutual fund or unit trust, you can arrange to have your principal (and interest) reinvested in new shares or units. This saves you from worrying about what to do with the income if you do not currently require the cash and you can gain the benefits of compounding. It also keeps you from spending your principal.

Though the minimum Ginnie Mae certificate is $25,000 and may be increased in $5,000 increments, the mutual fund or unit trust minimum is no more than $1,000, and IRA minimums are far less.

Real Estate Mortgage Investment Conduits (REMICs)

In the past few years, mortgages and other types of loans have been bundled into securities and sold to individual and institutional investors.

The most common of these are Ginnie Mae mutual funds (see above), but the market for "asset-backed securities" is much broader than just Ginnie Maes. Though there are other quasi-government agencies similar to GNMA that also offer similar securities, we now have, as a result of the 1986 tax reform act, REMICs.

REMICs are designed to act much like a Ginnie Mae mutual fund, only they are better because they can solve the problem for many investors in mortgage securities—early retirement of loans in the pool. And their yield can also exceed that of a Ginnie Mae.

A REMIC is a mortgage pool placed in a trust, then sold to the public. One key characteristic of these trusts is that the issuers can tailor the securities to individual needs. This is accomplished by breaking the trust into two to four segments called "tranches," the French word for "slice." Each tranche has an expected maturity. And each tranche, or REMIC, makes payments to investors on a monthly basis.

You can purchase REMICs through many of the larger brokerage firms. Beware: You may know about REMICs before your broker.

Tax-Exempt Bonds

Everyone wants to decrease his or her tax payments. Since municipal bonds offer interest with no federal tax—and no state and local taxes, if issued in your state of residence—it's small wonder that these bonds are one of the more popular investments today. They could be called tax-advantaged investments for the cautious. But you need to determine whether you should purchase a taxable or tax-exempt bond; therefore you must calculate the equivalent taxable yield for a tax-exempt bond. You make the conversion by dividing the return rate of the tax-exempt bond by the reciprocal of your tax bracket. (The reciprocal is 100 minus your tax rate—72 percent if your bracket is 28 percent, 67 percent if your bracket is 33 percent, etc.—and don't forget to include your net state income tax rate, if applicable.) So if the tax-exempt bond pays 7 percent, and your tax bracket is 28 percent, divide 7 by 72 percent (0.72). The equivalent taxable yield for this 7 percent tax-exempt bond, consequently, is 9.72 percent. If you're in the 33 percent federal tax bracket, the equivalent taxable yield would be 10.45 percent. This and other formulas can help you calculate the advantages of owning either tax-exempt or taxable bonds whose higher yields might be lost to taxes. But generally, because the yield spreads between tax-exempt bonds and taxable bonds have narrowed to record lows, municipal bonds can even make sense for you if you are in the 15 percent federal tax bracket, especially if you are also in a state where there is a state and/or local tax.

Municipals currently are issued in registered form, but most outstanding issues are in bearer form. The bearer form remains popular with many clients simply because of their anonymity. Interest is paid in six-month intervals for both forms, but paid directly to holders of registered bonds, while those who own bearer bonds must clip their coupons and personally redeem them for cash.

One of the unusual features of municipal bonds is their wide range of available maturity dates. When issued, bond maturities usually go from one to thirty years, and municipalities often offer bonds that mature in each of these years. This makes a municipal bond an excellent candidate for establishing a sequential maturity portfolio, which may reduce the risk of changing interest rates. Because the longest term bonds pay the highest income, most investors continue to prefer bonds with the longest maturities. But as I've mentioned earlier in this chapter, and elsewhere in the book, that's a dangerous gamble.

You should be aware that if you plan to purchase individual municipal bonds, the bonds are issued in $5,000 denominations. However, the general wisdom is that unless you have a minimum of $100,000, you should not purchase individual issues. You will not be able to gain enough diversification with a lesser amount of money, since any purchase below a $25,000-unit size is considered an "odd lot." You don't want to be considered an odd lot do you? With a smaller purchase you often pay above market prices when you purchase, as well as an "odd lot" penalty. And we all know that means you'll receive less money when you sell. If you do "qualify," and are a first-time municipal bond buyer purchasing individual issues, I generally advocate purchasing only insured or top-quality, triple-A-rated bonds. Though less than 1 percent of all municipal bonds issued since the Depression have gone into default, and an even smaller percentage never repaid their obligations, I recommend the above because of the "unknowns" due to tax reform. Stick to quality, and you'll never have to say, "I'm sorry."

And speaking of tax reform, a new class of municipal bonds has been created. Income from private-purpose municipal bonds (defined as Industrial Development Bonds if more than 10 percent of the proceeds benefit a private party such as student loans, commercial redevelopment, residential mortgages) issued after August 7, 1986, will be subject to the alternative minimum tax (see Chapter 15). For individuals whose income is high, interest on bonds subject to this tax may be hit by as much as 21 percent. Might this apply to you? A couple with two children and $50,000 of taxable income (after deductions) can have up to about $40,000 of sheltered income before they face the alternative minimum tax. With $150,000 of taxable income, they could have $73,000 of tax-preference income in 1988 before falling into the alternative minimum tax category. Translating that into market demand, the latter couple could buy up to $1 million of 7 percent tax-free bonds (regardless of whether the issues are subject to the minimum tax) before paying additional tax. Whatever your income, it is always wise to make sure that the tax-exempts you may want to add to your portfolio are in line with your expectations as to what portion of the income is tax-exempt.

Then there are taxable municipals—something else to complicate your choice. These include new issues for pollution control facilities, convention and trade show facilities, industrial parks and many tax-increment and redevelopment bonds that will no longer be federally exempt but will be exempt from state income tax. Several high-quality issues have come to the market with taxable yields at 1 to 1½ percentage points more than on comparable Treasuries, and slightly more than on comparable corporate bonds. Another attractive feature is that they are usually issued for only ten years and are not callable. But before purchase, you should calculate the equivalent taxable yield for a tax-exempt bond.

What are your risks? Most taxable municipals are revenue bonds, so your interest payments come not from the municipalities themselves, but from the ultimate users of the funds. If the money goes for housing, for example, and the builder defaults, you'd be the loser. Again, stick with the highest rated bonds.

If you think making municipal bonds taxable is bad, think again. What the government has accomplished is to create a new, exciting investment alternative. Now you can place taxable municipal bonds into a retirement account, maintain high safety levels, yet create a higher level of income than could otherwise have been had. Tax reform has even manufactured a new municipal bond that can be effectively used for your children's education costs: zero coupon securities that can be created to mature every six months. In the past, municipal zero coupon bonds were a popular investment for gifting or funding long-term financial goals, but they had drawbacks. They were usually very long-term bonds—25- to 35-year maturities—and had call dates in ten to fifteen years. Frequently, they were part of a housing bond issue. Since future housing issues will be sharply restricted, these zeros are probably doomed to extinction. But with some obscure language in the 1986 tax reform law (filed under the section dealing with taxes on alcohol, firearms and tobacco), baby zeros were born. (For a more complete discussion on this new type of bond, please see Chapter 7.)

There are so many different types of bonds available, and so many nuances to consider, that whole books have been devoted to the subject. You almost need a computer to keep track of all the variables. If you don't wish to get caught up in the details of municipal bonds, if you don't understand, or don't want to understand things like call features or the difference between general obligation and revenue bonds, then buy shares of a tax-exempt bond mutual fund or unit trust, investment pools whose managers should be able to pick the best credit risks. If sales are an indicator, hundreds of thousands of investors have already said the heck with it and are letting somebody else figure it all out. In each type of investment pool you have a professionally chosen investment, excellent diversification and greater liquidity than with a single bond, and with a mutual fund, besides being able to invest as little as $100, you also have ongoing portfolio management. (Since mutual funds can play such an important role in your financial plan, I discuss them in greater depth in Chapter 12.)

In contrast to mutual funds, unit-investment trusts are composed of nonmanaged or fixed portfolios. Each trust portfolio is made up of a single type of income-producing securities, and the portfolio will remain fixed until all the securities have matured and unit holders have recovered their principal. As an investor, a unit holder receives an undivided interest in both the principal and the income portion of the portfolio in proportion to the amount of capital he or she invests.

So, some unit-investment trusts are composed of corporate bonds, government bonds, preferred stock, mortgaged-backed securities and (surprise again) municipal bonds. The advantages of a unit trust are that the portfolio is known in advance and that the level of income is reasonably predictable. However, trust values are difficult to locate; reinvestment must be made into a different trust, which creates confusion, and the initial minimum investment size is usually in the $1,000 to $5,000 range. I definitely prefer municipal bond mutual funds.

Whether you choose a mutual fund or a unit trust as your investment vehicle, there remains yet another decision that should first be addressed. Do you want a multistate package or a package made up of municipal bonds from a single state, usually the state in which you reside (and have a state income tax)? Under the new tax bill, state taxes will account for a bigger portion of your total tax bite. So more than likely, you will gain maximum tax benefit by investing in single-state (your state) bond funds or trusts, since the income generated from these pools is usually exempt from all three taxes: federal, state and local.

Single-Premium Life Insurance

One of the big winners after tax reform is a new form of insurance called single-premium whole life insurance (SPWL). But don't let the term "life insurance" discourage you. With an SPWL, for an amount ranging from $5,000 to $1 million or more, you get a paid-up insurance policy. But the truth is, the insurance you buy is minimal, just enough to conform to the standards set by the 1984 tax law. A 40-year-old man who invests $100,000, for instance, might get only $250,000 worth of death benefits. So if it's family protection you're after, look for better values elsewhere.

Single-premium whole life insurance is primarily an investment vehicle, and because it's technically a life insurance policy under the law's definition, your investment can include some unusual features. Some people refer to it as four investment-oriented products rolled into one contract. It's like a CD, since the interest rates paid on your deposit (premium) can be guaranteed for one, three, five and seven years; no sales charges are deducted from the deposit; and loss of interest penalties only exist if the policy is surrendered prematurely. It's like a municipal bond since tax-free distributions are available. It's like an annuity since interest accumulates on a tax-deferred basis. And it's like a life insurance policy since a tax-free death benefit is available. Too good to be true? Perhaps, but it is legitimate until Congress says otherwise.

Quite apart from the wonders of tax deferral and compounding, as well as the advantages of having life insurance, the unique characteristic of an SPWL that has many people overly anxious is the tax free status awarded to distributions from an SPWL contract. Since these policies are, by definition, life insurance contracts, loans are considered tax free as well. Because the "loan" meets IRS standards for a transaction with the policy, the money is not taxed, and you may never have to pay it back. To top it off, insurance companies are making it attractive to borrow. A policy owner may borrow at a net one-half of 1 percent or even lower.

Let's see how it works. Assume you wish tax-free income. Before, your only alternative was a municipal bond, a municipal bond fund or unit trust. However, with municipal bonds, as described earlier, comes a degree of market risk. If an emergency arose and market conditions were unfavorable, you might have to liquidate at a loss. Not so with an SPWL. You can borrow against the value of the policy, and a $100,000 deposit into a SPWL could currently provide you approximately $7,500 of annual income tax free. The insurance company might charge you 7½ percent for the loan, but would also credit $7,500 worth of your account with 7½ interest. It would be a wash, and you'd wind up with tax-free cash. In addition, your principal is guaranteed at all times by the insurance company, not to mention the tax-free death benefit of perhaps two to four times the original deposit. The only time you would pay taxes is if you were to surrender the SPWL contract, but there are ways to overcome that. When you wish to surrender in order to reposition those dollars in other investments or for any other reason, you don't actually surrender, rather you borrow the principal. Many insurance companies will only charge you 2 to 3 percent when you borrow more than the accumulated interest, although some policies let you dip 10 to 15 percent into principal before that charge kicks in. (You can't deduct the "interest" on the loan.)

Ah, but there can be problems, too. If you retrieve all of the principal via a loan and fail to keep up with the interest payments, the policy will lapse—with dire consequences. All of the interest that built up inside the policy would retroactively lose its tax-free status and become taxable. Boom!

That potential tax burden is the company's built-in insurance that you'll hold on to the policy. To keep you from canceling in the first few years—before the tax consequences are too severe—most policies also have surrender charges. These charges usually begin at 6 to 10 percent of the cash value in the first year, then taper off each year until they disappear.

Tax realities and surrender charges make single-premium whole life and single-premium variable life insurance (similar to SPWL, except that an investor is allowed to direct deposits among numerous portfolios, in a manner similar to variable annuities) long-term investments —at least for part of the original deposit. However, the tax law will permit you to exchange one policy for another without triggering the tax bill, much as you may transfer funds in an IRA tax free. You might, however, have to repay any outstanding loans against the policy before you made the exchange in order to avoid tax on any funds you borrowed.

Is this for you? You should seriously consider the SPWL as a core or basic part of your portfolio at almost any age. When you are younger the insurance factor comes in handy. When you are older, the security is of primary importance. The single-premium life and deferred annuity products are available through most insurance salespeople, stockbrokers and financial planners. As always, shop around. Compare insurers' rates, the extent of rate guarantees and the stability of the insurance companies themselves.

Universal Life

If you want cash-value insurance, similar to whole life, yet you desire a more competitive rate of interest and a flexible premium, universal life is probably the policy you should consider. Its flexibility is its main appeal.

The premiums can be fixed or a variable amount paid monthly, quarterly or annually. You can increase or reduce it from time to time or even skip an occasional year if your family is in a bind. Cash values of universal life earn rates of return that are competitive with single-premium whole life or deferred annuities. The interest earned is at current Treasury bill rates, those of other government securities or other money market funds. The cash value earnings, however, generally reflect current economic conditions and, as with other insurance products, are not currently taxed to the policy holders.

The policy holder also has access to cash values. Within certain limits, he or she can draw funds or borrow against cash values without an interest charge, as one might do with a traditional policy, as long as he or she maintains sufficient cash value to pay the cost of protection. However, policy loans generally are at 6 to 8 percent. If you are primarily seeking a low-cost method to withdraw money from a life insurance product, then in my opinion single-premium whole life is the answer.

Tax-Deferred Annuities

Though you may not have heard much about deferred annuities, the concept is not new. As a matter of fact, it dates back to the days of the Roman Empire. A number of investors are turning to single-premium deferred annuities (SPDAs) for financial security in their retirement. The SPDA is especially attractive if you have an amount of cash from a maturing CD and want to avoid placing it in a taxable investment.

The SPDA works in a similar way to a pension plan or a nondeductible IRA, but with only one payment into the plan, usually a $2,500 minimum, with a maximum $500,000. I like tax-deferred annuities and recommend them often. These are accounts offered by insurance companies. Therefore if a high-quality insurance company is chosen, your investment should be secure. But SPDAs aren't really about insurance; they're about tax shelter. The big attraction lies in the fact that taxes on the compounding interest are deferred until money (as a lump sum or in periodic payments) is withdrawn at retirement. In short, the government keeps its hands off the cash buildup until you draw it out. This tax feature alone would make SPDAs an attractive alternative to CDs, even if the annuities pay a slightly lower interest rate. But to add to SPDAs' popularity, many are now out-earning CDs, before taking taxes into account.

The SPDA is great if you can afford to put your money away for a long time and have a low tolerance for risk. They must be considered a long-term investment because anyone who withdraws before age 59½ (except in the case of disability or death) must pay income tax on the distributions, plus an IRS penalty of 10 percent. Even for those who wait until 59½, distributions are taxed at your normal tax rate until all deferred income has been paid out. The nontaxable return of principal comes later.

The tax-deferred annuity is also a perfect complementary investment for someone with a portfolio that is heavily weighted to municipal bonds. Though municipal bonds are tax free, they do carry an interest-rate risk, whereas with a typical SPDA you can lock in an interest rate for three months, six months, a year or three years. Some insurance companies guarantee the current rate for as long as five years. Most plans then tie the deferred rate of interest to some sort of price index to remain competitive with other interest-bearing investments. Though insurance companies will levy a surrender charge of up to 10 percent of the accumulated annuity value for withdrawals over 10 percent, a return of your full principal is usually guaranteed by the insurance company, even if you take your money out the day after you've placed money with the company.

Once upon a time, annuities were able to be used as "temporary shelters" by high-bracket taxpayers. People were able then, as you can now, to place their money into an annuity and allow the interest to accrue tax-deferred. However, they were also able to withdraw money and declare those withdrawals to be a return of their original investment dollars. Thus, no tax due. Though the government several years ago said, "No more," all my clients who still have this option available have yet to use it. I suspect this is another example of the government screaming "Foul!" though there were too few players on the field to make a difference.

Still another point to consider is (more) tax reform. Life insurance has long had the benefit of tax-deferred cash buildup because Congress considered it a "social good." But if it believes the reason for the tax-deferred aspect of life insurance is abused—as it probably will be, considering the way it is being promoted lately—then the chances are good that the present advantage will be lost. While you could lose certain benefits from a new investment because of another tax law change, you will gain from existing benefits in the interim. Even if the tax-deferral feature is rejected (if ever), as with my clients who are still able to withdraw money from an annuity without taxation, you may also be able to continue to defer taxes if you had your money in one of these contracts before a law change.

What should you look for when purchasing a SPDA? You should first inquire, "What is the company's Best rating?" Make sure that you only consider annuities offered by companies rated "A" or better by A. M. Best Company, which tracks industry results. If an insurance company has not received Best's top rating for the past ten years, I say forget it. The Lipper Analytical Survey will also help you determine which companies have been (and currently are) doing well.

Then does the SPDA have an "escape" or "bailout" clause? Some annuities allow you to take out all of your money at no charge if interest rates fall more than 1 or 2 percent below the rate at the time of purchase. Look for a similar bailout clause if the renewal rate for your annuity lags more than 1 or 2 percent behind the rates of the insurance company's new annuity offerings.

Should you desire an alternative type of annuity, you might prefer a variable SPDA. You can choose to have your money go to work in several kinds of mutual funds within the annuity—common stocks, aggressive growth stocks, high-grade or junk bonds, GNMAs, zero coupon bonds, even money market funds. Your return then depends entirely on the performance of the underlying fund, and you are likely to be charged a yearly management fee of 1.5 to 1.75 percent of your assets.

Corporate Bonds

Another kind of debt vehicle you should consider is the corporate bond. And as you can probably guess, I'm going to tell you there are more types of corporate debt instruments (from equipment trust certificates to convertible bonds, to Eurobonds, to "bankbacks," to put-bonds) and strategies where they can be applied than you'll ever know what to do with. There's something for everyone, that's for sure—even maturities exceeding 100 years. The only thing to be aware of is that, in general, a corporate bond is likely to be riskier than the government debt instruments previously mentioned because the risk of default by a corporation is usually greater than that of a government. Since a corporate bond's safety is generally accounted for in the bond's ratings, I generally recommend an AA or AAA rating and maturity dates that do not exceed the intermediate term (three to ten years). Again, this is to reduce the chance of default and interest rate risk.

Like municipal bonds, corporate bonds can be purchased individually, through mutual funds or through unit trusts. Those that can be purchased through mutual funds, which actively manage the bond portfolio, are my preference. However, corporate bonds can also be purchased through "closed-end" funds, where a fixed number of shares are outstanding and are traded and valued on the open market. ("Open-end" mutual funds are those where you buy and sell your shares directly to the management company at a net asset value.) By the way, ask your broker or financial planner if he knows what a debenture is. If the answer is "a rich couple's teen-age daughter's debut," I suggest you find another advisor. A debenture is a general debt or an unsecured bond, backed only by the integrity of the borrower. A secured bond, however, is backed by collateral, and should therefore be safer.

Private Loans

Private loans are "investments" of lower security. You can't overlook private personal loans; most of us make them at one time or another. Very often my clients will have lent significant sums of money to friends or members of the family at less than the going interest rates and with no form of security other than a handshake. Most such loans are made because you want to help the borrower, not because it's a good investment. When push comes to shove, will you really be able to foreclose, even if the loan is secured? If you do make personal loans, I believe you should view this money as possible noncollectible funds. Any other view is likely to teach you a lesson you'd prefer not to learn.

Dividend-Paying Stocks

I'm going to detour here for a moment to discuss cash dividends paid by common and preferred stocks, which also provide safety like interest-bearing investments. As long as a stock pays a fixed dividend, be it a utility or a corporate stock, there is a point below which the stock will not usually drop. Someone, somewhere will always be interested in purchasing your holding just for the income. And its relative return will increase as the per-share market value falls. If the dividend is intact and secure, the lower security price will make its purchase more attractive. In short, it can work very much like a debt instrument.

I often recommend individual utility stocks (the exception to my "don't buy individual issues" rule) or utility mutual funds even if a client is not particularly enamored of the stock market. Utility stocks can "feel" like bonds because they are perceived as secure. But if you own utilities, you can also participate in dividend increases. Furthermore, with oil prices and interest rates at the lower end of the scale, many utilities are making a great deal more money and are not only able to increase dividend payouts, as is often the case, but these days the increases have been substantial. Of course, there are also utilities that got into trouble due to cost overruns when building nuclear power plants. Many such utilities were forced to suspend their dividend entirely. Which means, as always, you should carefully investigate the utility before you invest. Where income and safety are important, I believe known high-quality, dividend-producing investments, whether directly or through mutual funds, can be another highly liquid, possibly high-reward addition to a portfolio.

Money Market Funds

You may be wondering why I discussed dividends before I covered money market mutual funds. Well, there's a simple reason: even if 100 percent of the income from a money market mutual fund is interest, the government still calls it a dividend. But since both are taxed in the same manner, I'll just attribute the word "confusion" to another of the government's sleight-of-hand tricks.

A money market fund is a cash and cash-equivalent mutual fund that provides free check-writing privileges and seeks maximum current interest through investments in specified money market instruments. The fund can invest in a diversified group or specific group of high-yielding borrowings, such as CDs, Treasury securities, government agency issues, corporate promissory notes and other obligations. All these have short maturities, sometimes averaging as little as one day. Because short-term investments earn high interest rates, your return on a money market fund rate can be higher than those of savings accounts or certificates of deposit.

I'm frequently asked about the safety of money market funds. This is a consideration, since banks and savings and loans accounts are insured up to $100,000 by the federal government and money market funds do not have such insurance. However, in my opinion, these funds are still very low risk. They select short-term investments of low-risk issuers, and would incur losses only if these major issuers defaulted on their obligations. With diversification, even that would involve but a small portion of the portfolio. The other noteworthy risk, that of the fund management company's having financial problems, is negligible if you select a recognized major money market fund.

If you're still a little leery of money funds, you can further increase the already high safety by investing in a fund that invests only in U.S. government obligations. But since this is a very, very low-risk fund, the yields will be somewhat less than those of other money market funds. U.S. government and regular money market funds can be purchased through securities dealers or by dealing directly with the companies that sell and manage the funds. For many, the initial minimum investment is as little as $100, and there is no commission charge.

Bank Market Rate Accounts *vs.* Money Market Funds

In 1982, deregulation of the banking industry enabled banks to market accounts that compete with money market funds. The banks' market rate accounts initially paid higher rates than money market funds in an effort to regain the many billions of dollars that had earlier flowed out of the banking system and into the money funds. After that early period, bank rates fell and are still somewhat lower than money market fund rates.

The major competitive advantage of the banks' market rate accounts is that they are insured by the FDIC. The competitive edge of the money market funds comes in the form of lower minimum balances (bank account yields drop to passbook rates if the average balance falls below $2,500) and more flexible check-writing privileges (if you write more than three checks in any given statement month, bank account yields drop to passbook rates).

The Super NOW account, your third choice, was introduced by banks after the market rate account. It requires a minimum balance of $2,000 and allows unlimited check writing. However, it pays a yield approximately 1 percent below the market rate accounts.

These investments are appropriate for cash you want to keep immediately liquid for current expenses and emergencies and extra cash on hand while you consider other investments. The proper choice for you among these three depends upon your feelings about flexibility, safety and yield. The money market mutual fund provides the best combination of yield and flexibility, but it is not insured. In order to be fully insured, you have to make some sacrifice of either flexibility or yield.

How to Increase Your Income with Safety

One of the most asked questions these days relates to ways to increase unearned or passive income safely—in the face of declining interest rates. Over and over again I hear, "Without much risk it used to be so easy to obtain interest in the teens. But now I'm afraid to tie up my money long-term because I'm afraid of inflation. What can I do to increase my income and still feel secure?"

In fact, today's real interest rate is actually better than the net interest you were receiving a few years ago. When interest rates were 18 percent and inflation was 16 percent, the real rate of return was only 2 percent. If you then subtracted taxes, you went behind. But now, with inflation around 4 percent and some returns more than twice that figure, even after subtracting taxes you are at least keeping even. But I know you've heard that line before. And I know that it is the *gross* interest rate that pays the rent and buys the groceries.

Although I believe inflation will continue to be a nonevent for years, not just months, no matter how clear anyone's crystal ball, future interest rates are almost impossible to predict. No one knows where inflation, thus interest rates, will be just two months from now, let alone two years from now. But if earning a relatively high interest return without undue market risk is your goal, what can you do for the long haul?

Answer: Design a portfolio to work as a unit and be flexible. You could, for example, place your money in a money market fund, then systematically withdraw approximate equal amounts of money to purchase high-grade utility stocks or intermediate-term bonds or CDs (three to ten years) every time interest rates move up or down. If rates continue to decrease, your overall yield will remain higher than current rates. If, however, interest rates rise, you can also participate in the rise.

Another strategy (as discussed earlier) would be to place an equal dollar investment in Treasury notes and bonds with maturities commencing in one year and running at least ten and hopefully twenty years. Each year, when your note or bond matures, you have the option of using the proceeds for some other purpose or purchasing the next-longest maturity. If interest rates are rising, you could sell the shortest-term securities with far less investment loss than if you only had long-term securities to sell.

Whether you still seek an extra margin of safety or yet another method to increase your income, you could also purchase a mutual fund that is "fully managed." Whether it is a GNMA fund, a U.S. government securities fund or a fund made up of various types of interest-paying investments, a fully managed fund not only chooses which investment, but also attempts to call the timing of interest rates. If management believes rates are about to rise, it will shorten the average portfolio maturity, and vice versa. It's management within management, or a way for you to hedge your investment.

If your money is limited, or the need for simplicity is your goal, there are still other alternatives. Listed below are some of my favorites:

- Give Series EE U.S. savings bonds or Ginnie Maes a serious thought. As I pointed out earlier, both have unique features and provide flexibility unto themselves.
- As CD rates fall, corporate bonds begin to look more attractive if you want good yields and only moderate risk.
- Single-premium whole life insurance provides safety and a highly competitive tax-free rate of return. The rate chosen can either be fixed for one, three, five or seven years, or indexed to follow the Treasury bill rate.
- Single-premium deferred annuities also provide a high degree of safety and a high annual renewable rate of return. The rate paid is usually greater than that of CDs.
- Municipal bonds today are highly competitive with all other types of bonds, and in most cases are the winner. Even if you are in a 15 percent federal bracket, a 7½ percent tax-free bond is equivalent to a 9 percent taxable bond. If you are in the 33 percent federal bracket, it is comparable to 12 percent.
- Mortgage real estate investment trusts also pay a competitive rate of return. Many of them approach double digits.
- A high-yield (junk) bond portfolio can provide a double-digit return—and if highly diversified, should provide safety too.
- All cash-equipment leasing partnerships can provide 10 to 13 percent yields and a margin of safety if diversified with equipment that does not have a high obsolescence factor.
- A portfolio of utility stocks provides a level of income below that of CDs, but utility companies have a strong history of increasing their dividends. Thus, your return can grow along with a possible increase in stock value.

But probably the best way to obtain higher yields with safety is to construct a portfolio utilizing a combination of the above ideas as well as others presented throughout this book. Then you will have a variety of income vehicles, each performing various functions: some with variable rates, such as annuities, or single-premium whole life policies, or utilities, or U.S. savings bonds, or money market funds, MLPs, REITs or even all cash real estate partnerships, and some investments with fixed-income rates such as bonds with varying maturities, or preferred stocks, or CDs, or various Treasuries. If you follow any one of, or a number of, the above alternatives, you will probably not achieve the world's highest yield, but then again you will no longer have to feel the need (and risk) of chasing interest rates either. You will probably have to seek professional help in constructing such a portfolio, and you will, of course, have to track its performance. But you will have achieved that additional advantage that's worth a lot more than a few extra dollars in income—a good night's sleep.

Chapter 11

For Sale—Today's Real Estate as an Investment

Real property as an investment has always been alluring because it is perceived as safe: safe because it's tangible—it's "real." It's something you can see, touch, walk through, live in or rent out. Real estate is also familiar—most of you have bought or rented a single-family house or condominium. Furthermore, historically, almost all types of real estate have been excellent hedges against inflation. And for some people real estate has provided enormous amounts of money. As a matter of fact, most of the great fortunes in the United States were created by real estate investment. Somehow it "feels" that when you own real estate, you can't lose. However, many of the 16 percent of U.S. households that own equity in real estate other than their primary residences have already discovered (or will soon discover) that real estate ownership is simply not automatically profitable. The "sure thing" is no more.

Real estate investors did very well in the late 1970s because prices went up. Many people lay these price increases at the feet of inflation. Others claim it was due to all the tax incentives, and still others claim it was simply a tremendous amount of pent-up demand. I believe all three elements were contributing factors; however, none are nearly so prevalent today. If people are expecting major price increases to come from the return of any one or a combination of these three factors in the near future, they might as well wait for the Dow Jones industrial average to hit 5,000.

Inflation, of course, is down and will likely stay there for some time. The demand that came from baby boomers seeking housing no longer exists, and because of the Tax Reform Act of 1986, tax-oriented real estate syndications (which purchased up to 60 percent of all apartment buildings) have gone the way of the dodo bird. On the surface at least, it appears there is no longer any reason to purchase real estate. But on second thought most of those great real estate fortunes were made in the days *before* high inflation or baby boomers or favorable tax laws. And Congress hasn't outlawed ownership of real estate for investment or as a tax saver. It has just changed some of the rules, that's all. While there has been a lot of overbuilding, there will always be a need for the right kind of building in the right location. And if problems have been created for some investors, they will become someone else's opportunities. So, if you want to stay on the playing field, you'll need to become more knowledgeable about the new rules of the game. Neither profits nor tax sheltering will be as automatic. Now you'll have to make it the old-fashioned way—work at it.

The key to any investment success is value. And value, of course, is a function of supply and demand. While value in the more recent boom years of real estate often took a back seat to dreams of huge profits often generated from huge debts, value today is at the core of the economics of real estate. It has reappeared as the undisputed, essential characteristic of any property. The changes in depreciation schedules and the eventual elimination of the passive-loss provision mean that the quality and return on the investment will be almost the only reasons for selecting a real estate investment.

There's no shortage of investment opportunities in real estate—nor is there a shortage of opportunities in just about every type of investment. As with every investment possibility, you need to investigate thoroughly all of the relevant factors that affect the deal: everything from the economics to the safeguards, from your liability to the type of (real estate) property; from questions of management to location, and so very much more. Even the expected holding period can be a major item when viewing real estate due to its illiquidity. Do you have staying power? Over the years I have learned that you have to have a lot of patience as well as a great deal of staying power. My clients who have made the most money through real estate have fully learned that valuable lesson. They are primarily conservative people who shop for value, invest for the long term, then have the staying power to realize potentially handsome returns.

As for tax advantages, if you listen to the doomsdayers, you'll never consider real estate as a tax saver again. But for most people, real estate is *still* a superb tax-cutting investment vehicle despite what others might have you believe. Certainly it is not as enticing as it once was, but then nothing is. I have to repeat what one of my real estate oriented clients recently said: "They've changed the tax law and depreciation schedules so many times in the last ten years it's hard to count. I'm still doing what I've always done, buying good properties at fair prices." Amen.

Real Estate Tax Benefits—Alive and Well

What are some of the continuing investment real estate tax benefits? There's still the Section 1031 tax-deferral exchange. The disposal of property through a reciprocal transfer for a similar piece of property is a nontaxable event. You can't own appreciated shares of IBM and make a tax-free exchange for shares of Apple.

Straight-line depreciation of 27½ years for residential and 31½ years for commercial property is still shorter in most cases than actual historical averages. O.K., so the depreciation deduction isn't as terrific as it once was. It's still not horrible, especially when you consider that the property might be appreciating in value rather than deteriorating. That's what a depreciation allowance is *supposed* to cover—the wearing out of an asset.

There are still tax credits for rehabilitation of historical structures. Although they have been reduced to less than half, and have other restrictions, the credit can be subtracted from the value of the structure after rehabilitation to determine the depreciation base. Historic properties continue to have tax benefits that other types of properties and other types of investments no longer have.

As for "passive" loss limitations, you will be able to deduct passive losses (by definition, all rental property activities will be considered passive) only against passive income and not your salary, interest or dividend income. However, you can accumulate the passive losses. When the property is sold, if there is insufficient gain to offset all the accumulated losses, you may then deduct any remaining losses from your other income, regardless of type.

There is an important exception to the small real estate investor who is actively involved with his or her property. This exception won't apply to the person who simply turns over all the details of the property management to an outside firm. If you are "actively participating" in the rental activity of your rental properties (making management decisions or arranging for others to provide services, such as repairs, etc., but not rent collection), and your adjusted gross income is under

$100,000 a year, you can deduct up to $25,000 worth of losses a year from your rental properties against your nonpassive income (earnings). If you have more than $25,000 in excess losses, the excess can be offset against other salary or investment income, or else carried over to future years when it can be used. If your income falls between $100,000 and $150,000 annually, you can deduct a portion of your excess losses. And if it is above $150,000, you cannot deduct any of your excess losses.

That's an important exception, especially for the small real estate investor who starts out with one or two properties. Over the years you will find you can still build up quite a bit of equity in your properties, and when you operate at a profit, perhaps the earlier mentioned 1031 exchange might then make sense.

Another real estate advantage occurs if you own a rental house or another relatively small investment piece of property with mortgages, but have a low amount of debt against your home. You may then want to consider moving the debt from your investment property to your home. If it's within certain interest limitations, the interest on the new home mortgage would be fully and currently deductible against your other income. Also, since you have reduced or eliminated the mortgage interest expense on your investment property, the amount of your passive loss that couldn't be currently utilized would also be reduced or even eliminated.

Of special note: Another way to escape the passive loss limitation rules through the ownership of real estate is not own it personally but to own it through a corporation. This is because the passive loss limitations do not apply to corporations, a provision that could become the biggest income property investment benefit (loophole) of the Tax Reform Act of 1986. For instance, if you have a corporation that sells rubber baby buggy bumpers at a profit, you should consider having it also invest in real estate as an alternative to paying out your profits in taxes.

Of course, the benefit of the mortgage interest deduction for the homeowner, as discussed in Chapter 6, presents other significant tax-planning opportunities. Then the opportunity for tax-free withdrawal of equity through refinancing your investment remains as a real estate opportunity. Congress still allows investors to withdraw their equity tax-free, without selling, as the value of the asset increases. You can refinance all or part of your original investment to take advantage of future growth.

Yes, the new law also retains several other important real estate benefits. So you can see, real estate investing is not dead at all. It remains a solid opportunity and one that can still find a place in most portfolios as long as your expectations do not exceed what it can deliver.

The Real Estate Investment Right for You

If you have available cash to invest and find real estate appealing, as always, you have two fundamental decisions to make. The first concerns your portfolio: what proportions of your discretionary income and savings, if any, should be in real property. The second is whether you wish to be a landlord or to invest in group ownership with professional management.

My response to the first decision is that I believe just about everyone should have some amount of real estate as part of his or her portfolio. Even if you are retired, you can still select conservative types of real estate investments where no mortgage exists and it primarily produces income. It still has an opportunity to appreciate. I don't believe you should forever swear off growth opportunities, no matter what your age. If real estate constitutes 10 to 20 percent of your investment worth in younger years, it can still constitute 5 to 10 percent in later years.

As for the "how" of participating in real estate, if you have the necessary down payment, expertise and time to pursue it, individual ownership of property can be quite an emotionally and financially satisfactory investment. You have a lot of control over the property and its eventual sale, particularly if you're the sole owner. Most of the time, however, I do not recommend individual ownership, simply because most people don't have the time and/or expertise to make it a successful proposition. This is especially true in today's investment real estate climate. There's an old saying about choppy waters favoring strong swimmers.

Then there are the problems of being a landlord. Do you want to be bothered with such problems as the roof possibly blowing off, or the boiler not working, or flooded basements, backed-up toilets (discovered at 2 A.M., of course), tenants repairing their motorcycles in the middle of the living-room carpet, litigious tenants?—you know what I mean.

Another possibility is to create a joint venture with one or more other investors. But this alternative also requires a substantial down payment and limits your diversification. Initially it's just as much work: you still need to research, evaluate and negotiate the property, and then someone has to manage it.

Real Estate Limited Partnerships (RELPs)

Another way to invest in real estate is to find a stand-in swimmer or landlord. A real estate syndication, also known as a real estate limited partnership (RELP), could fulfill that function. A limited partnership is made up of a general partner who manages the project, and limited partners who invest money, but have limited liability and are not involved in the day-to-day management of the property. Most such syndicates buy and manage anything from a single piece of property to as many as ten or more pieces. In the larger partnerships, the properties are often diversified by geography and sometimes by type of real estate. Many earlier partnerships can be thankful they diversified geographically, so that all their investments weren't, say, in Houston. Regardless of how the partnership performs, the limited partners only risk their original investment, which might be as little as $2,000.

The problem many sponsors of RELPs now face is that investors, bombarded by an almost daily barrage of stories about real estate developers, lenders and syndicators going bust, are now clamoring for all-cash (therefore no debt on the properties) offerings that produce income. The extent to which any offering has a good shot at generating the income it promises will hinge, of course, on the same basics that have always governed sound real estate investments. Therefore you, as an investor, also have to be more nuts and bolts oriented, for if your partnership is mismanaged, as a limited partner there is not much you can do about it.

You can reduce or eliminate several of the risks and difficulties of real estate investing by taking care in choosing the specific syndication. Try to find a sponsor who has a proven track record through good and bad markets, managing *both* leveraged (mortgaged) and unleveraged (no mortgage) real estate. Too many of them are simply redesigning their products to meet today's needs in light of the new tax laws and investor demand. They are moving to transform loss-structured tax shelters into income-producing investments and have little experience in managing these kinds of real estate investments. A review of past performance will demonstrate if the general partner has that capability and how he or she has performed managing various types of real estate. Do not blindly trust the "new kids on the block" until they have proven their abilities. I admire pioneers, but it must be remembered that they are Marines, not Boy Scouts. Go by what they have done, not by what they say they will do.

Locating a good real estate syndication is not an easy task. The prospectus isn't always easy to understand; the document is crammed with legalese. But readable prospectus or not, you still need to make a choice, and I suggest the best way to start is by getting answers, with the aid of your financial or tax advisor, to these questions:

1. Who is the general partner? What is his or her expertise, experience and reputation in partnership programs? What is the expertise of the management staff, and is it given to playing musical chairs?
2. How big is the sponsoring company? What are its financial resources? I believe the sponsor should have, at the minimum, 5 percent net worth related not only to the current offering, but also to the collective capitalizations of all programs still active under that management. I also like to see a minimum $250,000 liquid net worth.
3. How much money has the general partner(s) invested in the partnership? During difficult years the general partners may have to or want to dig into their own pockets in order to maintain their reputation. And it's always nice to know the general partners don't make money if you don't. That's why if they are also substantial investors, you can rest assured they will walk that extra mile.
4. How do the front-end, middle and back-end fees compare to industry averages? In general, look for lowest loads. In RELPs, front-end fees should be under 20 percent, middle fees 4 to 6 percent for property management, and back-end fees should be payable only after you have received your original investment plus a (low) cumulative 5 to 6 percent, to twice that, annual return. When the deal is solid and you cash out, let the general partners make a well-deserved profit on the back end. This subordinated sharing to the general partners can range from 5 to 25 percent for public programs and even higher for private programs. The latter are programs not registered with the Securities and Exchange Commission, and which can accept up to thirty-five investors and usually require a minimum investment of $25,000 or more. Private programs offer potentially higher rewards, but the risk is higher, too. Unless you are experienced at reading prospectuses or have a competent advisor, stick with public programs.
5. Is the deal compatible with your overall financial goals and your ability and desire to tie up money? Ask about the sponsor's projected holding period. I suggest it should be between five to seven years. Also ask or check the prospectus to see whether the sponsor, in the past, usually sold the properties for "paper"—that is, provided seller financing rather than negotiating for straight cash. The latter is better for the investor. If the

sponsor takes paper—in effect, acts as a lender—your grandchildren may receive all the real investment rewards.

There is more, of course, but if this sort of close analysis is not your cup of tea, you could start your investigation from a different angle—with still another shopping list. This list, however, is a simple one, consisting only of the names of reliable partnerships you've run across from one of several monthly newsletters. Two of my favorites are *The Stanger Report* (1129 Broad Street, Shrewsbury, NJ 07701) and *Brennan Reports* (Suite 200, P.O. Box 882, Valley Forge, PA 19482). Armed with these names, you can query your advisor for his or her advice—that's what you pay him for. My "surefire" guide (in Chapter 16) to selecting financial professionals, I might add, can also help you find reputable partnership names.

There are, however, other sources for locating reputable limited partnerships. Recently the SEC issued a "No Action Letter," permitting partnership sponsors to list a rating of the fairness of the terms of their offerings by another Robert A. Stanger Co. publication. The Stanger ratings are listed in the $225-a-year *Stanger Register,* P.O. Box 7490, 1129 Broad Street, Shrewsbury, NJ 07701.

Real Estate Investment Trusts (REITs)

Another way for you to participate in a diversified portfolio of properties is through a real estate investment trust. REITs, as they're called, are companies that purchase a variety of properties or lend money to developers. Shares in these trusts are traded on stock exchanges and resemble mutual funds. But instead of a portfolio of stocks, REITs hold a variety of real estate investments. Equity REITs provide shareholders interest with income from rents and capital gains when the properties are sold. Mortgage REITs make loans to builders and pay shareholders interset income. Some trusts are a combination of the two.

The law requires that 95 percent of the REIT's income must come from passive investments, 75 percent from passive real estate investments and that 95 percent of its net income must be distributed annually to shareholders. The fact that REIT shares can trade publicly has remained one of a REIT's most potent attractions to investors who also feel more at home in the stock market. Indeed, the liquidity of REITs often is used as a primary marketing tool. Yet it must be remembered that the trading price of a REIT is often lower than the price for which the share was originally sold as the REIT was being organized. And it may be far below the actual value of the underlying real estate. Thus a REIT's liquidity is best viewed as an emergency escape exit, not as a revolving door.

Returns on REITs, which generally have hovered in the 8 to 10 percent range, are appealing. And you can get into REIT for very little money: as little as $500 can bring you a percentage of a diversified group of properties across the country. That too is appealing, and today REITs are very popular indeed. But it's not necessarily because they are better investments. The new tax bill just made other investments worse than before. I recommend them, but a REIT, like any other investment, should be judged on its merits and on your needs.

Finite Life Real Estate Investment Trusts (FREITs)

Still another real estate trust you may wish to consider is called a finite life real estate investment trust (FREIT). These investments are an alternative to real estate limited partnerships, for they also either purchase properties (with or without debit) or make mortgage loans. The FREIT, however, is scheduled to be liquidated within a designated time frame, whereas a limited partnership only suggests a time frame as a goal. Similar to the REIT, another FREIT advantage over the limited partnership format is that a FREIT is also liquid (the shares are traded on an exchange), and they are usually of lower risk.

I suggest if you are thinking about either a REIT or a FREIT, you consider an income-oriented REIT or an all-cash FREIT. These entities pay cash for properties and so carry no debt, thus producing relatively high income with relatively low investment risk. But there is another reason: *déjà vu*. Back in the early 1970s, real estate trusts were opening at a rate of three a month, and the real estate market was heading for a recession. In the mid-1970s there weren't any new public offerings as a result of so many REIT failures. Today, initial public offerings are again almost climbing to the early 1970s' rate. The more things change . . .

Master Limited Partnerships (MLPs)

Merger mania is poised to strike your real estate limited partnership holding. Although you probably won't hear the names of Carl Icahn, Irwin Jacobs or T. Boone Pickens associated with the merger of your investment, if your limited partnership is affected, you will nonetheless detect major changes. Not the least of which is that you will suddenly own a share of a much, much larger partnership, now called a "master limited partnership" (MLP). And since I believe MLPs might well be the wave of the future, I want you to become aware of them now. I not only feel they could provide a safer and often better way to invest new money through real estate limited partnerships, I also think the investment outlook of current partnerships might be improved if they were part of an MLP.

There are two primary types of MLPs. They are formed either by the consolidation of existing limited partnerships or through a corporate reorganization or liquidation. In the most popular form, the consolidation type (called a "roll up"), interests in numerous existing limited partnerships are exchanged for interests in a giant or master limited partnership. The new MLP interests are then represented by units that may be listed on stock exchanges and traded. The other type of MLP is a "roll out." This is where corporate-owned assets are transferred to a newly formed partnership in exchange for partnership units. A portion of these units are then sold to the public and can also be listed on exchanges.

An increasing number of real estate sponsors are searching for ways to offer investors a combination of liquidity and possible tax benefits not available in REITs. Unless the rules of the game are changed, you can shelter MLP taxable income with "passive losses" in other partnerships. No doubt that tax break will be reconsidered at the IRS's insistence. But if it is eliminated, it would seem that outstanding MLPs or MLP investors could be grandfathered (not suffer from any change in the law). And even if the break is eliminated, the public is clearly very interested in this type of investment. The MLP is not only here to stay, but in my opinion will be the wave of the future.

In the traditional limited partnership, those limited partners have money tied up for (supposedly) five to seven years. Today, more limited partners are finding that time period extended to ten or fifteen years. By placing properties into an MLP, which is publicly traded, partners can take their money out at any time. You make your own investment decisions to buy, sell or hold. Also, as with the REIT and FREIT, you own a security that can be bought on margin.

Buying and Selling "Used" Limited Partnerships

There is still one more real estate investment opportunity of which most of you are probably unaware. It's a rather complex arrangement in which a real estate partnership purchases your limited partnership interest, sort of a limited partnership of limited partnerships. These real estate partnerships do just one thing: They acquire partnership units from investors who wish to cash out of their investments before the investments have gone full cycle and the partnership has sold all its properties. Units in these so-called "used" real estate limited partnerships are then offered to investors.

Publicly offered real estate limited partnerships, when new, have relatively high start-up costs, and that means the investor must hold his units long enough to allow the properties' value to appreciate and overcome its initial expenses. If, however, you purchase a unit in a limited partnership that has purchased someone else's older partnership interest, much of the risk and up-front expense has already been dealt with. Although most older limited partnerships are sold as five- to seven-year investments, because many such partnerships take back a mortgage when a property is sold, as mentioned earlier, the average life can be in the ten- to fifteen-year range. An investment in a "used" limited partnership, however, since some of the risk has been eliminated, is usually at the halfway mark in terms of performance. These can be purchased primarily through financial planners, although there are a handful of brokerage firms that are also creating these partnerships. If you are interested in either purchasing "used" partnership interests or selling yours, contact a financial advisor who can give you a prospectus that will tell you more about these partnerships and their minimum purchase or sale qualifications.

Still another place where you can both purchase and liquidate used real estate partnership interests is the National Partnership Exchange (NAPEX) located in St. Petersburg, Florida. The exchange provides a computerized secondary market in partnership units. Though the exchange is only a few years old, the basic partnership auction concept is beginning to catch on.

If you are considering an investment in real estate, it would only confuse you if I attempted to detail and compare the various merits (or demerits) of various types of real estate: shopping centers, apartment complexes, office buildings, industrial parks, miniwarehouses, agriculture, raw land and the like. Nor would I be helping you if I set out to describe the "best" regions in the country in which to invest. As always, "best" depends upon your goals. Each kind of investment and each geographical area can fulfill a different objective and carries different rewards and risks. If you are aware of your own investment profile, and are fully informed about the nature of the various real estate investments, you can't go too far wrong.

But is this a good time to invest in real estate at all? I expect real estate, at best, to be only a so-so opportunity at present. It is, however, a good time to be planning and adjusting your involvement in investment real estate without worrying too much that you'll miss the boat. In fact, one of the ways to tell when the bottom of the market has been reached (when time does become a factor) is when all those around you are rushing to abandon ship and no one even wants to talk about real estate investing. That may very well be the time for you to consider climbing on board.

Life Among the Bulls, Bears and Chickens—How to Turn a Gamble into an Investment

The daily fluctuations of the stock market are reported religiously in the business sections of our newspapers and on the TV news. You read, you watch. But how often has it occurred to you that most of the time no one has any idea why the market goes up or down?

It's true.

A few years ago, a broker I knew at the New York Stock Exchange was asked by a television reporter why the market went down that day. The broker wasn't quite sure what to say, so he told the reporter that he would ask other professionals for their views before he went on the air. The best response the broker could get was "Today, there were more sellers than buyers." The answer that ended up on television was different, of course, but you get the idea. While a rationale for stock market activity certainly exists, people have been spending their lives trying to find it, especially when it moves in a direction that defies all logic. I sometimes think the stock market is like a bumblebee—all the rules of aerodynamics say it can't fly, but it does.

Holding Individual Stocks: Is This Best for You?

When you are buying a stock, you are buying equity or ownership in a company and its potential growth. Therefore, you are now investing directly in the economic system, sharing in both its risks and benefits. That seems very logical and straightforward, but in fact the stock market rarely is. It can be awfully frustrating when the company in which you've invested your hard-earned money shows a substantial increase in earnings, but the stock drops like a rock. Why? Because the entire market declined due to something as silly as lower-than-expected earnings at IBM or an "expert's" prediction that a market downturn was about to occur.

Almost 50 million Americans now own stocks either directly or through mutual funds. That represents approximately 20 percent of the entire U.S. population. Though the number of indirect shareholders is rapidly growing, there are still a very sizable number of shareholders with direct securities holdings. And in my opinion most of that latter group has no business directly purchasing securities.

I'm convinced most people who choose individual stocks purchase them for one, or a combination, of four major reasons. First, they buy stocks in this manner because they find old habits are difficult to break: their generation was taught to believe that people *had* to invest extra cash in the stock market. A second reason is that people want to do *something* besides sock their money away in a low-interest savings or money market account, and individual stocks seem the easiest, most liquid and most available alternative—perhaps the only one. A third reason is ego: owning shares in a company can not only make a person feel good, but can also provide good country club, barber or beauty-shop conversation. Finally, individual stocks can be exciting: the thrill of "winning" money is more attractive than the boredom of *making* money.

I sincerely believe over the long term that most people who choose their own stocks or have a broker "assist" with that choice rarely make money in the market. I tell that to everyone, whether the listener is a serious investor, a casual investor or an experienced trader. Though one person's investment history hardly constitutes a thorough study, let's look at the track record of one investor I know.

About seven years ago, the president of a company listed on the New York Stock Exchange came into my office shaking his head. He had invested seriously in the stock market for more than twenty years, owning many individual issues and following them very closely. He had an accounting background, kept meticulous records and was very confident of his performance—until someone challenged his results. The president, taking up the gauntlet, carefully reconstructed his stock market activity, noting additions of new capital and withdrawals of older capital (something most people would have great difficulty re-tracing). He also took into account all dividends received and taxes paid. After twenty years (from 1960 to 1980), he discovered he ended up only breaking even. He was shocked! He hadn't made any money.

Further calculations revealed that if he had pulled out of the market completely in 1978, he would have been seriously behind—and that's not even taking inflation into account. If *you* are a serious individual stock investor, you should check your long-term record as well. You too might be surprised.

Serious investors often belong to the first group I mentioned above: those who trade in the stock market because they "always have." Then there are those who see the stock market as his or her only alternative, which is frequently correct because they haven't got much motivation to look around. What happens? Usually these people lose money, not understanding that individual stocks require a great deal of time. In addition, they don't realize that the cost of buying and selling stocks, especially with a full-service broker, can be high. If a full-service firm or broker is used, you have to have an approximate 75-point rise in the Dow Jones industrial average to just break even when purchasing a typical blue chip stock. Thus, thinking of the market as just someplace to put their money, such people turn a potentially viable investment opportunity into nothing more than a gamble, and a bad gamble at that. Sad, I know, but true.

Since these people are unable to relate to the activities of the market and unwilling to research and follow the stocks they buy, I have an idea for them. Instead of investing $10,000 in the stock market, they might be better off investing $500 in any kind of business in the neighborhood. At least this way they will probably pay more attention to the soundness and progress of their investment because the investment will feel more tangible.

If an investor needs his or her ego massaged—our third group—the stock market can be the perfect place. The price may be unusually high, however, and the massage often leaves bruises. Besides, it's no fun to compare losers in the locker or powder room. Chances are your ego will be rubbed the wrong way.

Finally, there's the trader. I could never believe a trader sincerely expects to make money. As a matter of fact, a recent study about securities trading has confirmed my impression. The research concluded that in any tax bracket, over time, high appreciation is required to achieve even a modest return. Why? Primarily commissions (again), which add up very quickly. The research concluded, "The clearest indication of the difficulty of trading for profit is what it takes simply to break even. Assuming discount commissions and no taxes, if a stock were held for only one month, the trader would require a 19.7 percent annual appreciation just to break even." While trading may be appropriate for short periods, only the most clairvoyant traders will be able to accumulate wealth over time.

During my more than twenty years of involvement with the stock market, the only people I know who have made significant amounts of money through individual stock ownership are those who owned private companies that favorably merged with public companies, or those who have vast holdings in such a company before their company went public. Oh yes, and then there's Ivan Boesky. If you cannot or do not wish to follow footsteps like those, but still wish to end up with $1 million by purchasing individual stocks, then start with $4 million. Of course, another method to achieve success through the purchase of individual stocks involves starting with a more modest amount of money. If you desire trading experience, you then work closely with a broker. When your lesson is complete, you will probably learn that you have accomplished the ultimate trade. Your broker now has the money—you now have the experience. As a matter of fact, you'll hope you live long enough to use all the experience you've gained.

I won't even bother to comment on people trading stock options, except to say those people are just as short-sighted as options are short-term. Trading options is pure gambling.

An eternal truth: Save time and emotional energy. Try to understand *why* you're buying individual stocks. If you're in the market in a casual way—to have a little fun, or for your ego and maybe to get lucky—that's fine if that's what you *want* to do. But if you're serious about providing for your future security, about attempting to achieve your goals, then you do what that president of a New York Stock Exchange listed company did: hire professionals to help out.

The Professional Money Manager

Because I discuss the problems most people have with individual stocks, it doesn't mean I don't like the stock market as a place to invest; far from it. Over time, if you employ professional management, and do so intelligently, you *are* often well rewarded through investing in the stock market, especially since the average return from stocks has historically been higher than the average return from "safe" investments, like interest-bearing bonds.

For those of you who meet minimum dollar investment requirements, where that minimum is an appropriate percentage of your asset base, there is a professional money manager called an "investment counselor" or "money manager." These counselors are registered investment advisors with the Securities and Exchange Commission, and manage *only* stock and bond portfolios, usually on a discretionary basis. Normally their minimum asset requirement is $250,000 but some investment counselors will consider a lesser amount as long as a minimum fee is met.

The professional money manager's full-time job is to study the market and select the companies whose shares he or she believes will perform to meet your goals. The counselor is motivated toward good performance because the more money you make, the more money he or she makes, as the fee charged by most money managers is a fixed percentage based on the value of your portfolio. The percentage will depend upon the amount of money being managed, but typically ranges between ½ percent to 2 percent of the assets under management per year. If the money under management grows, the counselor's income increases, and vice versa.

Generally, an investment counselor will (or should) inquire about your financial goals. You might want aggressive growth, mostly income with some growth, something in between or something else. Investment counselors will then construct a portfolio specifically for you, based upon the securities they follow. Securities and money are held in your name at a bank or at a brokerage firm, but never directly by the advisor. Also, investment counselors do not receive commissions; in fact, they will often save you commission money as one of their functions. It is part of their job to direct the transaction, thus the commission, to the brokerage firms that charge the lowest fees, while also providing the best order execution. On the other hand, if you specify that you wish a particular person or firm to execute your various trades, the counselor must oblige you.

I'm sure it will come as no surprise when I say that all investment counselors are not terrific. Just because a counselor spends all of his or her time selecting and monitoring stocks and bonds, it doesn't mean those investments are sure to perform any better than if you had picked them yourself. Furthermore, it's not easy to determine a counselor's past performance. Though they will provide you with representative information about the history of their accounts, the portfolios they will show you are not, and cannot be, exactly similar to a portfolio that might be designed for you. They will also reflect a different era, and the performance record will only include clients who have remained with the money manager, not those who have left due to unhappiness or dissatisfaction. But perspective is still necessary. I once asked a money manager for his performance history and he flatly refused, claiming each client's investment performance was different. Though his statement was valid, obviously I could not recommend his services.

There are a large number of excellent money managers who will indeed consistently outperform most do-it-yourselfers. So even a representative portfolio performance can provide valuable insight. There are numerous companies that continuously track the performance of money managers and that, for a price, would be more than happy to share the information (see Chapter 16). It's a starting point when trying to determine who some of the better investment counselors are. Then you should shop around carefully and make your final decision only after considering the following factors—in addition to previous performance:

• Does his or her investment philosophy match yours?
• Are you comfortable with his research methods?
• Are you satisfied with the frequency as well as the quality of the information he or she will provide you about your investments?
• Will your individual income tax situation be taken into consideration?
• Most important is the "chemistry" between you. If at all possible, meet with a prospective counselor and his or her firm, then ask yourself how do you "feel" about them. Trust your first impression.

I know a person whose first impression was that the counselor seemed to have an attitude of "I'm doing you a favor." Despite being uncomfortable—and just barely able to meet the minimum dollar requirement—he nonetheless engaged the counselor's services. At the conclusion of the first quarter, his portfolio was down by 4 percent. When questioned, the money manager fired his client because the client no longer met the minimum portfolio size. Yes, there are certain choice words to describe that manager, and I'll leave them up to your imagination. But the client should also have known better. Even though the manager was known to have an excellent performance record, the client still should have trusted that negative first impression. For my "surefire" method for selecting good investment counselors, as well as financial planners and other professionals in the field, see Chapter 16.

Mutual Funds Can Spell Mutual Fun

There may be a less expensive and easier way you can secure professional management for your investments: Invest in a mutual fund.

Some 25 million people have turned to mutual funds to simplify investment strategies while also hiring top-quality professional money management. The nation's mutual funds now have assets of almost $800 billion. That's talking big.

Mutual funds are open-end investment companies (they continually create new shares on demand) that pool their capital (your money) in investments monitored and managed by staffs of highly trained professionals. This pooling of capital reduces your risk substantially by enabling you to enjoy instant diversification for as little as $100, because your investment is spread over a portfolio that may contain 100 or more holdings. You can spread your risk even further by diversifying among funds that have similar investment objectives, as well as those funds with different objectives. Mutual funds are "objective oriented." You can select from a wide range of funds, depending on the risks you are willing to take and the loftiness of your desired return.

In addition to providing professional management to locate, research and follow individual investments and to worry about what to buy and sell—and when—mutual funds offer an abundance of other services that are difficult to match elsewhere. If you wish, periodic payments will be made to you monthly, quarterly or in any time frame you desire. Numerous funds also offer check-writing privileges against your account. And if your investment objective changes, you can switch your investment to other mutual funds managed by the same investment company, for each fund within the "family" serves a different investment purpose.

Mutual funds are also a very liquid investment, since the management company is obliged to redeem your shares on request. Redemption can either take the form of withdrawing your investment or, if you are not satisfied with a fund's current performance, you can, as just mentioned, switch your shares to another fund within the family. Most such exchanges occur when your goals change or market conditions warrant. If you hold shares in a stock fund and the market is declining, you can move your entire investment into cash overnight, at the current market value of each of the shares you own. And if the market makes an "about face," you may do the same, overnight, again at the current market value of your shares. I don't believe you would have the same degree of flexibility, much less the courage to be so flexible, if you held individual securities.

There is still another time when an exchange is appropriate. Mutual funds can be either load or no-load; that is, they either charge a commission to invest in a fund or they do not. For more than fifteen years

I have been recommending that when investing in a load fund, clients utilize the exchange method to obtain an immediate tax write-off of the sales charge. Few people are aware of this "tax-smart" use of the exchange. Since sales loads are not deductible as an investment expense, this strategy can provide an immediate deduction approximately equal to the sales charge paid. You initially purchase one of the funds in the family *other* than the one you wish ultimately to own. Very shortly thereafter you switch into the fund you *do* wish to own. The redemption counts as a sale for tax purposes, resulting in a realized net capital loss. For example, if you invest $10,000 in a load growth fund, your investment is actually worth only $9,150, the difference of $850 having been charged against your account as a sales commission. So if you promptly exchange your shares for the income fund you wanted in the first place, you create an $850 capital loss. Since the loss doesn't exceed $3,000, the full amount can be deducted against other types of income. Alternatively, you could also use this exchange technique to offset a capital gain. In either event you will now be able to make use of an advantageous tax treatment, where previously for tax purposes a load charge would simply increase the cost basis of your fund shares.

When it comes to track records, mutual funds stand rather naked in the wind. Their performance is a matter of public record and can be tracked during any period of time you choose. Even the neophyte investor can follow the fund's progress daily in the newspaper. Furthermore, there are a large number of independent services that measure the absolute and relative performance of mutual funds. There can never be a question, as there sometimes is with privately managed accounts, of "best or average" account performance, for a mutual fund can only demonstrate one set of figures—it's always their best. And for their sake, it had better be good.

How to Select a Top Mutual Fund

Since there are more than 1,700 mutual fund companies out there (the number has quadrupled in ten years), an excellent and easy starting place when you are seeking to invest is to look for the annual review of mutual fund performances in the latest August or September issues of *Forbes, Money* or *Business Week* magazines. *Changing Times, Financial World,* and the special fall issue of *Fortune* also have excellent annual reviews. For a quarterly survey, you can read *Barron's*. In addition, your local public library should have a copy of the *Mutual Fund Source-*

book or the *Wiesenberger Investment Companies Service,* both of which list the name, address, investment philosophy, fund size, sales charge and minimum investment amount of every mutual fund. There is also the "Lipper Mutual Fund Performance Analysis," which provides weekly year-to-date performance figures for over 1,000 funds. And now Standard & Poors also tracks mutual fund performance.

Then there are the mutual fund newsletters published by various and sundry analysts and experts. After surveying its shareholders recently, a large mutual fund discovered that newsletters were their second most important source of information, after newspapers and magazine articles. There probably are some fifty or so newsletters in existence today, which is almost four times the number in 1982 when the bull market began. And because there are so many, it's hard to comment on their specific value. Before you follow investment advice from any source, be sure it makes sense for your own financial situation and investment goals.

If you hunger for more information about mutual funds, all of which can be considered reliable, the trade group called the Investment Company Institute (1600 M Street, N.W., Washington, DC 20036) publishes useful material on mutual funds, including a $2 Mutual Fund Fact Book. There is also the No-Load Mutual Fund Association (11 Penn Plaza, No. 2204, New York, NY 10001), which will send you a free list of publications from which you can buy its own $2 Guide to Mutual Funds. Not bad—only $4.44 spent on research, including the expense of driving to the library for some of the above material, and you'll learn more than you could ever want to know about mutual fund performance.

Speaking of expense, as earlier stated, you may or may not have to pay a commission to purchase a mutual fund. The highest commission allowed by law is 8.5 percent of invested funds, which is called a full "load." The greatest number of funds today still charge a full load. However, the commission can be lowered through volume discounts (and use of the above "tax-smart" idea). All full-load funds have what is called "breakpoint" sales. If you can invest enough money to reach a certain breakpoint, the commission is lowered—the more money you invest, the lower the commission. By the way, if you believe you can invest enough money within a thirteen-month period to reach a certain breakpoint level, all full-load funds have a nifty "letter of intent" form you can use. Once signed, this unilateral contract (*you* can cancel it at any time) allows your current investment money to receive the discount commission you would have been charged had you invested the full breakpoint amount. If you can't or don't choose to fulfill the letter of intent within thirteen months, there are no penalties. The fund simply takes back the extra number of shares purchased as a result of the lowered commission.

Full-load mutual funds can only be purchased through stockbrokers and financial planners. "Low-load" mutual funds can also be purchased through these two sources as well as, in many cases, directly from the fund itself. Low-load mutual funds are so called because they charge less than the maximum commission, usually 2 to 4.5 percent of your investment. But in contrast to full-load funds, most low-load funds do not offer breakpoint sales.

Loads are usually charged when fund shares are purchased. A charge for withdrawing shares from a fund is called a "back-end" load. Then there are the "12(b)1" loads, or the so-called "inside loads" allowed by the Securities and Exchange Commission to cover advertising and sales costs. To date, not many mutual funds charge back-end loads. However, a growing number of funds do levy 12(b)1 charges. While the 12(b)1 ranks are rapidly increasing, still the type of fund second in popularity only to the full-load fund charges none of the above-mentioned fees. It is called a "no-load" fund, and shares can only be purchased directly from the fund. Though more than 50 percent of all non–money market funds are no-loads, as the second most popular type of fund they still only account for around 25 percent of all mutual fund sales. Nonetheless, a debate has raged for years between the load and no-load funds. Which are the best types of mutual funds—those that impose a sales charge or those that do not?

Answer: A recent survey of mutual fund performance says you are *not* better off paying a sales charge. Funds without a sales charge have actually performed better than funds charging one, though the difference is razor-thin. For example, a current one-year performance period demonstrated that no-loads returned an average of 27.5 percent, full-loads 27.15 percent, and low-loads 26.03 percent. But in any given year the overall performance of no-loads depends on the type of funds that do well that year. The reason: No-load funds generally are those with focused, clear-cut investment strategies, such as investing only in foreign companies.

However, lengthening the time frame recently to ten years, no-load funds still outperformed the others, returning an annual rate of 16.06 percent, while full-load funds returned 15.13 percent and low-load funds increased only 13.53 percent. And those figures did not factor in any of the loads that were levied, which would, of course, decrease the rate of return for investors in full-load and low-load funds. So if those sales charges were included, no-load funds would come out substantially ahead. If you think about it, that's not really a surprising piece of news. Sales charges are simply a way of doing business and in no way add to the wisdom or inspiration of fund managers, who are the people who control performance.

So you should go with no-load funds—if you are prepared to spend some time on research. And that does *not* mean you'll get a gold star simply by locating the best performing funds of the past. Numerous studies have shown that very few funds consistently perform in the top ranks year after year. And past records alone contain no guarantees with regard to future performance. Yes, it means work! Remember those important items you should consider when seeking a top-quality private money manager? Why should this assignment be any different?

Portfolio. To help you choose the mutual fund or funds that are right for you, probably the most important place to start is with their latest financial reports. Read over the list of their holdings. What you see is what you get. All of those statistics about past performance help, but future performance is based upon what they own today. Are you comfortable with the selection, the diversification, the concentration, the amount of cash? Compare the cost *vs.* market values of each security (usually found in the annual report) to determine if you are buying too many losers. The portfolio is the litmus test.

Philosophy. Many funds say in the prospectus simply that they invest in a broad range of securities seeking capital appreciation, but you need to look for a more specific strategy for how they aim to achieve results. The better funds have a precise, strict and disciplined approach to investing.

Historical Performance. A general rule can be deduced from studying the past: The top and bottom performers often change places, but those below the median usually stay there. However, the best performing funds can be found between the median and the top twentieth percentile.

Statistical Risk. Over longer time periods it has been established that the greater rewards evolve from the lower risks. Funds that promise you the moon may never get off the ground.

People. As is true with private money managers, it's the people who manage the fund who are responsible for its performance. Who are they and are they still there? How are they compensated, and what is the turnover and attrition rate? Do they use a committee, team, manager or computer for decisions? Maybe you can't visit their offices, but a telephone call will answer many of these questions, and most portfolio managers are accessible.

Expenses. The annual costs of managing a fund (also found in the prospectus) should not be overlooked. Fees for management tend to be smaller when the fund is larger.

Size. If you're interested in a growth fund, look for those with assets between $50 million and $500 million for best results. Large growth funds can have difficulty adapting readily to market changes and following, say, 150 stocks when 40 would be more suitable. And if it is a $5 billion fund, to whom are they going to sell their stocks in a declining market? The bond market is seven times larger in value than the stock market, so that problem is not as prevalent with a large bond fund. Nor is it a problem with other types of large income funds whose investments are far less volatile than growth fund investments.

Portfolio Turnover. Your investigation must also include an examination of a fund's rate of portfolio turnover (also described in the prospectus). For example, less than 20 percent per year may indicate there isn't much management, while 100 percent implies the added risk of market timing. Look for turnover in the 20 to 80 percent range. Most successful funds have made their records with stock positions held from eighteen to thirty months.

Service. Good shareholder service doesn't just happen. It requires a costly commitment by the fund to deliver timely and meaningful reports and statements, as well as prompt check-cashing and exchange services. Without such a commitment, there may be delays in withdrawal requests, incorrect and late statements, busy phone lines, computers that might be down and so on. If you know another shareholder, ask that person about service, or ask your financial advisor. From time to time various financial magazines will also report on the quality of shareholder service—listing some of the better mutual fund management companies.

Once you have considered these specific aspects of a fund's operation, match your own needs with the overall objectives and strategy of the fund. That should not be difficult since virtually every fund adver- tises its investment objective, strategy and specialty. You will find that you have a wide choice. There are, for example, bond funds that invest only in certain types of government or corporate bonds, even certain maturity periods. And there are now stock funds for every taste too: aerospace and defense funds, energy funds, financial services funds, gold funds, health care funds, leisure and entertainment funds, natural resources funds, service economy funds, socially conscious funds, technology funds and utility funds. Though this list is by no means complete, I should also mention closed-end funds, which are a cross between a stock and a mutual fund. A closed-end fund issues a fixed number of shares that are traded like individual stocks on major ex- changes. Professionally managed closed-end funds can also offer you either a diversified or specialized portfolio. So your choice widens. However, remember that the most common mutual fund is the least specialized—the money market fund I discussed in Chapter 10.

Enlisting the Aid of Your Financial Advisor

Now, and only now, are you ready to choose the particular fund or funds that fit your personal financial philosophy, needs and goals: growth, income, tax savings and so on. If you haven't either the time or the inclination to do this kind of research, then enlist the help of a stockbroker or a financial planner, not only to provide advice, but also to bring to your attention funds you might never have heard of in today's overcrowded marketplace. But your advisor needs adequate compensation to do the job properly. So if that compensation comes from the commission on your purchase either of a full-load or low- load fund, insist upon seeing the research that went into the recom- mendation. It might have come from the *Forbes* "Honor Roll," which simply is not enough research. If, however, your advisor can demon- strate that the above guidelines have been followed, you should find that the addition of professional expertise is well worth the extra money spent—without overplaying the issue of load *vs.* no-load. Re- member, there are many outstanding load funds and many poorly managed no-load funds. And remember too, when it comes to choos- ing the best time to purchase your shares, you'll want to follow master investor Bernard Baruch's advice: It's "when you have the money."

"Sure" Market Timing

Despite Mr. Baruch's advice, your gains or losses utilizing mutual funds as part of your strategy will ultimately depend on how much you paid for them. Yes, we all know cheaper is better, but since no one, including your favorite economist, market analyst or tarot reader can accurately predict the absolute best purchase date, you'll have to put that thought aside. There is, however, a method whereby I can assure you that you won't always be paying the highest per share price. It's called "dollar-cost averaging."

Dollar-cost averaging calls for you to invest a fixed amount of dollars in the mutual fund at set intervals. Because the market generally rises, you will be buying more shares when the price is low and fewer shares when the price is high during any given period of time. And your average cost per share will always be lower than the current market price. But it is essential to the success of your dollar-cost averaging program that you stick with it—at least to the extent of ignoring all market fluctuations. You will also find a secondary value in dollar-cost averaging: it is literally a forced savings plan.

Does dollar-cost averaging work? Let's look at the Great Stock Market Crash of 1929. If I remember my statistics, there were twenty-four mutual funds in existence in 1929 (the first fund started operating in 1924)—and all are around today. Well, let's say you dollar-cost averaged those funds each and every month for almost four years. In 1933 the stock market was still down by more than 80 percent from its 1929 high. But you continued to dollar-cost average (it took real courage) for yet another year. At that time, though the stock market was still off more than 70 percent from its 1929 high, if you had liquidated your holdings, you would have already broken even.

Because the system requires a long-term commitment, the choice you make of a given fund is especially important. Averaging won't save you from poor results in a fund that is poorly managed. Even a well-managed fund will test your faith at some point along the way, for during a span of five to twenty years, you can count on periodic bear markets. And when this happens, I hope the old story of emotion winning out over intellect, which causes many investors to make foolish and often costly investment decisions, doesn't occur. If you don't set your expectations too high, and hang in there, all will usually be well.

The Great Mutual Fund Myth

If, however, you think you have a "sure thing" by investing in *any* mutual fund, you will be in for a rude awakening. This was dramatically demonstrated to a large number of people back in the early 1970s, which was the last time mutual funds were enormously popular. Highly aggressive funds were created in the red-hot market of the 1960s, and some of these funds appreciated as much as 100 percent in just one year, attracting hordes of money both to themselves and to other types of funds. But a funny thing happened on the way to cashing the profit check: the stock market started to drop and so did the share value of most of the mutual funds. In fact, the market value of the aggressive funds declined far faster than the value of the market averages. That "sure thing"—the easy money—was no more. Disillusion set in, and people scrambled to recoup what they could, selling their fund shares at a loss as quickly as possible.

When shares in any fund are purchased as a result of overoptimism about past or current performance figures, and/or without an understanding of the role that investment should play relative to your other assets and your investment goals, and/or without a method or game plan of purchase, the same thing could happen to you. Furthermore, if you purchase a mutual fund or place your money with an investment counselor without taking the time to research fully your final choice, and if you fail to monitor your selection, then it is likely that your investment performance in mutual funds will appear no different than had you purchased individual securities. In short, you will have taken a fine investment opportunity and turned it into a gamble.

Chapter 13

Having It Both Ways—How to Double Your Assets and Minimize Your Risk

I know it's hard to believe, but if you had $1 million in assets, most of you would *still* not feel wealthy. If you had $10,000 in cold, hard cash, however, you would feel *quite* wealthy. Similarly, if you suddenly began to make money by the carload, you would lose identity with it. The same holds true with a quick $100,000 profit. You would remember the days when you had to count in terms of years to make that kind of money, and this windfall would seem as though it had happened to someone else.

A new client entered my office not long ago declaring he had a net worth in excess of $15 million and his personal income exceeded $1 million a year. What he went on to say underscores my point. What makes him so unusual is that he went to such an extreme in order to be able to identify with money. Because his earnings and net worth seemed as though they were "Monopoly money" dollars, he actually bought a piggy bank—a *big* one—and decided to save "real" money. So each day, after arriving home from the office, he would put his "spare change" into the piggy bank. You guessed it, he quickly accumulated more than $10,000. Feeling very good about his accomplishment, he now wanted more. So he went to a commercial bank and asked for envelopes in which he could regularly mail them money. Soon he had over $100,000 put aside, and for the first time in many years felt terrific financially because *this* was real money and he had a direct hand in accumulating each dollar.

Who hasn't dreamed of becoming a millionaire like TV's J.R. Ewing or Blake Carrington—better yet Donald Duck's Uncle Scrooge, who owns two cubic acres of money. Perhaps that's why so many people buy lottery tickets or attend those get-rich-quick real estate seminars. Yet the goal remains elusive because most of us are unwilling to take the risk that instant high rewards require. We probably should not get involved in high-risk money situations anyway because we cannot afford the potentially high loss. Wouldn't you rather let someone else take out a mortgage on his or her house to buy a roomful of lottery tickets, or purchase the Empire State Building with no money down?

But that doesn't mean you should never try for the brass ring. I believe you should go ahead—as long as you *risk only as much money as you can afford to lose.* This is money that will in no way jeopardize the food you put on the table today or your financial future, cash you can say good-bye to without breaking down in tears. If you get the ring, it can be very exciting, and we sometimes need more of that in our financial lives. As I said earlier, there are times when the thrill of "winning" money is more attractive than the boredom of making money.

Does that mean by investing more speculatively some of you will become millionaires? I certainly hope so. But more realistically, there is a greater likelihood that you can become a multithousandaire.

To start you on your way, I'll show you how to grant yourself more money by giving your portfolio a bit of a boost, using various levels of risk. All you have to do is make an investment from $25 to $10,000 or more, and within one to ten years try to double it—at the very least. Along with the assets you will acquire as a result of your working and saving, if you don't quite achieve that $1 million figure, you will nonetheless be likely to have a high six-figure net worth, which isn't too shabby.

Easier said than done? Perhaps. But here are seven of my favorite ways to possibly double (or better) your money in ten years or less. I will be moving from the ways most likely to succeed within the longest time frame (ten years) to those most likely to succeed within the shortest time frame (one year). You will observe there is little need to "go for broke." There are methods of investing the money you have earmarked for more speculative investments that can result in major financial rewards without the extreme risk of losing all of it. Yes, even speculative investments can be made safer.

DOUBLING YOUR MONEY
The safest way to double your money is to fold it over once and put it in your pocket.

—FRANK MCKINNEY HUBBARD

In Ten Years

U.S. savings bonds (Series EE) are my choice to double your money in ten years or less. Though at this writing these bonds are guaranteed by the federal government to double your money in twelve years, I believe a double in ten or less years is more likely, due to rising interest rates within the ten-year time frame.

U.S. savings bonds were once considered the ugly duckling of investments because their interest rate was always well below the prevailing market rate. But today that ugly duckling has become a lovely swan and everyone, young or old, should find a place in his or her portfolio for this intelligent investment. Here's why:

In November of 1982, Congress finally allowed the Treasury Department to index interest on new EE bonds to a floating rate. Investors who hold the bonds at least five years will receive an annual investment yield that is the greater of either 6 percent, or 85 percent of the average yield on outstanding U.S. Treasury notes and bonds with remaining maturities of about five years. The yield is adjusted twice a year, and the EE bonds have a twelve-year maturity period. This means that the interest rate actually paid on the savings bonds may rise during their lifetime if market rates increase. And if inflation rises, usually interest rates follow. Though the previous minimum investment yield was 7½ percent, if you had purchased EE savings bonds in 1982, after the first five years your average return was in excess of 9 percent. If that average rate continues, the original bond holders will double their money in less than eight years.

Interest on U.S. savings bonds is not paid until the bond is cashed in (although the interest is figured and compounded every six months). Nor is federal tax payable until the bond is redeemed. To this advantage add the fact that there are no state or local income taxes on the bonds, no sales or redemption fees and no management charges. There is also instant liquidity at virtually any bank, the Federal Reserve Bank and some savings and loans (where you can also purchase EE bonds). Then there is the safety factor. The bonds are backed by the full faith and credit of the U.S. government.

EE savings bonds are sold with face values large and small, ranging from $50 to $10,000. They sell for half their face value; therefore, they may be purchased for as little as $25 or as much as $5,000, with a limit of $15,000 per Social Security number per year. By the way, the holding period is flexible, and, as discussed earlier, can be extended beyond the EE bond twelve-year limit by rolling the funds over into HH bonds in a nontaxable event somewhat similar to an IRA rollover. HHs can serve as a retirement annuity, with taxes due only on the HH's 6 percent interest payments, which are paid twice a year.

In Seven to Eight Years

A zero coupon bond can equal at least a 10 percent annual return, or an opportunity to double your money in seven to eight years. Zero coupon bonds are simply U.S. Treasury bonds sold in "stripped" form. To understand how they work, picture a Treasury bond with all the interest coupons cut off. By holding a zero coupon security you don't receive any semiannual interest payments the way you would if you owned the entire bond. Instead, the bond becomes a separate security that increases in value as it approaches maturity. As with any bond, you are locked into a given interest rate until maturity. So if rates rise, your investment will be earning less than it could elsewhere, and if you have to liquidate, you will probably lose substantial money. Because zeros don't pay interest or principal until maturity, the resale value of the bond will decline more than the value of conventional bonds. A 10-year zero is nearly twice as volatile in price as a 10-year conventional bond, a 20-year zero is about three times as risky as a 20-year conventional and a 30-year zero is about four times as risky as a bond of the same maturity.

That's the bad news. Now for the good. Worst case: If you purchase a $1,000, 10-year zero coupon Treasury bond yielding 7 percent, because of the convenient way it compounds, at the end of the ten-year period, your investment would be worth $1,967, guaranteed by the U.S. government. Holders of zero coupon securities must pay taxes on the interest each year as if they were actually receiving cash payments, but if the bonds are held in a tax-deferred account such as an IRA, Keogh, variable annuity or life insurance contract, qualified corporate retirement plan or even in the hands of lower-tax-bracket children, that return can be a true figure. So if you don't have to sell the bond at a time when its interest rate is lower than prevailing market rates, hence decreasing its resale value, you will still be sure of doubling your money. If, however, the interest rate on your bond is higher than prevailing rates, which would increase the resale value, the time it would take to double your money could possibly be cut to as little as three to four years if you decided to liquidate your bond(s) prematurely.

Treasury zeros (there are also corporate zeros) are usually sold with face-value amounts of $1,000 and in multiples thereof. A $1,000 face security with a 10-year maturity and a 7 percent yield would sell for about $510 and can be purchased through all brokerage firms, most financial planners, and there are even some mutual funds specializing in holding zero coupon bonds.

In Six to Seven Years

If I were to ask you to define "junk," you would probably answer with one of the following words: worthless, valueless, unsalable, unserviceable, unprofitable or unneeded. And if the word "junk" is combined with "bond," you would probably conjure an image of a very high-risk investment.

But beauty is only skin deep, and junk bonds can indeed be beautiful if you look beyond the words. In fact, these holdings, by yielding an annual 10 to 12 percent, can double your money in six to seven years. As with zeros, the income is taxable, so in order to achieve this doubling rate, you either have to have your bonds in a tax-deferred vehicle or utilize a combination of high income with appreciation at time of resale or maturity.

Junk bonds are those about which the bond graders—Standard & Poors, Moody's and other rating companies—have serious doubts whether the issuer has the ability to pay the interest or principal when due. On a scale in which the highest rating is AAA, junk bonds are rated BB or lower, which means there is a greater risk if you buy them. Consequently, they can be purchased at great discounts—often more than 50 percent off face value. But that is also an opportunity. The facts show that a portfolio of junk bonds can rate very highly as a genuine investment portfolio, too. A New York University study of default rates on bonds from 1974 to 1984 found that, even including losses from defaults, junk bonds outperformed Treasury bonds by an average of about 5 percent a year from 1978 to 1983. In fact, the losses from credit downgrading in Ford Motor Credit bonds during 1981 to 1982 (about $400 million), or nuclear utility bonds in 1983 to 1984, have dwarfed all the bankruptcy losses in the junk bond market since 1977.

Additional confirmation of junk bond performance is available in a number of academic studies. For example, an analysis by the Wharton School at the University of Pennsylvania on investment returns for the period of January 1980 to June 1984 found that below-investment-grade bonds produced a total return of 13.5 percent a year, almost double the 7.2 percent return for triple-A corporate bonds. The Wharton study concluded that, "In the context of a well-diversified portfolio, the risk of lower-quality bonds was no greater than the risk of high-quality bonds."

Today, however, defaults are growing. The default rate of all junk bonds issued since 1980 has increased to an average 3.4 percent from less than 0.2 percent of the bonds available in the last forty years. Though "default" doesn't necessarily mean the issues legally defaulted, only that they didn't keep up their interest payments on schedule, it still points to the fact that the diversification offered by a mutual fund portfolio of junk (most companies prefer to call them "high yield") bonds makes more sense than purchasing them individually. In addition to low initial minimum investment requirements (often as little as $100), you also gain the professional management I deem necessary.

Do you still shudder when you think of junk bonds? You may indirectly have a junk bond relationship and not even know it. If the thought of a passbook account at a savings and loan seems secure, think again. Scattered S&Ls invest in junk bonds, as do many life insurance companies. So with the kind of returns available with a junk bond portfolio, you might wish to consider this opportunity for 5 to 10 percent of your intermediate-term investment money.

In Five to Six Years

Opportunities to make money are not always packaged in forms we readily recognize. Sometimes the best investments appear foreign— and they are. Foreign currencies or foreign stocks are two investment areas that I believe could grow at a *minimum* 13 percent annual rate, with a possible doubling of your money within six years. The dollar began its decline in March 1985. I believe as long as the United States keeps stacking up gargantuan trade deficits, the primary trend for the dollar will be down. It will take several more years—and much lower values for the dollar—to stop the flow of red ink in America's balance of trade.

If you have a yen to invest in one of the two above areas, then I suggest you first consider foreign currency. For one thing, investing is easy and you can begin with a very small amount of cash (a prudent starting place for most people). Another advantage is you'll also be able to sell your investment quickly if you have to, with no penalty for haste. Best of all, however, you can see how your investment is doing every day just by reading your newspaper's business pages and tracking currency exchange rates against the dollar. You'll soon notice, too, how the news affects exchange rates, and that may give you a fair idea of which ways the currencies are going. And purchasing them is usually not a problem. You can buy most investment-quality currencies through a foreign exchange broker or certain brokerage firms for usually only a 3 percent markup.

An additional way to purchase foreign currency is by purchasing traveler's checks denominated in another country's currency. I particularly recommend the use of traveler's checks because most people can better identify with the fact that they represent an investment. Though the language might seem a little strange, a traveler's check makes your investment seem more like real money, whereas if you hold the actual currency of a foreign country it might seem like play money.

How does a foreign currency investment work? Let's suppose you purchased a $100 traveler's check denominated in yen at an exchange rate of 200 yen per dollar. You would therefore be purchasing a 20,000-yen traveler's check. Although some companies charge a 1 to 2 percent service fee, a number of banks require no service charge, so you might be able to purchase your 20,000-yen traveler's check for a grand total of $100. Then if the yen strengthens to, say, 150 yen to the dollar, by dividing your 20,000-yen figure by the new divisor of 150, you will now have the equivalent of $133.33 in U.S. dollars. If you wish to realize your profit (which will be taxed as ordinary income), all you would have to do is convert your yen back to dollars. Not bad for a day's work. By the way, foreign currency denominated traveler's checks can make an excellent gift. I've purchased them as wedding, bar mitzvah or divorce gifts and always receive a lengthy thank-you note.

You can also hold foreign currency investments that produce income. There is an active market in foreign bonds, which pay interest and can be bought through a number of U.S. brokerage firms. And now available are foreign bond mutual funds and unit trusts, which could, for example, hold a diversified portfolio of government bonds denominated in a range of international currencies. Unit trusts retail for about $1,000 apiece, including a 4 percent sales charge. For additional foreign income-producing sources, you could talk to your financial planner about foreign currency endowments and annuities.

In recent years the soundest foreign currencies or investment vehicles paying a foreign currency have been the West German D-mark, the Swiss franc and the Japanese yen. Since pure money instruments can be volatile, I strongly recommend, as a novice investor, that you stick with "the big three" and don't bet the house. With even the most stable or soundest of currencies, the dynamics of the world currency markets can move so fast and are so complex that you could get your head handed to you if you have too much invested in foreign currency and have made the wrong choice.

If you would like to invest a larger sum of money and require greater safety, then you should consider another low-cost foreign opportunity. A less direct way to invest in foreign currency is through the purchase of stock in foreign companies. While many investors proclaim that they are investing internationally in order to diversify their portfolios into equities backed by foreign currencies, the actual motivation has been the extraordinary investment performance of foreign stock markets. They now account for a little under 50 percent of the world's stocks, and more than 60 percent of the world's entire stock market value. For the past fifteen years the EAFE (Europe, Asia, Far East) index has outperformed the S&P index in all but two years. On average, it has more than doubled in the past two years, and more than tripled since mid-1982 (in U.S. dollar terms). Even with increases of this magnitude behind us, I still believe another double in five years is possible, for foreign markets will continue to achieve superior performance, but relative foreign currency performance will also be a significant contributor. If you want to assemble your own foreign stock and bond portfolios, an investment of $50,000 is generally considered the minimum needed to achieve adequate diversification. However, as mentioned in Chapter 12, there are numerous open- and closed-end mutual funds you can invest through. For as little as $100 you can purchase a highly diversified portfolio of foreign bonds, stocks, or both. As I state in Chapters 12 and 14, I believe foreign securities should represent approximately 35 percent of monies allocated for all stocks in your portfolio.

In Four to Five Years

If only you had invested seed money (pun intended) in Apple Computer some ten years ago, at one point you would have realized an approximate 50,000 percent profit. One investor I know actually achieved a staggering 177,000 percent profit through venture capital investing. Just think of all the spare money he now has! Well, I'm certainly not suggesting those kinds of profits are readily available, but I do believe through intelligent venture capital investing you have a reasonable opportunity to double your money in four to five years, or an average annual 20 percent rate of return.

How many people invest in the right companies at the right time? And how many of you would be doing nothing more than guesswork? Most people who do well through individual investments in start-up companies have been, in a word, lucky. But that doesn't mean, of course, that venture investing is not viable. It will always be risky business, but it can be well worth your while.

If you wish to invest in an individual start-up company, odds will be long—but that, of course, is what venture capital is all about. In order to reduce your risk, you need to investigate the field, separate the good prospects from the phantoms, and target a return rate of as much as 100 to one in five years if you are considering funding new start-up operations with seed money. Here you'll be joining the founder's family and friends by putting money into Big Mom's latest idea.

A somewhat less risky venture capital investment (as well as less potentially rewarding) can be made during the next funding period in the growth of a new company, which is called "the first round." This is when the management team is established and a product prototype is developed. The next investment stage is called "the second round." It begins when a commercial product becomes available and sales commence. Of course, with each financing round there is less investment risk as well as lower potential reward. Therefore the third investment round, when there is now positive cash flow (or the capacity for it), bears even less risk and reward. The last or lowest risk investment round is the mezzanine level. It is when the company demonstrates sustained profitability. It is also the final stage before a company is about to go public or merge. Regardless of the investment state and risk/reward level you choose, there must be intensive investigation. And investigation means research—research usually far beyond the capabilities of most investors. Good research is not reading about a company in the morning paper or a tip from a friend of a friend. You can count on the fact that 99.9 times out of 100, by the time you hear about it, you'll already be at the end of the investment pack. Furthermore, don't put all your venture capital investment dollars in one basket. You need to invest in a number of these companies because most of the new companies seeking venture capital are going to fail. Yet high technology—the largest area for this type of investment—has many winners. Despite the losers, the average annual investment return over the past twenty years has still been 22 percent and 25 to 30 percent for the past ten years.

Venture capital investing can also involve less risk or not be nearly so speculative if you can afford to accumulate a well-balanced portfolio. Today, due to the broad portfolio approach, venture capital investments have achieved enough respectability that pension funds, insurance companies and banks are large investors. The state of Michigan, for example, is now one of the nation's largest venture funders, setting aside over $650 million of its Employees' Retirement Pension Fund for venture capital.

Professional venture capitalists have a good working knowledge of the area, a full-time commitment to the business and know how to diversify. Usually, a very small group of portfolio superstars is responsible for the overall success of a portfolio. A few years ago a study probed eight portfolios, consisting of over 200 investments managed by seven leading venture firms. The resulting composite profile revealed the following: Approximately 33 percent of the individual portfolio investments lost money; 34 percent broke even or had minimal returns; 23 percent provided returns between two and five times the invested capital; and 10 percent of the investments returned ten or more times the invested capital, generating up to 70 percent of the total profits. So unless you have the time, temperament and a lot of money to invest, you are likely to need professional management for your venture money.

Several methods exist through which you can gain professional management and still choose the level of risk you wish to take. There are registered limited partnerships available that lower risk by investing in a number of ventures. They have greatly expanded investor participation in high technology, for example, and at affordable prices, too— you can invest in several public partnerships for as little as $5,000. But a private placement minimum investment often starts at $100,000.

You can also invest in high technology through specialized venture-oriented mutual funds that invest mostly in companies that are already public. That means, of course, you won't be getting in on the ground floor. But then again, you will probably have something more solid to stand on. Some of these funds have done well, doubling or tripling their share value while the stocks of the companies they have invested in were hot.

There are still other ways to invest a relatively small number of dollars in high-tech companies while acquiring a diversified portfolio. Closed-end funds, for example, are required by law to invest most of your money in the shares of companies that are already public. And there are also limited partnerships, SBICs (small business investment companies) and BDCs (business development companies) that offer shares or limited partnership interests to the public. Though each is technically different, all can invest in a diversified portfolio of companies that have not yet gone public.

Before you venture into the world of venture capital, more than ever you probably should seek professional advice. But as a general rule, I recommend you seek venture capital investments having potentially unlimited up-side potential due to the high risk. Some programs "cap" the investor's return after a certain percentage has been made; for example, four times the investor's money back. I also recommend that you seek an investment that does not have a potential conflict of interest between you and the development and promotion of their own venture(s). And select a program that will invest in a variety of ventures. There are numerous single-venture programs—sort of one-well oil deals—and those should be avoided.

It is easy to get caught up in the glamor and excitement of venture capital investing, particularly in high-tech industries. If the automobile industry had moved as quickly as the computer industry, we would today be able to buy a Rolls Royce for under $3 and get 1,000,000 miles to a gallon of gas (highway driving—the actual mileage you may get—might be more or less). But high technology, despite all the hype and hoopla, is subject to the same economic trends and business principles as the more mundane industries. That's why the quality and competence of the professional management of your venture capital investment—your business partners—are especially important.

In Three to Four Years

Penny stocks, properly diversified, are perhaps the best "crap shoot" for your spare $1,000. These are stocks that trade from less than 5 cents to $3 a share and that may rise to as much as $10 a share after the initial public offering. Penny stocks are issued by companies with a short or erratic history of revenues and earnings, and therefore such stocks are more volatile than those of large, well-established firms traded on the New York or American stock exchanges. For that reason many brokerage houses have special precautionary rules about trading in these stocks.

Because of the low share price, you have an opportunity to buy a large number as well as a wide variety of shares with little money. Not only does it make you feel good owning so many shares (You really feel you have a "position" in a company!), but you will also possibly double or triple your money within three to four years if just one of those stocks takes off. Smallness offers tremendous leverage, so the theory goes. It is easier to grow from $2 million to $10 million in sales than from $2 billion to $10 billion. In 1980 and 1983 everyone was so struck by this appeal that the result was a major bull market for penny stocks in each of those years.

When investors are enthusiastic about the penny stock market, that is the time to be in it—you can probably multiply your investment profits by just throwing darts and buying a variety of stocks. There is also the possibility of a bust, but in today's market you don't have to worry as much about that. If you are selective, you can now hold a penny stock for as long as three to four years and approach it like any other investment. Your goal is to double (or triple) your penny stock portfolio if one of your "investments" or the market catches fire.

All penny stocks are traded over the counter (shares not traded on an organized exchange), many in the local markets of Denver, Vancouver or Salt Lake City, all of which have had a history of boom and bust. The speculative fervor for oil, gas and gold-mining stocks in the Denver penny stock market in the late 1970s, for example, turned to bust by the early 1980s. Companies that went public at a dime (with a book value of 5 cents) would see their shares bid up to 50 cents and more, but quite a few investors were burned when prices of those shares, many of which were in oil and gas exploration firms, plunged as a result of the oil glut. Some share prices have yet to recover, even though book values are now often higher than market values.

A young client of mine was one of those victims. He once purchased $2,500 of a very low-priced oil stock traded on the Denver exchange. The company hit and so did he. Within six months the value of his stock had jumped to $13,000. Ironically, but typically, it was the worst thing that could have happened to him. He learned just as quickly that his magic touch was nothing but luck, for only six months later he was right back where he started.

If your interest is to purchase individual penny stocks, then I recommend shares priced at $3 or less. Long-term winners selling at $1 or $1.50 are extremely rare. They tend to be very speculative companies with spotty histories. The younger you are, the higher the percentage of your portfolio that can be devoted to low-priced stocks. Never, however, would I suggest these stocks represent more than 10 percent of your total investment worth.

If you've always wanted to invest in penny stocks, but feared that you would pick the wrong ones, you can invest in a penny stock mutual fund. There are both open- and closed-end funds available (see

Chapter 12), and because of the diversification and professional management they offer, not only will you instantly acquire less volatility, but also gain people who know when to sell. For only then with penny stocks will you have an opportunity to double your money in three to four years, and be able to stay ahead.

In One to Two Years (or Minutes)

By now you must have surmised that trading commodities fits into this last time frame. With commodities, or futures contracts, you can indeed double your entire investment in one or two minutes or hours, let alone one or two years. But they can be very highly speculative and you can lose your investment—and your shirt—in just as brief a time.

None of the other six methods for doubling your money are as potentially dangerous to your wealth as commodities trading. Even penny stocks, if purchased through a mutual fund, hold a reasonably limited loss risk. But with commodities you have fewer alternative forms of investment and a greater opportunity to lose all your money. Some 300,000 people trade commodity futures every year, and as with individual stocks, only even more so, the vast majority of them lose money. Commodities, however, are much more dangerous, for you can also lose *more* money than you started out with.

The odds are against you to begin with, and sink even lower when you consider your fellow traders. Many of them are full-timers who do nothing but trade commodities: they win the futures game more than most other people. They succeed, in large part, by outfoxing inexperienced traders, which is most of us. In order to play the game, the commodities investor must know a lot about what he or she is trading and do so at the right time. It's difficult to predict the future, of course, but if you happen to have some expertise with some kind of investments, you may be able to turn commodities trading into something more than a blind gamble.

The secret, and danger, of trading futures is *leverage*. When you buy a futures contract—whether for traditional commodities like pork bellies or for other investments like silver—all you need part with is 10 percent of the purchase price. Many investors are attracted to futures because of that low deposit or "margin" needed to buy a contract. With little of his or her money involved, the investor stands to make a lot of other people's money, or if things don't work out, lose his or her shirt, shoes and socks because this leverage places you at personal risk.

When you buy a contract, you agree to buy something at a given price at a future date; you're betting that the price will go up, so you can sell your investment later, at a profit. When you sell a contract, you're betting on the opposite—that the sale price you agree to today is higher than the market price of your investment at the specified sale date. The typical contract lasts only three weeks, and the buyer rarely takes delivery, so you don't have to worry about having thousands of pounds of pork bellies delivered to your home. Although they were created as a business hedge and are still effectively used for that purpose, commodities are mostly regarded as a quick means to make or lose money.

Aside from understanding the nature of the investments you want to trade, there is little you can do to gain an edge over other traders. Commodities trading, in fact, is as much art as science; temperament and intuition are probably as important as timing and knowledge. For that reason, beginning traders should trade on paper for a time, keeping track of gains and losses, before entering the market. (This advice also applies, of course, to almost every highly speculative investment.) If you are successful in the safety of your home or office, you may have what it takes. The real futures market is far more challenging, however, so if and when you play for keeps, you should start out using less leverage and perhaps only one-eighth of your earmarked commodities capital to keep your losses (and gains) small.

If you make a plan and stick to it, you may be able to become one of the few traders who profit in the futures market. Those who do follow a few simple rules of thumb.

Create stop points for all your purchases, so if prices fall to that level, you'll sell the contract and take the small loss. Trade only when you have the right opportunity, not just when you have some extra cash. Be wary of commission costs, don't trade on every rumor and keep your wits about you. And remember that successful traders can distinguish trending markets from trading markets, moving at once when they've spotted a sure trend.

Above all else, don't take a position you can't handle—for most people it should be less than 5 percent of their investment dollars. A dramatic adverse price movement can be ruinous and can turn an exciting investment into a disaster. You would therefore do well to consider creating a commodities pool completely separate from your other investments and also consider getting into the market by purchasing one of the publicly traded commodity funds. The advantage is that the funds are professionally managed and diversify your investment among many types of commodities. More important, any losses are limited to the amount of money you put up; you are never subject to a margin call (a demand that a customer deposit enough money to bring a margin account up to minimum maintenance requirements). But before you invest, because commodities are likely to be by far the most speculative and dangerous element in your portfolio, be sure to check out the funds or any professional manager's past performance. Be sure also to include the other material factors I mention in Chapter 12, when determining the quality of professional management.

How Fast Do You Want Your Money to Grow?

Finally, in plotting your strategies to make your money grow in the years ahead, don't forget to factor in the plus or minus effects of compounding (definitely a plus; see Chapter 9), interest rates (a plus if they rise, a minus if they fall) and your tax liabilities (definitely a minus). In addition, there are a couple of simple formulas you can use to help you with the arithmetic.

The Rule of 72 (Doubling). How long does it take $1 to become $2 at various rates of return? Simply divide the rate of return into 72. For example, at 5 percent per annum, an investment will double in 14.4 years (72 divided by 5).

The Rule of 115 (Tripling). How long does it take $1 to become $3 at various rates of return? Divide the rate of return into 115. For example, at 5 percent per annum, an investment will triple in 23 years (115 divided by 5).

When Serendipity Strikes

No matter what your circumstances, each of you will probably come into at least one financial windfall during your lifetime. Though we are conditioned to think of a financial windfall as a large amount of money from an unexpected inheritance, or from winning the lottery, it could simply be more money than you're used to handling at one time.

Windfalls can be created many different ways—not all of them unexpected. They can include that old limited partnership investment that suddenly pays off, or a merger that creates a sudden and substantial profit in a stock you own. It can be a stock option that pays off due to market appreciation, an early or a normal retirement payoff, or a "golden parachute" payoff (a lucrative contract given a top executive of a company, which provides lavish benefits in case the company is taken over by another firm, resulting in loss of job). A financial windfall can even include an offer to purchase your company at a price you can't refuse. It could also come in the form of sudden fame and fortune after years of struggling, or a real estate investment purchased long ago that just sold at a profit. Or money that really did double as a result of following this guy Krause's advice. And of course there is always the expected inheritance, unexpected insurance benefits or a divorce settlement, expected or unexpected.

All can create a windfall or "rush" of money, and all usually also create money anxiety problems: what to do with it, and the fear of losing it no matter what you do. This fear is based in reality. The insurance industry some years ago found that among people who had received a financial windfall, 90 percent had absolutely nothing left after five years. Though the figures are not current, they are certainly indicative of a major peril that seems to exist: losing all or a major part of your money.

So the first step is to lessen your anxiety by taking the time to figure out what to do. Until you have a plan for dealing with your windfall, for six months or so place the cash in a taxable or tax-free money market fund, Treasury bill(s) or short-term municipal bond(s). You must treat this blessing with great care and not allow it to burn a hole in your pocket. You must understand that the amount of lost income or opportunity during those extra few weeks or months while you're taking the time to decide is not going to alter your long-term financial security picture. But by moving in haste, because "this is your last chance to . . . ," could not only cost you a great deal of money, it could cost you everything. Please remember, there will always be opportunities—as long as you still have the money.

Keeping in mind that your goal should be to preserve your capital and make it work for you at the same time, there are several different approaches you can take. That's what this book is all about. Before starting on any of them, however, you should figure how much tax (if any) liability you might have, since windfalls usually have tax consequences. This money will have to be put aside into a highly liquid investment that bears no risk. And if your windfall has substantially increased your net worth, you should immediately take out an excess liability or umbrella insurance policy (see Chapter 5). Because now if you run into that nice little old lady while riding on your skateboard, you have even more to lose than your life. With an increase in assets, you are a prime target for lawsuits.

Now, where should you invest your money? I hate to harp on this again, but you need to diversify your investments. Simply placing all your money in the bank or in Treasury bills is no longer the thing to do, particularly with interest rates so low—unless, that is, these are the only investments that make you feel secure. As a rule, I believe today, with so many economic unknowns, as I stated earlier, it is riskier not to diversify your money than ever before. As for the investment areas in which you should diversify, that will depend upon your specific situation. In addition to all the information I have provided throughout this book, I have also prepared six sample diversified portfolios for your consideration, which can be used at various stages of your life. The purpose of each is to preserve the purchasing power of your assets —always keeping in mind the balance between today's needs and to-morrow's wants. The portfolios are listed on pages 271 through 280.

I ask but one thing. When your windfall does occur, take the time to prepare. Turn your windfall into permanent sunshine.

PART FOUR

Guarding Your Assets

Chapter 14

Unclouding Your Crystal Ball—
How to Hedge Your
Investments Against Economic
Unknowns

The sky is falling! The sky is falling! A few years ago doomsdayers advised you to load up on silver and gold and store your food in a cellar. Some even asked you to buy farms so that you could grow your own food.

Does that seem silly today? Maybe, but unfortunately those predictions frightened a lot of people into overreacting. Some actually followed the doomsdayers' advice to the letter, which cost them money. I am working with such a couple now, who do not want to do themselves in a second time.

A few years ago they had overreacted to the predictions of a few financial gurus by purchasing a great amount of silver at very high prices, and a farm in the state of Washington where they could retreat to grow their own food after The End came. No doomsday. They still have their silver, which has fallen in value, but they ultimately sold the farm at a $25,000 loss, money they could ill afford to lose.

Many of us recall what happened to so many Americans in 1929 and a stock market that was not supposed to crash. Or we recall the government telling us inflation would never hit double digits. Or that an energy crisis could never happen in the United States. Or that the budget will be balanced next year . . . next year . . . next year. Or that a balance of trade is just around the corner. I guess in some ways I don't blame anyone for fearing the economic unknowns: They can be frightening. But there are better ways to fill a half-empty glass than drop it into an ocean.

You should consider purchasing "asset insurance." These assets should typically represent between 3 to 10 percent of your investment worth, are held for the long term and will help guard against the possibility of a future economic loss due to inflation or deflation, recession or depression.

Precious Metals

I recommend you either initiate or continue accumulating a precious metals position in your investment portfolio. Precious metals like gold, silver and platinum are a prudent hedge against bad times brought about by political upheaval, future domestic or international economic dislocations, inflation, disinflation and the like. They can, for example, be an excellent hedge against inflationary pressures that usually devalue the worth of fixed-income investments such as savings and bonds. Frequently, the very same factors that cause many investments to erode in value cause precious metals to increase dramatically in price. A precious metals position can thus be viewed as asset insurance, as well as being a reasonable investment in itself.

Investing in precious metals in general, and (my favorite) gold in particular, has been viewed, at least in this country, as a highly speculative endeavor. And there is a reason for that perception: Gold's short-term price volatility has been quite pronounced since 1971, when it became a freely floated commodity no longer restricted to a $35 an ounce price. More recently, however, most investment advisors have become aware of gold's usefulness as an investment vehicle, principally because of its ability to maintain purchasing power.

Yes, gold is volatile, but still there exists a 4,000-year historical uptrend for this precious metal. I therefore recommend that you consider purchasing gold on a very long-term basis, not as a trading vehicle. You should hold on to your core position through good *and* bad markets. Even the metals experts have difficulty deciding when to get in and when to get out.

I also recommend that you accumulate your position in gold or the other precious metals with periodic purchases over time in order to "dollar-cost average" this potentially volatile hedge or investment. Stick to a disciplined plan, such as investing monthly, quarterly, semi-annually—name your pleasure. Another recommendation: If the price of metals increases or decreases enough to unbalance the rest of your portfolio, you should add to or reduce your position to bring the percentages into line.

Your investment can consist of purchasing the actual metal through coins or bullion, or certificates representing ownership of metals stored in the United States or abroad, individual mining stocks or a mutual fund that invests in diversified mining stocks. The advantage of owning mining stocks is that they pay dividends, and that can provide some protection against the price volatility of a metals investment. The disadvantage of mining stocks (or certificates of ownership, for that matter) is that they represent ownership of metals-related assets, not the tangible metals themselves. If you actually own metals, you are investing *directly* in metal, and that may be a significant advantage in a doomsday emergency, when gold or silver coins are likely to be more useful to you than paper. But its also true that in a really dire emergency, coins may well be less marketable than food or ammunition anyway.

You should also take into consideration the fact that most of the world's gold comes from South Africa and that its mining stocks (thus mutual funds investing in these stocks) bear political, thus economic, risks that are not present in U.S. or Canadian mining stocks. Furthermore, many of you may have a socially conscious sensitivity with regard to South Africa. If you do not, then the fact that South African stocks pay much higher dividends may partially offset the disadvantage of the political risks.

From the various choices available to you, I recommend you invest in a precious metals mutual fund that buys mining stocks. In my opinion, a fund has several advantages over the other metals investment vehicles. First, the fund is composed of a diversified group of metals stocks that (as mentioned before) pay dividends. Metal coins (such as the U.S. Gold Eagle), bullion and certificates, by contrast, pay no current income, and bullion usually has storage, assay and insurance costs. Second, the fund is liquid and can be converted to cash easily. Third, you are gaining professional management that not only closely monitors the political situation and the stocks, but also physically visits the mines. Furthermore, you can start or add to your mutual fund metals portfolio anytime for as little as $5; metal coins and bullion purchases, however, must be in greater dollar amounts.

Now that I've said that, let me put this metals business in perspective. If you're like most people, you probably have a difficult time thinking of gold as a hedge and purchasing it for that reason. It is therefore usually at the bottom of your priority list, and will remain there unless you get caught up in "gold fever" or later think it's a good speculation. Nevertheless, I really believe you should still purchase *some* precious metals. The how and why is up to you. If you can't get motivated to do so, I suppose the world won't collapse. However, if you don't, and it does, you will be sorry you didn't.

Gems

Like precious metals and other noncurrency assets, gemstones can also hedge your other investments. But hedging with gems—blue sapphires, emeralds, rubies, diamonds and the like—is not something I generally recommend, for a number of reasons. There is no central exchange that records gemstone prices; there is no equivalent of the watchdog Securities and Exchange Commission around to monitor gemstone activities; there is no universally recognized grading system such as the Gemological Institute of America grading (GIA scale) for gemstones other than diamonds; and there is no adequate pricing system. The result of which is that in most cases you would be fortunate to get back half of what you paid for a gemstone in five or more years. When considering any investment as a portfolio hedge, it does not seem rational to purchase something *likely* to decline in value as an offset to a portfolio which is (you hope) increasing in value. In short, there is very little reason to hedge your portfolio with gemstones unless you envision the need to flee your burning house or a political revolution with your entire net worth, sometimes a fortune, in your pocket. Failing that, if you would still like to consider gemstones for investment or hedging—or fleeing—purposes, stick with investment-grade diamonds. Always purchase Round Brilliant (shape), flawless or VS2 (clarity) and colorless or slight to faint blue. Stay with quality. If you can't afford to, you're probably better off sticking with gems for their beauty.

Collectibles

Runaway inflation—and the fear of it—kept the collectibles market hot for years, and many people used them as a portfolio hedge. That market is not as hot today; however, collectibles, like precious metals, can still be an excellent investment—with emphasis on the "can."

The dictionary defines a collectible as something that is gathered for a hobby, but there are, of course, many collectors who buy and sell solely to make money. Collections begun just for the fun of it today, if bought intelligently, however, could turn a profit when they're eventually sold. Though most collectibles are status symbols capable of appreciating because of their intrinsic beauty and perceived rarity, they nevertheless can have a legitimate financial purpose and can be considered as part of portfolio planning.

Almost anything can be considered a collectible: Shirley Temple dolls, fountain pens, comic books, campaign buttons, autographs, baseball cards, shells, mugs, telephones, doorknobs and matchbooks, to name just a few. As part of a portfolio, the fact that these and other collectibles are in ever-diminishing supply, and hence prove valuable, can indeed provide a powerful hedge against loss of value due to inflationary pressures over the years. And during periods of high inflation or inflationary expectation, collectibles can even bolster portfolio values.

Obviously, all collectibles are not advisable investments. Therefore, I will provide you with what I consider key factors you should observe when considering collectible investing.

Size of Market. The market for a collectible should be large, well organized and preferably international. This is important because market size defines liquidity.

Availability of Expertise. The more organizations, books, magazines, trade journals and dealers concerned with a specific collectible, the easier will be authentication, establishing current market value and tracking of investment performance. It's a relatively simple matter to appraise or authenticate a rare coin. But if you want to invest in antiques, signatures or coffee cups, expertise will be progressively harder to find.

Storage, Maintenance and Portability. Ideally, you should store collectibles off-premises to safeguard against loss or theft. While some collectibles (such as vintage cars) require special storage, other collectibles are often kept at home because you want to keep them near you to enjoy. In that case, the collectibles should be insured (see Chapter 6), especially if they have a value of several thousand dollars or more. Too often, people enjoy their hobby so much, they fail to realize that it represents *real* money.

Long-term Performance History. Any collectible you might consider should have a minimum five-year history of appreciation, ten or more years being preferable. By looking at the long term you will eliminate "fad" collectibles, since their performance is characteristically sporadic and short-lived. Collectibles such as artwork, antiques, classic cars, coins, stamps, Chinese ceramics, Tiffany glass, Roman glass pieces, Oriental rugs, photography and vintage wines have a very long-term appreciation history and thus can usually be classified as investments.

Sometimes, however, you have to redefine the word "investment" when viewing many of the relatively shorter-lived collectibles. For example, one collector came to my office soon after he had sold *part* of his baseball card collection for $200,000. Despite the sale, he says, he still has one of the largest such collections in the world.

His experience, of course, is highly unusual. Most of the time there is a real risk in collectibles, primarily because investment collectors must be extremely knowledgeable about their chosen field. Most of us don't have the time to gain that knowledge, so it becomes difficult for us to buy right in the first place. Sizable commissions and fees are involved, too, which means that your profit may be quickly eaten up by buying and selling costs. Lastly, there can be an additional risk because investment collectibles often tend to become personal assets rather than financial assets. Many people buy paintings as investments —or at least say they do—and then can't bear to part with them. If it has appreciated in the meantime, the art has become an appreciated personal asset, like a home, and should no longer be viewed as part of your financial portfolio. And what do you call your "investment" after you break open a bottle of your vintage wine?

Keeping the above in mind, I also have to admit that collectibles are one of the few areas of investing that also can consistently provide a great deal of enjoyment. You collect primarily out of a deep interest in the objects you are purchasing, but that deep interest can go far to ensure future economic rewards as well as be a reward in itself.

Probably the most suitable investment collectible for most of you are rare coins or stamps. Coins and stamps have the widest markets, the widest availability of expertise, the greatest ease of portability, storage and maintenance, and the most firmly established track record of long-term performance.

When evaluating particular coins or stamps as an investment, you (as always) should consider diversification and liquidity. The price of any one coin or stamp should not exceed 25 to 30 percent of your total collectible portfolio. A large portfolio of inexpensive coins is safest, but rare (and expensive) collectibles tend to appreciate at higher rates than more common ones. Prices also affect liquidity. Think of the marketplace as resembling a pyramid, with most buyers at the bottom spending $1,000 or less per coin and only a few buyers at the top spending more than $10,000 per coin.

A tip: Studies show that the highest priced (or rarest) collectibles become available on the market primarily four months before and two to three months after the peak of a price cycle. Therefore, this is the period for liquidating at the optimal price. Afterward, prices weaken due to a lack of interested buyers, so then you may have to wait months or years until the next cycle peaks to gain optimal collection value.

Numismatic Investments

The supply of any given coin or currency note is limited to the total number struck during a particular year at a specific mint. Mintage figures are published, verifiable and precise (quite a contrast to the numbers bandied about in the gem market). These figures only give us a yardstick for measuring the actual current supply of coins and currency, however, for it constantly diminishes over time. Many experts believe that 95 to 99 percent of all original rare coins have been lost, destroyed or melted down to metal once again.

When you look into purchasing a numismatic investment, keep in mind that, though the rare coin industry is advanced when compared to most other investment collectible areas, the biggest problems it still faces are consistent grading and arbitrary value-setting. However, there have been recent attempts to regulate and standardize the U.S. rare coin market, and more coin dealers are now using certification procedures to take the mystery out of rare coin ownership.

As with any investment collectible, it again is important to buy the best you can afford, and to think in terms of a long-term commitment due to the markup and markdown. And again diversify, purchasing not only gold but also copper, nickel, platinum and silver coins, as well as coins from different years, mints and nations. Also remember that the worth of a particular coin or bill is determined by its condition and rarity, and often has little to do with its face value or age. And since there is virtually no public place where the average numismatic investor can pay for, or otherwise get, good advice, it is imperative that you work with a well-established, reputable dealer.

Philatelic Investments

After a couple of stagnant years, the stamp market is again heating up. Stamps have been called "the rarest commodity on the market for their size and weight," so perhaps that might be one of the reasons why they have again become so very popular.

Philately, or stamp collecting, has been a favorite of hobbyists around the world for many years. Since 1840, when Great Britain became the first country to issue adhesive postage stamps (1847 for the United States), stamps have fascinated men and women, young and old, common folk and royalty. It has been estimated that there is now a collector base of over 20 million people in the United States and some 50 million people worldwide.

If you desire better stamp issues (nineteenth and early twentieth century), less than 2 percent of the original printings are available in the marketplace today; and those, of course, can cost thousands of dollars each. But philately doesn't have to be so costly. While you should always purchase the best quality you can afford, like so many other collectibles, most stamps don't require a large initial investment; after all, you probably started collecting as a child, using your allowance money. Stamps, like coins and other investment collectibles, should be held for at least five years. And sometimes even that isn't long enough. I *still* have a numbered block of four stamps I purchased more than thirty-five years ago for $3.60. A genuine expert told me at the time, "Hold on to them, kid, they'll make you rich someday." I'm still holding. Last time I checked, about three years ago, my block was worth $36. Fortunately, I'm a patient sort.

If you're serious (or optimistic) about this type of investing, it is vital to learn the basics about stamps before putting any serious money into them. What makes one stamp valuable and another not? As with coins, there are many factors that determine a stamp's condition and thus contribute to its value.

Stamps are graded extremely fine, very fine, fine, very good and average. Mint stamps have never been used for mailing purposes, but could nonetheless be damaged while being handled. While used stamps don't bring the prices that mint stamps do, they still have an aura (like rare coins) because of their history. Owning a stamp that anyone from a President to the garbage man might have used is part of the mystique of stamp collecting. Here are some of the other considerations that influence value:

Centering. A stamp's condition is governed by several factors. The most important is centering. While perfectly centered stamps with even margins on all four sides are the norm today, early equipment often perforated stamps imperfectly. Therefore an early day, well-centered stamp will bring a premium.

Color. Color is another important factor in grading stamps. A stamp that is crisp, with sharp, unfaded colors, is a better buy. The paper should also be firm and of an even thickness. Also, a used stamp with a light postmark will bring a higher price than one with a heavy mark that obliterates much of the stamp's detail.

There are many other factors to be aware of when buying stamps as an investment hobby, such as whether or not the stamp has been hinged, or attached to an album using a strip of gummed paper, or if the gum is the original. It may be worthwhile to hire a knowledgeable advisor or agent to make acquisitions for you. These advisors charge a 5 to 10 percent commission for each purchase.

Art

Once upon a time it wasn't fashionable to buy art. My, how fashions have changed. One expert states, "There are more people collecting art today as a percentage of the population than ever before, even during the Renaissance." Some observers contend that collecting some forms of art has become so trendy that the boom has reached a level of hysteria, almost guaranteeing a bust. Over the past decade, in fact, the art market has become huge, sophisticated and competitive. So if you think you can casually collect investment art without doing at least as much research as you would (and should) for an equity investment, you are only asking for trouble.

Purchasing art is not like buying stock: you don't phone your broker and ask to buy a hundred old prints. So whatever you do, read up on specific artists and genres, attend schools of art, visit museums and attend auctions and exhibitions before purchasing. And again, get expert help, dealing only with reputable galleries and dealers who know the business of art—what, where and when to buy and sell. Here, too, *never* compromise on quality. Buy works of established artists. And don't speculate until you're knowledgeable about art values and understand risks. Remember, you're up against well-seasoned people, like a woman I met a few years ago. She was a major collector who certainly understood the art market. She explained, for example, that in order to obtain premium money for an "important" work of art, she would simply "hint" that it might be available and there were so many hungry amateur art collectors out there that her "system" assured her of top payment.

Keep in mind that you are buying art for your own esthetic appreciation as well as for capital appreciation, so wait for what you want. If your purchase appreciates significantly in value, consider that a bonus—especially if you intend to sell it. For only then will that landscape become a hedge of another color. While contemporary art by well-known Americans is commanding huge sums, it remains the biggest gamble of all due to rapid shifts in fashion, compared with paintings dated before 1900.

By the way, it's so important that I'm again mentioning that you insure your most valuable collectibles. You should have them appraised every year, as that kind of information is almost essential if your collectibles are stolen or damaged. At the very least, take pictures; a description, no matter how detailed, hardly takes the place of a photograph. A picture of a picture is worth more than a thousand words; it could be worth thousands of dollars.

Natural Resources

A hedge-oriented investment in natural resources can be a double-edged sword. Because natural resources, like collectibles, are finite investments, they will theoretically become more valuable as they are consumed. Land, for example, has always been singled out as "they don't make any more of it." However, as with so many adages, a statement like this needs to be examined further. While it's basically true that there is only a finite amount of land available, you should keep in mind that if every person in the United States moved to the state of Texas, the population density of Texas would still be less than that of England, and the rest of the United States would still be available for habitation. Of course, land in and near urban areas has generally appreciated tremendously over the last two decades because you really can't create new, centrally located parcels. As always, with real estate, it seems to come down to location, location, location.

Then there are some natural resources that really are finite. For example, oil and gas wells won't pump forever, and their returns will eventually cease. The curious contradiction in natural resources is the fact that the *demand* for them almost always increases. In that sense, oil and land are unlike gold or diamonds, which can also be considered natural resources; gold and diamonds are valued for their *traditional* worth, while oil and land are valued for their *actual* worth. Without natural resources, this country grinds to a halt, as we saw during the Arab oil boycott of 1973.

If you believe, as I do, that existing energy resources will always be in demand—particularly oil and gas for at *least* the next ten years—you should seriously consider these natural resources as both a portfolio hedge and an investment opportunity. During inflationary times, oil prices have been at the forefront of the spiral. Therefore, oil should be included in your portfolio as a hedge. But it can also be considered an investment because certain types of oil and gas purchases can provide an excellent, partially sheltered, high rate of income. Now is a good time to buy, too, because oil prices are down. As the aforementioned Bernard Baruch once said about timing one's purchases, "Buy straw hats in the fall."

Despite considerable discussion and hope for alternative sources of energy, many of the highly touted ones have not proved to be viable or good investments. Nuclear power is currently in disfavor, solar power has yet to live up to its potential and the development of wind and geothermal energy sources is still experimental and done only on a very small scale. Therefore, the United States consumes all of its domestic oil and will continue to import about 25 to 35 percent, or approximately 6 million barrels, of its oil daily.

Therein lies the problem. For a number of reasons, including the fact that energy consumption in the United States is beginning to increase with oil reserves remaining flat, and the fact that an increasing number of U.S. wells are being shut down or abandoned, it is likely that oil imports will rise as much as 50 to 100 percent over the next three to five years. As a result, in the best case we will return to a significant dependence on foreign and Middle Eastern oil sources, and in the worst case we will be forced to live with the greatest dependence ever. In both cases, we all will see the day when OPEC regains control of the market. Thus we all will feel the pinch of sustained increases in oil and natural gas prices.

To invest in oil and gas now is to be a contrarian. We all believe in the concept of "buy low, sell high" and we all realize that the only way to do this is to sell when others are buying and buy when others are selling. But no one can know where the bottom really lies. Contrarians already made that mistake in 1984 when oil was selling for $28 a barrel, down from a high of over $35. Prices are now substantially lower from what they were at that time. The same mistake in timing was also made in 1983 and 1985. We are all getting an opportunity to guess the bottom again. Maybe we've seen it; then again . . .

So rather than try to achieve perfect timing, I strongly recommend that if you are considering investing in oil, you diversify. This means diversify between investment types and within the different types. It also means that you should diversify over time, investing a portion of your dollars regularly into each area. Despite its simplicity, dollar-cost averaging really works (see Chapter 12). In addition, you should always consider your personal need for liquidity and your risk tolerance.

How can you participate today in an oil and gas investment? You can buy oil stocks, of course. If you don't have enough money to invest in a diversified stock portfolio, then perhaps you might want to choose one or more mutual funds that concentrate their portfolios in energy issues.

There are also a number of types of public and privately offered drilling oil and gas investments. For example, there are drilling limited partnerships where the write-offs can be as high as around 70 percent but are considered a passive loss, which means the loss must be deductible against your income. A direct interest in a well, however, allows the "loss" to offset your earned or portfolio income (see Chapter 15).

Then there are royalty funds and royalty trusts, which buy nonoperating interests in oil and gas wells. In effect, your fund buys a percentage of the gross revenue of a well without any liability for capital costs or operating expenses. With income funds you are not only a passive owner of producing oil and gas reserves, you also own an operating interest. Therefore, changes in operating expenses and capital costs are your responsibility.

There are also combination funds and master limited partnerships (MLPs). Combination funds acquire existing, producing oil and gas reserves with part of your capital contribution and drill with the balance. And MLPs are mergers of a number of smaller partnerships that are producing oil and gas reserves. One type of MLP redirects some production revenue to drill more wells in the hope of generating growth in income and capital value. The other type pays out all of the cash income. Both types can often be purchased as stock through one of the exchanges.

Although some people regard these investment vehicles as highly questionable, the best ones don't have to be. We've all heard about Florida swampland and oil-drilling lottery scams, and in truth there are a number of charlatans in this area. But if you investigate thoroughly, you'll find a number of reliable investment companies and partnerships. If wisely selected, these investments should not only provide a portfolio hedge, but can also provide growth, and in some instances even significant income. All of the above possibilities, however, require research time on your part. And, of course, discussion with your financial advisor.

International Mutual Funds

International mutual funds are an important hedge as well as an investment opportunity. Diversification of your growth portfolio with global and international mutual funds can be very useful because national stock markets often fluctuate independently of one another. The U.S. stock market, for example, may be declining at the same time the Japanese market is posting advances. By dividing your holdings into securities of both countries, you would reduce the overall volatility of your portfolio and lower your risk. I typically recommend that clients place 25 to 35 percent of the money they have earmarked for a stock market investment into international mutual funds.

Why else should you invest abroad? I believe there are a number of other reasons for investing at least a portion of your assets overseas. In the first place, you can diversify your risk by owning stocks backed by currencies other than the dollar. Many experts point out that although this is changing somewhat, the movements of international markets tend to offset those in the United States.

The other chief advantage of investing abroad is the potential to earn returns greater than those available in the United States. This is based, of course, on the expectation that these foreign markets will continue to achieve the superior performance they have enjoyed for the past ten to fifteen years (see Chapter 13).

Still another advantage is the increase in the number of securities from which you can choose. The U.S. stock market represents only 40 percent of the stock market value from around the world (down from 70 percent twenty years ago). Obviously, with more markets from which to choose, you will have a greater variety of stock choices. The

Japanese markets offers stock in many automobile manufacturers and Sony, as well as other electronics companies, while the Australian market offers stock in many natural resource companies.

If you choose to invest in individual securities, you have a number of ways to do it. You can buy shares through local brokers on the markets in the home countries. Additionally, some international shares trade on the London and New York exchanges. And a number of foreign companies have listed their securities or American depositary receipts (ADRs) on the New York Stock Exchange.

ADRs are certificates that are surrogates for the underlying shares. They are easier to trade than the actual securities, and are quoted in U.S. dollars. But since I believe most people don't make money purchasing individual securities (see Chapter 12), why then would I now recommend the purchase of individual foreign securities? I don't. Instead, I recommend the purchase of global or internationally oriented mutual funds. Many have done well over the past years, outperforming most of their purely domestic counterparts. You have a choice of more than thirty-five international funds, which invest chiefly in foreign securities, or twenty-five global funds, which invest in both foreign and U.S. stocks. The minimum investment is typically $1,000. Again, you can learn more about these funds (both load and no-load) from a broker, investment advisor or financial planner.

By the way, there are also more than a dozen closed-end, specialized country funds traded on the major exchanges (see Chapter 12), and if you feel strongly about the outlook of a particular country, such as Korea, this is the way to participate, although diversification is a far better strategy.

Though most U.S. investors have limited their foreign investments to international stocks, many people are also beginning to show interest in bonds denominated in foreign currencies. In the recent past, investors have done well as certain foreign bond markets have advanced and their currencies appreciated against the U.S. dollar. And I have already mentioned the opportunities of investing in foreign currencies, either directly or through the purchase of foreign denominated traveler's checks. (See Chapter 13.)

Finally, it has been said you can always tell the house where the prudent investor lives, for he or she has a "hedge" around it. Regardless of our country's economic future, the world political situation or even your personal goals, a modest investment into one or more of the above-named hedges can indeed protect your "house."

Chapter 15

The New Tax Laws—How to
Make Them Pay Off

It doesn't even have a name. Other major tax bills have always had acronymic labels like ERISA (1974) and TEFRA (1982). So far, the sweeping tax reform bill that recently became law has only a nondescript generic name: the 1986 Tax Reform Act. But it deserves better, for it is positively historic. It altered more than 4,000 sections of the frequently amended tax code first adopted in 1913; it is over 1,800 pages in length; and it is a true change that affects all taxpayers and places in question all tax-related decisions you have made.

Worse yet, the whole hand hasn't been played. While the 1986 Tax Reform Act rounded out ten years of unprecedented policy changes (major laws were enacted in 1976, 1978, 1982 and 1984), Congress is now committed to tinkering with the tax laws forever. That was clearly demonstrated by the fact that an amendment *not* to alter the 1986 legislation for five years was quietly dropped in conference. So there will be no further misconceptions, I propose to rename the most recent act TRANFA (Tax Reform Act Now and Forever After).

As a professional financial planner, I am often asked, "How do you do it? How do you keep up with so many changes?" Even more far-reaching is the question: "Larry, after ERTA, TEFRA, DEFRA and REA, do you really believe in tax reform for fairness, simplicity and economic growth? And how do you think I can defend myself against all this?" To them and to those of you who are also wondering, I have but one answer. "I sleep like a baby. I sleep for an hour . . . I wake up and cry for an hour . . . I sleep for an hour. . . ."

Though 6 million low-income people are being removed from the tax roles, the new tax laws are nevertheless assuring that nearly everyone else will now pay something. Unfortunately, that "something" for many of us means we will see a bigger tax bill—despite the government telling us that tax revision was designed to be revenue neutral. In other words, just when you thought you had this tax thing licked, you will discover that you haven't quite yet finished the job of guarding your investments and income.

It's true that income tax rates have been in a long-term downward trend, and that 28 percent is a relatively "mild" rate. During World War II, for example, the top tax rate for individuals hit a record 94 percent. The maximum rate on individual incomes was cut to 77 percent in 1964. The top rate on earned income dropped to 50 percent in 1969. The Tax Reform Act of 1976 and Revenue Act of 1978 sliced the top rate on capital gains to 28 percent from a maximum of 49 percent. The Economic Recovery Act of 1981 cut the top marginal rate on unearned income from 70 to 50 percent, while it reduced the top capital gains rate to 20 percent, while it reduced the top capital gains rate to 20 percent. And yes, now the top individual rate has been lowered to just 28 percent. It sure sounds as though tax rates are heading in the right direction. So why, since we have been paying income taxes at increasingly lower rates, have the annual taxes paid by the average family increased *thirty-two times* faster than its income? Misadvertising, that's why. The numbers are misleading, for we are being taxed in more ways and in more categories than ever before, with fewer and fewer ways to offset these taxes.

But take heart, Congress has and will continue to provide many convenient techniques for minimizing tax liabilities, many of which I've mentioned in previous chapters. In addition, while the 1986 Tax Reform Act cunningly attacked tax shelters and various other tax-planning opportunities, it did not offer us an obituary, but a whole new set of rules—and with them new planning strategies and opportunities, some more obvious than others.

No-Risk Tax Reduction Procedures

The best way to reduce taxes is not to make money. The second best way is to avoid taxes on the money you do make. And the best tax avoidance method is not a tax shelter but a tax procedure. Where do you buy them? You don't. They are techniques. A tax procedure is a noninvestment, low- or no-risk course of action. Have you ever noticed when you see your doctor with a problem, he or she will first consider the lowest risk solution, such as a change in diet, before higher risk approaches, like surgery? So it should be with tax reduction: Only after all procedural solutions have been exhausted should you turn to the more aggressive tax reduction methods.

So let's go procedure shopping. Actually, I have already mentioned a number of procedures. IRAs and Keoghs are considered tax-saving procedures. Though many people mistakenly assume these retirement plans are specific investments, they are in fact shells that will hold an investment. If applicable, an IRA or Keogh can first provide you with a tax deduction, then shelter your investments until retirement. Furthermore, an IRA rollover (the movement within sixty days of the proceeds from a distributed qualified retirement plan to another investment without tax consequence) is also a tax-saving procedure. Your currently unneeded money has an opportunity to grow and compound tax-deferred, and you don't have to pay taxes on the income until you withdraw the money at retirement. Similarly, the nontaxable transfer of money from EE government savings bonds to HH savings bonds saves tax money and bears no risk. Other previously discussed tax (as well as retirement) procedures are the various pension, profit-sharing and deferred compensation plans. (See Chapter 3.)

Income Shifting

Gifts of income-producing assets are related procedures. They do not produce tax deductions or defer taxes; instead, they are "tax smart" in that they can shift taxable income from a higher tax bracket to a lower tax bracket within the same family. Who are usually in a lower tax bracket? Children. If a child is age 14 or older, his or her (dividend, interest, rent, royalty, etc., but not wage) income will be taxed at his own bracket. Even if the child is under 14, he or she gets the first $1,000 taxed in his own bracket. You can also shift income by setting up a 2503(c)—also known as an "age-21 trust"—for your children. For a child under age 14, money or property placed in this trust can earn up to $7,550 and be taxed at the trust's tax bracket, which might still be lower than that of the parent(s).

Shifting income from one year to another is still another procedure. If your tax rate is likely to be lower next year, ask your boss to postpone your year-end bonus or raise until then. Another procedure is to buy Treasury bills or a bank certificate of deposit that matures in the next (lower tax) year. However, the CD must be the type on which interest is neither credited nor made available before the maturity date.

Treasury bill interest, which is not subject to state or local taxes, is not taxable by the IRS until the bill is redeemed. Or, if applicable, you may find it makes sense to shift your income into the next year by putting off billing your services until January, or sending bills out so late in December that you won't get paid until the next year.

And speaking of shifting, you could consider taking out a home equity line of credit to pay off consumer debt. The interest you pay on all loans secured by your house, including a mortgage, is fully tax deductible up to the purchase price of the house plus the cost of improvements, whereas interest on a consumer debt is only partially deductible now, and in 1991 will not be deductible at all. You should also immediately take excess money from savings and pay off all consumer debt. I often have clients with $10,000, say, in a money market fund, asking where they should invest some of their money. Meanwhile, they have $5,000 of 19 percent consumer debt outstanding. No question about it, pay off that consumer debt. If you could only deduct 40 percent of the consumer debt interest, earn a 6 percent return on your savings and were in the 28 percent federal tax bracket, the paying off of your debt would be equivalent to making almost a net 13 percent after-tax profit on your money. A simple, no-risk, high-investment-return procedure. The early payment of your state income taxes beyond salary withholding and estimated taxes is also a no-risk procedure. Why? That payment can be taken as an itemized deduction on your federal taxes. If the current year is a higher tax bracket year, that is the best time to use this procedure.

Capital Gains and Losses

If you have sold an investment at a profit, yet have another asset on which you are behind, you should sell the loss investment asset to offset the gain. If it is an exact dollar match, then no tax will be due. If the match results in an excess gain, then the gain will be fully taxed. If, however, the loss is greater, losses can be deducted against your income up to $3,000 a year. Excess losses can be carried over to future years when they will be applied to profits for that year. Once again, any excess (up to $3,000) will be deductible.

As with the timing of other income, you may wish to postpone taking capital gains on investments until the next year, when you might be in a lower income tax bracket. Of course if you could, you would first want to offset your gain with a loss. For some people, however, taking a loss presents an ego problem. They find it distasteful to sell an investment at a loss, because they see that as an admission of some sort of failure. In my opinion, the failure is in paying taxes unnecessarily. Sometimes losses aren't used to offset gains simply because the idea never occurred to anyone. Recently, a client whose tax bill mostly consisted of gains taken in the stock market learned this valuable tax-saving procedure. No one had told him he could avoid the high tax bill if he started taking losses. Once he did, we reduced his taxes by over 80 percent. If he really liked the stocks he sold, he could repurchase them after a short wait. He could not, however, buy back the exact same security or a similar one issued by the company until thirty days after the selling date. The IRS considers a shorter waiting period to be a "wash sale" of assets and will disallow the offset. If you're afraid the market will rise during this waiting period, here's another available procedure to "double up" on your loss shares: buy the same number of shares you already own, wait the thirty-one days and then sell the half of the stock with the higher cost basis.

A loss and repurchase is particularly easy to establish with municipal bonds. If you want to increase your municipal bond yield, consolidate your holdings or just establish a new maturity date, you can sell the bonds at a loss and replace them with the desired bonds whether issued by the same municipality or not. This is called a "swap" but don't let the word confuse you. It is not a tax-free exchange. It is a sale and repurchase. I've known people who have gotten into tax trouble because they misunderstood that important point. Bonds issued by different corporations can also be swapped to avoid the 30-day rule. This is more difficult with corporate bonds than with tax-free bonds, however, because fewer maturity dates are available from the private sector, so the time match might be more difficult. But all such bond swaps are not considered wash sales by the IRS.

The important thing to remember is that a swap, or sale and repurchase, should make economic sense whether it creates a loss or not. The cost incurred in a bond swap, for instance, generally should be returned in less than one year due to the extra yield of the new bond. Likewise, if you've moved into a lower tax bracket (and have less need for the tax-free qualities of municipal bonds), your sale of a tax-free bond and purchase of a corporate instrument should result in a higher after-tax yield. Only a broad review of your tax status will tell you how best to deal with gains.

As mentioned earlier, another outstanding tax procedure is the mutual fund switching technique (see Chapter 12). Remember, if you invest in a load mutual fund, you can immediately establish a loss in the amount of the load by switching from one mutual fund to another within the same family of funds. The IRS considers each switch within a fund family to be a sale and new purchase. If, for example, you desire the municipal bond fund (which is part of the Hedda Lettuce family of funds), you could instead purchase the GNMA fund, then quickly switch your shares for those of the municipal bond fund. What you have then created is a tax loss the size of the amount of commission, which could either be used as an offset against another gain or as a tax deduction of up to $3,000 in the year of the exchange.

Still another gain or loss procedure is to sell mutual fund shares with an eye toward taxes. When liquidating fund holdings, sell the shares that have risen least in value. The IRS customarily assumes the shares you sell are the ones you have owned the longest. These are often the shares with the greatest price appreciation, and thus the ones that will be taxed the most. By keeping careful records of the purchase dates and prices of your fund shares, you can then sell only the shares you wish—and thereby postpone taxes you would otherwise owe. Similarly, if you decide to sell a portion of the shares of an individual stock holding, and you had purchased shares at various prices over a period of time, by specifying exact purchase dates at the time of sale, you are able to choose the profit or loss shares that best suit your tax circumstances.

The best gain or loss procedure of all is one you never hear about, yet it's the most obvious, and that is: Don't sell. While you hold an investment that is showing a profit, unless you sell it you have no tax to pay. Only when you sell will you have to report the transaction on your tax return.

Charitable Contributions, Please

Congress encourages private citizens to support their favorite charitable institutions. Many of you make such contributions as part of your personal philosophy or your belief in community responsibility, sometimes even as a response to social or business pressure. You might allocate money to your church, synagogue, college or university, the heart and cancer funds, Goodwill, the Salvation Army, Girl Scouts, Boy Scouts, etc. And that donation is tax deductible in the year it was made, so it is to your benefit to give in years when your tax rate is highest. Those tax benefits are still another riskless procedure as long as gifts are made to IRS-qualified charities or institutions (the IRS has a book, *Publication 78,* that lists each and every organization that is qualified to receive your tax-deductible contributions).

There are, however, various limitations on the amount of charitable contributions you can deduct, and you probably don't want to exceed them. The general limitation is that you can deduct no more than 50 percent of your income in charitable contributions in any one year, but excess amounts can be carried over to future years. If your gift is that of appreciated property, such as securities or real estate, the amount you can deduct is limited to 30 percent. So if your adjusted income is $100,000, you can deduct no more than $30,000 in any one year. But you may still want to give more than that because the law allows you to deduct the excess over the next five years. For example, if you contributed $50,000 in securities this year, you could deduct $30,000 this year and $20,000 next year.

The tax law does, however, throw a curve when you make a donation of appreciated property. It's called the alternative minimum tax (AMT), and if you're not careful, it could be expensive.

The law has long subjected certain individuals to the alternative minimum tax. These are people who have effectively avoided paying tax on most of their income through various tax loopholes and special preferences. Congress didn't think that was fair, so they passed a rule intending that everyone pay at least something. The alternative minimum tax rules provide that everyone who itemizes deductions must compute their income taxes two ways. First, you go through the regular system, where you add up all your income, subtract your deductions and personal exemptions, and apply the applicable tax rate. Second, under the alternative minimum tax system, you *add* to your regular income certain other items that have not previously been subject to income tax. These are called "tax preference" items. From this total you subtract an exemption amount ($40,000 for married couples filing jointly; $30,000 for singles; $20,000 for marrieds filing separately), and to this result apply a 21 percent tax rate. You then must pay the higher of the two computations.

The alternative minimum tax can apply when giving appreciated property to a charity because that appreciation will be a so-called "tax preference item" that could subject you to the alternative minimum tax. Ah, but where there's a will, there's a (procedural) way for donors of appreciated property to increase their current deductions to 50 percent of adjusted gross income and also avoid the alternative minimum tax. The contribution of appreciated property can, in effect, be treated as a cash contribution. To do this you elect to reduce the claimed appreciation by 40 percent—the portion that would have been taxable at ordinary income tax rates had you sold the appreciated property and given cash instead.

I will illustrate, using one of my clients as an example. This client had an adjusted gross income of $100,000 a year and donated securities acquired for $200,000, now valued at $400,000, to the American Cancer Society. Under the basic 30 percent limit, she could deduct no more than $30,000 for each of the next five years—a total of only $180,000. But it's possible to increase the total deductions to $300,000 in the same period on the same $400,000 gift. She simply reduced the value of her deduction to $320,000—subtracting 40 percent of the $200,000 appreciation. She could then immediately deduct $50,000 and a similar amount for each of the next five years.

Trusts can be used as tax procedures, too. A charitable trust lets you give away an income-producing asset, such as a bond portfolio, and deduct at your current tax rate the amount of income the asset will produce over the term of the trust. Charitable trusts, however, are mainly for philanthropists who can afford to give away an income-producing asset worth at least $50,000. That is because annual fees for administering these sophisticated trusts can cost hundreds of dollars, in addition to the $1,500 to $3,500 setup charge. The most common type is called "a charitable lead trust." You put an asset in the trust and designate a charity to receive the income generated during the trust's term, usually five to ten years. You also designate an individual who will receive the asset when the trust dissolves. You will not owe any gift or estate taxes when the asset goes to your beneficiary. Another type, which works in reverse, is the charitable remainder trust. Here, the asset in the trust produces income for your beneficiary during the trust's term. When the trust dissolves, the asset belongs to the charity.

Your Home and Other Individually Owned Real Estate as Tax Havens

Keep records of all improvements on a house you own. Then when you sell your house, you can reduce any taxable profits by adding the amount spent on improvements to your original purchase price. You may also need such records if you want to deduct the interest on a home equity loan.

When you sell your home, another procedural consideration is available if it is your principal residence. Your profit will escape current tax if you use the proceeds to buy a new home, generally within two years. Just be sure the new house costs as much as or more than the sale price of your former residence. And if you are 55 or older and have lived in your house three of the past five years, you can exclude from tax up to $125,000 in profits from selling your house. But it is a one-time exclusion; you can't buy and sell future homes with the same exclusion. If you are considering marriage, and both you and your amazingly lucky other-half-to-be are 55 or over and own houses, you should both sell your homes before that "big day" occurs. Each of you will get the exclusion. If, on the other hand, it looks as if you must sell your house at a loss, renting the property for a reasonable period of time before the sale might convert your nondeductible selling loss into a taxable loss.

Another "tax smart" procedure can apply if you own a vacation home. By staying in that home more than fourteen days or 10 percent of the time the house is in use, you can deduct 100 percent of the mortgage interest and property taxes, regardless of the amount of passive income you have.

As discussed in Chapter 11, if your adjusted gross income is less than $100,000, by owning rental real estate, you can write off the first $25,000 of losses from real estate you actively manage. You can still deduct some of those losses, regardless of passive income, if your adjusted gross income is between $100,000 and $150,000. Furthermore, with investment real estate, as with your home, you can consider making a tax-free exchange. This procedural tactic can save you taxes if you want to sell rental real estate you own and buy another investment property. As long as you do not get any cash or other property, and your new mortgage equals or exceeds the amount left on the mortgage of the property you are swapping, you will defer paying a capital gains tax on your first property until you sell the second one.

The Shape of Your Business

Don't forget the form in which you do business can have important procedural tax consequences, too. You can fully deduct the cost of owning and operating a business. Fees for accounting advice, financial planning advice, legal services, wages, salaries, tax payments, utilities and more are all tax deductible. In an S corporation—a business with thirty-five or fewer shareholders that is organized under Subchapter S of the tax code—profits are passed through to shareholders and taxed at their rates. Both entrepreneurs and self-employed professionals can have S corporations. In businesses that are not S corporations, profits are taxed first to the company and then, once paid out as dividends, to shareholders as well. In most cases the tax rate for individuals will not exceed 28 percent, compared with the higher maximum corporate rate of 34 percent. Also, S corporations are not subject to the alternative minimum tax.

Under the new tax law, the top corporate tax rate is higher than the highest individual tax rate (34 *vs.* 28 percent), so your corporation may no longer be an effective tax shelter. Perhaps you would be better off liquidating the corporation or choosing Subchapter S status. Corporate income below $75,000, however, is taxed at only a 15 percent or 25 percent rate, so if you are in the top 28 percent tax bracket, you can still reduce taxes by incorporating a small business with income of less than $75,000.

Still another business positive is that like-kind exchanges can be made. As with real estate, you can exchange similar businesses for each other without recognizing any taxable gain on the trade. And a non-qualified, deferred-compensation agreement is a terrific tax procedure that can allow corporate owners to defer salary (and taxes) for years. When a nonqualified plan is used, the nondiscrimination rules and other pension plan restrictions don't apply. The plan can cover only one employee and you can contribute as much money as you want. One doctor I know managed to defer 90 percent of his annual income through this method.

Another thought: Perhaps you could try to turn your money-making hobby into a business. By doing so, you will be able to deduct any of your related expenses and taxes. You can claim such deductions if the activity you engage in was profitable for three out of the last five consecutive years.

Tax Details

In the income tax deduction department, you also have a number of potential procedural income tax-saving opportunities. Some are built-in deductions already figured into the year's tax tables. For example, there is no floor for itemized deductions and you can take the standard deduction even if you do not have enough expenses to equal that amount. In addition, you get an exemption for yourself, and if applicable, your spouse and each dependent. You can bunch miscellaneous deductions such as unreimbersed business expenses, tax preparation and investment advisory fees, union dues and more, and deduct such costs to the extent that the total exceeds 2 percent of your adjusted gross income. And of course there are always your medical expenses. You can deduct the portion of unreimbersed costs that exceed 7½ percent of your adjusted gross income.

I could go on and on, but I'm sure by now you are more than getting the idea that there are an awesome number of procedural methods to reduce your tax bill. I suspect the person who is under the impression there aren't any safe methods to reduce taxes simply hasn't taken the time to look. Or else he or she actually enjoys paying as much tax as possible. In that event, I wouldn't be surprised if a thank you note from the IRS is "in the mail."

Now You See It . . .

Of course the best procedural tax savings idea is the worst one if it isn't used. But first you need to be aware of its existence. Even your accountant or professional tax preparer or financial planner can't be expected to be aware of all available procedures. That is the reason you also need to keep your eyes open. A good idea: Every time you spot a tax-saving procedure in *The Wall Street Journal, USA Today, The New York Times,* your local paper or *Money, Forbes,* etc., or hear of one through the broadcast media, if it applies to you tear it out or write it down. You should then file it in one place. For convenience and ability to locate that information quickly, break your file down into subcategories that follow this book's procedural headings, such as "capital gains and loses," or "charity," or "home," etc.

As the government changes the rules, either consult with your financial professional or determine for yourself if the new procedures apply. In either event, you need to take advantage of as many appropriate procedural tax savings ideas as possible to accomplish the goal of saving substantial tax dollars without risk. The dollars saved are your own, and they can speed up your journey to financial security.

The Tax Shelter Dinosaur

The 1986 Tax Reform Act knocked down the many ingenious tax shelters that were built around the provisions of the old tax laws. Now nearly everyone will pay something. Except for a very select few, no one will mourn the passage of tax shelters. It's "Tax Shelters, R.I.P."

What is a tax shelter? It's an investment that creates artificial paper losses that can be taken as tax deductions against other types of income, such as salaries, profits, interest, dividends, etc. In years past, an investor in a "three-to-one" shelter could invest $10,000 and find him or herself with as much as $50,000 in deductions. That $50,000 was then used to offset one of the types of income listed above. As a result, the investor didn't care if the investment ever turned a profit. He or she had already made out very well indeed.

A few years back I received a phone call from a Hollywood producer asking me to locate a "ten-to-one" tax shelter for him. He explained that he was making in excess of $2 million a year, had lots of apartment buildings and other investments, and now wanted a highly aggressive tax shelter to wipe out his tax bill. I told him to lower his sights; he told me to go to hell. Needless to say, he never did become a client, and, needless to say, the IRS probably had him in mind when it shut the door on tax shelters.

The new law wipes out most of these arrangements by creating a new "passive activities" category. Losses in these activities are called "passive losses" and can only be deducted against income from the same type of activity, called (surprisingly) "passive income." Since acronymic labels seem to be a necessity, and financial types are sometimes known to have a peculiar sense of humor, we now help you find "PIGs" (passive income generators) for your "PALs" (passive activity losses).

Tax shelters are considered passive investments, as are rental activities, even though you are actively involved with your rental investment. Stock market activities, however, are considered active investments. There are a few exceptions to the new rules—but not many. For a number of people, the most important exception is the one applying to rental real estate, described earlier in this chapter and further described in Chapter 11. Working interests in oil and gas properties (described in detail shortly) are exempted from the rule, but only if the form of ownership does not limit the investor's liability, which rules out limited partnership arrangements. There are a few more specialized exceptions, such as historic real estate, but for the most part, interest in creating artificial losses to offset noninvestment income has virtually disappeared. For the last several years our phone lines would light up like a Christmas tree around the end of the year. The callers had a severe case of "tax-itis" and required a fast cure. Now that Congress has found a cure, the last few year-ends have produced but one phone call dealing with that dreaded disease.

Though the battle is won, apparently the war is not over. IRS Commissioner Lawrence Gibbs recently said that the agency's crusade against abusive tax shelters will go forward, even with tax reform and concerns by some that the agency is burdened with a backlog of tax shelter cases. Gibbs said, "There will be no retroactive pardon for abusive tax shelter investors and promoters."

If you were an investor in a nonabusive (where the value of the acquired property was not inflated beyond its fair market value) tax shelter, you probably don't have much more to worry about beyond what to do with your PALs. In fact, you will be able to phase them out. Those net losses from tax shelters purchased on or before the date of enactment are 65 percent deductible in 1987, 40 percent deductible in 1988, 20 percent deductible in 1989 and 10 percent deductible in 1990. In 1991 and later years, none of the losses can be deducted, but rather will have to be offset against PIGs, or carried forward indefinitely, until used. It bears repeating. The excess passive losses that an investor is unable to use in a given year are only "suspended," not lost.

I am reminded of the words "Opportunity is nowhere." But repositioned, the words read, "Opportunity is now here." There is indeed opportunity each time the tax rules change. These suspended losses, for example, can be used to offset a gain recognized upon the sale of the passive investment and, if excess losses still remain, can be used to offset net income or gain for the taxable year from *all* passive activities. What that does is create an interesting side opportunity. If you can find a PIG to go with your PAL, you could create, in effect, as much as a 10 percent after-tax yield in today's market.

Tax shelter promoters are helping out by pairing a high-income passive investment with a loss-generating investment. A low-leverage, high-income real estate investment such as a parking garage could be paired with a highly leveraged apartment building. Publicly traded master limited partnerships or non- or low-leveraged equipment-leasing partnerships may also generate passive income to take advantage of otherwise unusable passive income losses.

Another opportunity in the passive loss limit is that it doesn't apply to corporations other than personal-service corporations. Corporate owners can sell their tax shelters to the corporation (but be careful of the tax consequence of such sales) and let the losses offset corporate income instead of personal income.

Still another opportunity: for those of you who invested in real estate tax shelters, the 1986 Tax Reform Act is expected to reduce new construction, thereby increasing the value of existing properties. Though sometimes the picture looks bleak, from an economic point of view you still may have made a wise investment considering the sheltering of income achieved in prior years.

Oil and Gas

Still thirst for a tax shelter? The shelter I like the most (from the few that are left) is the oil and gas shelter. Besides the tax benefits, I'm contrarian enough to like it as an investment opportunity, too.

Changes in taxation of the oil and gas industry in general, and in oil and gas investments in particular, are less severe than in many other areas. This is in large part due to the current depressed state of the domestic oil and gas industry, as well as the necessity of providing real incentives to defray the inherent risk of oil and gas exploration. Domestic energy self-sufficiency remains a critical priority both from a national security and a balance of payments standpoint.

Thus, the deduction for intangible drilling costs (IDCs), the primary source of deductions in drilling ventures, remains largely unchanged. If a drilling partnership is used, then the deduction of IDCs is restricted to passive income under the passive loss rule. If you are an owner of a direct interest, also called a "working" interest in oil and gas, you will be allowed to deduct as much as 100 percent of the IDCs against personal service or portfolio income. But, unlike a limited partner, working interest owners are also exposed to full liability in the transaction.

An owner of a working interest has yet another tax advantage called "the depletion allowance." This is a cost recovery concept analogous to depreciation, and it will shelter a significant portion of cash flow in the early years of the investment. So you see, from a tax sheltering standpoint, oil and gas investments have strong benefits. Now it comes down to a question of economics, where it always should be in the first place. In Chapter 14, I state why I believe oil and gas prices may face a substantial increase within the next five years. But if you want to invest, do your own homework and come up with your own conclusions. Perhaps a Louisiana billboard summed it up best: "Please Lord, give us another oil boom. We promise not to mess it up this time."

The same might be said for all the tax reduction procedures. Congress has given them to us to use, if we promise the IRS not to mess them up.

Chapter 16

Action!—Putting Your Financial Plan to Work Now

Financial planning is a deliberate process for achieving your economic objectives. It is a process, not a product, so it never ends. But the work it demands is more than offset by its considerable rewards.

In my many years as a financial planner, I have seen only one kind of financial plan that I would consider bad. The common flaw in such plans has nothing to do with the goals of their creators or their financial status or their intelligence; it is solely that the plans remained *unimplemented,* fallow, useless. The hard work was already done, but the most important step—action—had been left undone. In short, an unimplemented plan is no plan at all. If it isn't put to work, your plan is useless: a road map you won't look at, let alone follow, even though you may feel lost.

The biggest problem most people have with their financial planning —as with most things—is getting started. By this time I'm keeping my fingers crossed, hoping that you've done something in that direction. I hope, too, that you've had a will professionally prepared (or updated) or (at the very least) composed a temporary holographic will. What you need to do next is set a specific date on which to begin thinking about what you want out of life and consider the financial plans necessary to achieve your goals. A good target date might be the next time you write your rent check or mortgage payment and pay your bills—great tangible reminders that what you now have and what you want out of life will always require money. Most of you balance your checkbook every month. So after you've done that, get started on a financial plan that will "balance" your life.

Putting It All Together

Organize your thoughts and goals in the way you find most comfortable.
Discuss them with your family and/or your significant other. If neither
situation exists, then talk to yourself. Think about them before you fall
asleep at night, tape them to the refrigerator, ponder them while you
drive to work, write them backward in Esperanto. Do what it takes to
dredge out the goals that you truly want to achieve in this life; it will
prove to be a very liberating and exciting experience. And that done,
you will have the foundation on which your financial plan can be built.

*Think about how you can achieve your goals and whether your choices reflect
your personality and abilities.* A common reason that a financial plan goes
unfulfilled is that it does not make sense for the individual, even though
it may be theoretically perfect. Recognize and account for your personal strengths and limitations. In order to succeed—and in order to
be personally rewarding—your plan must reflect your personality.
Don't kid yourself about what you like and don't like, what you can
and can't do. If you're honest and realistic about yourself, your plan's
achievements will be a great source of pride as well as value.

Prepare a laundry list of your financial assets and liabilities. Follow the
guidelines in Chapter 1 to determine your net worth, and this sum will
provide you with the foundation for your financial plan. Now consider
ways to increase your assets and decrease your liabilities. How much
money can you reasonably expect to earn—and how much can you
reasonably expect to save and invest? This, and the money you may
already have invested, are the building blocks of your financial plan.

Determine how best to get from today's situation to tomorrow's goals. Now
you have a starting point—your current worth—and an end point—
your goals. You also have an idea of the means available to you to
achieve these goals. With that information you can now consider the
investments you can make that will be tailored to your own particular
means, your personality, your age, your tolerance for risk and the time
needed to achieve your goals. *Voilà!* You now have a financial plan.
That plan is not carved in granite. It will change as your needs and
circumstances change. But there is one thing that will never change: If

you do nothing to implement your financial plan, you might as well be keeping your money in your mattress. And that is not my idea of the way to get a good night's sleep.

To help you put together your own financial plan, in the following pages I've described five possible financial strategies for five various stages of life, both for single and married individuals. The purpose in each is to preserve and enhance the purchasing power of assets while keeping in mind the balance between today's needs and tomorrow's wants. Please look at these plans carefully, with an eye to your individual assets and goals. But if you are ready to perform certain investment maneuvers of your own, and have considered them carefully, you should not limit yourself to the specific investments listed for your age and phase.

Subject:	Age 30–40, SINGLE, earns $40,000 per year, has $15,000 to invest. Can save $1,000 monthly.
Goals:	Highest priority is to buy a house in 5 years and accumulate $40,000 for that purpose.

Amount	*Recommendations*	*Reasons*
$2,000	IRA in a utilities stock mutual fund	Tax deduction; tax savings can be added to growth mutual fund. IRA offers tax deferment and utility fund offers predictable results with appreciation potential.
$3,000	Government money market fund or tax-free money market fund	Safe emergency money. When combined with other liquid investments, equals 73% liquidity. Need high liquidity because of unsure future plans. May need quick money.
$5,000	Growth mutual fund investing in both domestic and foreign stocks	Investment for potential growth, professional management opportunities both inside and outside U.S., and can be a hedge against further dollar decline.
$3,000	REIT or master limited partnership (MLP) in oil or real estate	If REIT, recommend an equity trust to acquire and hold income properties of all types. If an MLP,

Amount	*Recommendations*	*Reasons*
		could have possible high reward if in oil. If in real estate, recommend a high–equity MLP.
$1,000	Education	Investment in self. Take courses to improve job skills (or investment courses).
$1,000	Mutual fund investing in gold shares	Will provide income and can act as portfolio hedge if high inflation or deflation.
		Use excess cash flow of $1,000 month per month for additions to mutual funds (dollar-cost average). Also periodically add to money market fund. When sufficient size, use for next year's IRA (if eligible for deduction) or add to REIT, MLP or education.

Portfolio ⎱ Growth oriented: 40%
breakdown ⎰ Income oriented: 60%

           Fully taxable: 20%
           Tax advantaged: 80%

Will add: $2,000 per year to IRA (if it is deductible)
             $4,000 per year to growth fund
             $4,000 per year to REITs, MLPs
             $1,000 per year to self-improvement
             $1,000 per year to gold mutual fund

Result: Possible 5-year accumulation for house: $45,000
             Possible additional accumulation of assets: $40,000

Subject: Age 30–40, MARRIED, family income $75,000, has $30,000 to invest. Can save $1,500 monthly.

Goals: Maintain sufficient liquidity for potential purchase of home in 5 years. The figure: $50,000. To have $40,000 set aside for retirement in 5 years. Accumulate $70,000 for children's education expense in 5 years.

Amount	*Recommendations*	*Reasons*
$4,000	Pay off consumer debt	It's the equivalent of making an almost 13 percent net after-tax return on the "investment."

Amount	*Recommendations*	*Reasons*
$6,000	Fully managed mutual fund investing in growth domestic stocks	Investment for possible appreciation. "Fully managed" means manager can move freely among investments for growth, stability and income.
$3,000	International mutual fund investing in growth-oriented foreign stocks	The fund can take advantage of opportunities outside the U.S. and could rise in value if the dollar falls.
$5,000	Government money market fund or tax-free money market fund	Safe emergency money. When combined with other liquid investments, equals 83% liquidity. Should still have one income if partner can't work.
$4,000	Income-oriented real estate limited partnership	Can provide reasonably secure sheltered income of 4% to 8% and have growth potential. Plan to hold 5 to 7 years. Could be an inflation hedge.
$5,000	EE savings bonds	Gift to oldest child. Income will be taxed at child's bracket in 5 years. EEs offer a safe, relatively high minimum interest rate if held 5 years. Are tax-advantaged now since child is under age 14 (and has more than $1,000 other passive income). To be used at later time for college expenses.
$2,000	Mutual fund investing in gold shares	Will provide some income and can act as portfolio hedge in high inflation or deflation.
$1,000	Invest in self-improvement	Your number-one investment. Use excess cash flow of $1,500 per month with $750 for monthly additions to mutual funds (dollar-cost average) and additional $9,000 to $10,000 per year, which

Amount	Recommendations	Reasons
		should be a combination of EE savings bonds, zero municipal bonds and gifts to children (under UGMA), where money is invested in managed growth mutual fund. Also periodically add to gold fund, but only $1,000 per year.

Portfolio breakdown }

Income oriented:	63%	
Growth oriented:	37%	
Fully taxable:	17%	
Tax advantaged:	83%	

Will add: $9,000 to $10,000 per year for children's education expense
$9,000 to $10,000 per year to both growth funds
$1,000 each year to gold fund
$1,000 each year toward improving job/investment skills

Result:		
Possible 5-year liquid accumulation for house:	$52,000
Possible 5-year accumulation for retirement:	$40,000
Possible 5-year liquid accumulation for college:	$72,000

Subject: Age 41–55, SINGLE, income $100,000, has $60,000 to invest. Can save $2,000 monthly.

Goals: To purchase or upgrade to a larger residence in 2 years using $50,000 as a down payment or as additional money.
To set aside $75,000 toward retirement over and above qualified retirement plans.

Amount	Recommendations	Reasons
$10,000	Tax-free money market fund	Safe emergency money. When combined with other liquid investments, equals 83% liquidity.
$10,000	Fully managed mutual fund investing in quality growth-oriented domestic stocks	Investment for possible appreciation. "Fully managed" means manager can freely emphasize portfolio growth or income, but always stability.

Amount	Recommendations	Reasons
$6,000	Mutual fund investing in international quality growth-oriented stocks	For diversification and opportunities outside the U.S.
$10,000	Income-oriented MLP	Opportunity for tax-free income, plus appreciation potential. Possible inflation hedge. High liquidity.
$10,000	Municipal bond mutual fund	Should be a fully managed portfolio of short- to intermediate-term securities.
$10,000	Single-premium variable life insurance policy	Should be in a government bond fund. Income is tax-deferred; interest can be borrowed without taxation.
$3,000	Mutual fund investing in gold shares	Could provide some income and can act as portfolio hedge if high inflation or deflation occurs.
$1,000	Invest in self	Improve job/investment abilities. Use excess cash flow to add to mutual funds, MLPs, municipal bond mutual funds, EE savings bonds and no more than $1,000 per year to gold fund.

Portfolio } Income oriented: 68%
breakdown ⌡ Growth oriented: 32%

         Fully taxable: 0%
         Tax advantaged: 100%

Will add: $8,000 per year to mutual funds ($5,000 to domestic and $3,000 to international)
               $6,000 each year to municipal bond funds
               $5,000 each year to EE savings bonds
               $4,000 each year to MLPs
               $1,000 each year to gold mutual fund
               $1,000 each year in "number one" best investment

Result: Possible accumulation for residence purchase: $50,000
            Possible accumulation for retirement: $80,000

Subject:	Age 41–55, MARRIED, family income $100,000, has $60,000 to invest. Can save $1,750 monthly.	
Goals:	Getting two children through college (2 years); possible job change (2 years); accumulate $70,000 for both. In 5 years put $150,000 aside for retirement, in addition to qualified plans.	

Amount	Recommendations	Reasons
$10,000	Government money market fund or tax-free money market fund	Safe emergency money. The choice depends upon best current interest rates and tax bracket. Liquidity is 100%.
$15,000	No-load GNMA mutual fund in name of children under UGMA	Withdrawal program would be established to deplete funds within 2 years. Yield would be taxed at children's bracket.
$10,000	No-load municipal bond mutual fund	Withdrawal program would also be set up to deplete funds within 2 years for education costs.
$10,000	Fully managed high-quality growth mutual fund concentrating in domestic stocks	Can be liquidated at any time if needed. No penalty other than market risk. This type of fund was chosen for its safety features and opportunity to grow.
$5,000	International high quality growth mutual fund	Need further stock market diversification. Good opportunities exist to make money outside U.S. Also opportunity to make money if dollar falls.
$7,000	Municipal bond mutual fund	Should be short- to intermediate-term and a fully managed portfolio. Dividends can be reinvested until retirement.
$2,000	Mutual fund specializing in precious metals	Can act as a hedge against inflation or deflation.
$1,000	Invest in self	Upgrade job skills or investing skills to get the best return on your money. Use excess cash of $1,750 per month for monthly additions of $700 to the domestic growth fund, of $400 to the international

Amount	*Recommendations*	*Reasons*
		fund, of $50 to the gold fund and continue to seek to improve your earning skills.

Amount	*Recommendations*	*Reasons*
Portfolio breakdown	Income oriented: 55% Growth oriented: 45% (not including assets given to children) Fully taxable: 0% Tax advantaged: 100%	

Will add: $8,400 each year to domestic growth mutual fund
            $4,800 each year to the international growth mutual fund
            $600 each year to the precious metals mutual fund

Results: Possible investment worth in 2 years (not including
          college funds): $65,000
          Possible investment worth in 5 years: $185,000

Subject: Age 56–65, SINGLE or MARRIED, family or individual income $125,000. Has $150,000 to invest and can save $2,500 monthly.

Goal: Retirement in 5 years; accumulate $550,000 in addition to qualified retirement plans.

Amount	*Recommendations*	*Reasons*
$15,000	Tax-free money market fund or government money market fund or Treasury bill	Need safety of government fund whether taxable or tax-free. Which to choose depends on current rates and expected future tax brackets. Total liquidity equals 93%.
$15,000	Combination of income-oriented real estate MLPs and limited partnerships	Tax-sheltered income with growth potential. Can also be considered an inflation hedge.
$15,000	EE savings bonds	Guaranteed by government tax-deferred, relatively high interest rate if held 5 years. Can later make tax-free exchange to HH savings bonds if need the income distribution.
$25,000	Single-premium whole life insurance	Allows the investor to deposit funds and get high current interest rates. Can take out interest each

Amount	Recommendations	Reasons
		year as tax-free income or leave to accumulate tax-deferred.
$40,000	Single-premium variable deferred annuity	Funds accumulate tax-deferred. Recommend $25,000 in fully managed, high-quality domestic growth mutual fund and balance in high quality international mutual fund.
$33,000	Municipal bond mutual fund	Should be fully managed portfolio of short- to intermediate-term bonds.
$6,000	Mutual fund investing in gold shares	Could provide income and act as "portfolio insurance" if high inflation or deflation.
$1,000	Invest in self	It's never too late. Explore opportunities for new activities in retirement. Use excess cash flow of $2,500 per month for $1,500 monthly additions to municipal bond fund, with the balance going into the money market fund until there's enough money to purchase a $5,000 EE savings bond, to add $2,000 to gold fund, and to purchase a $10,000 single-premium deferred variable annuity using junk bonds as the investment.

Portfolio ⎱ Income oriented: 69%
breakdown ⎰ Growth oriented: 31%

Fully taxable: 0%
Tax advantaged: 100%

Will add: $1,500 per month to municipal bond fund
            $2,000 each year to the gold mutual fund
            $5,000 each year for EE savings bond
            $10,000 for the first 3 years in single-premium variable annuity using junk bond fund, but last 2 years use government bond fund

Result: Possible additional retirement money: $580,000

Subject:	Age 65 and over, SINGLE or MARRIED, retired, has $200,000 to invest.	
Goal:	A balanced portfolio to produce high income with a high amount of safety.	

Amount	*Recommendations*	*Reasons*
$25,000	Utility stock mutual fund	Utility stocks offer good income that usually increases. In addition, there is also appreciation potential. The mutual fund offers professional management, safety and convenience.
$30,000	Government money market fund, or tax-free money market fund, or Treasury bills, or CDs	Must have very high safety and availability. Since this is meant to be short-term money, high yield is not main consideration. Total liquidity is 100%.
$70,000	Fully managed government bond fund	Manager may move freely among government bonds, notes, bills, etc., for the highest yield along with interest rate risk.
$25,000	Quality growth world mutual fund	Fund management can invest anywhere in the world, which improves diversification and safety. Even when retired, need some growth opportunities.
$20,000	REITs	A public organization that owns and manages real estate investments for its shareholders. Recommend an equity trust to acquire and hold income properties of all types. Can provide high income that can increase.
$25,000	Municipal bond mutual fund	High current tax-free yield competes favorably with Treasury bonds. Fund should not be longer than intermediate term. Fund offers advantage of flexibility and diversification.
$5,000	Mutual fund investing in gold shares	Portfolio insurance. Portfolio is geared for safety and

Amount	Recommendations		Reasons
			for convenience. Income has an opportunity to increase. If not needed at present, most can be reinvested. Also, taxable income level is higher due to lower tax rates since retirement.
Portfolio breakdown	Income oriented:	85%	
	Growth oriented:	15%	
	Fully taxable:	58%	
	Tax advantaged:	42%	
Result:	Possible portfolio total return:		8% to 10%

Put your own plan in action. Then monitor your investments carefully, looking for weaknesses that can be eliminated and opportunities that can improve performance. Two of my most basic rules of financial management are protecting what you already have and keeping your investments performing ahead of inflation on an after-tax basis. And remember, your investments are not the only items in a comprehensive financial plan. Do you have a will? Would a living trust benefit you and your heirs? Are your insurance policies up to date? Are you sufficiently protected, or are you perhaps wasting money through overprotection? Can refinancing make your home mortgage less costly? By tracking all of the items in your financial plan and keeping them up to date (When will your kids need money for college? When do you plan to retire?), you'll be able to spot those areas in which your money could be doing a better job.

Plan ahead for this year's income taxes, and think about future taxes. The most common way of wasting money may be giving away more of it in taxes than you have to. As Calvin Coolidge once said, "Collecting more taxes than is absolutely necessary is legalized robbery." Sure, we all acknowledge that it's foolish simply to give money away, but the realities are if you wait until August or September to study your tax situation for the current year, you have probably already wasted a lot a money. If you do your tax planning at the beginning of the year, you are more likely to find procedural alternatives for protecting your income. The sooner you estimate and act on your tax bill, the better chance you'll have of lowering that bill through both procedures and investments.

Do You Need a Financial Planner?

Hiring a financial planner costs money. But if you get sound advice, it should more than pay for itself by pointing out money-making or money-saving opportunities that you were unaware of. If you work with a person with whom you feel comfortable, who is client oriented, knowledgeable, follows through and motivates you to take action, then it will be money well spent. But that does not mean you actually need and should therefore hire a financial planner. That depends on what kind of person you are. If you intend to spend more time planning your vacation than your finances, then you do need to find and hire a good financial planner. But then again, if you are a do-it-yourselfer, or are in a moderate income bracket, a complicated financial plan may not be what you need at all. If, for example, you can come up with positive answers to the following questions, that may be all the financial planning you require. Ask yourself:

- Do I have three to six months' take-home pay in a secure savings account?
- Do I know how much life insurance I need, and have I bought it?
- Do I have a retirement savings program, and am I funding it regularly?
- Do I know how much I'm spending and how it compares with income?
- If I have children and plan to send them to college, do I have a plan in place to save for it?
- Do I have a will?
- Am I completely satisfied with the way I am managing my assets?
- Am I aware of all the investment opportunities that are available to me?
- Am I informed about the investment strategies that could lower my taxes?
- Do money worries keep me awake, or do I get a good night's sleep?

If your honest answer to any one of those questions was no, or if you feel you need help in translating what you do know into constructive action, then you probably should seek professional advice.

I have a good friend who is financially successful. He insists he doesn't require my services. And you know what? He's probably right. It's not because he's made a lot of money—he'll always be better at that than I am—but because he has a plan to keep his money and make it work intelligently. It's simple, and best of all he implements it. He divides his assets into three categories: one-third are his business assets, one-third go into real estate and the final third is placed into liquid, secure investments such as municipal bonds. If one part of his assets grows or shrinks out of proportion to his other assets, he'll either subtract or add assets to keep the balance roughly equal. He has provided for his family by creating a thoughtful estate plan and has made sure, to the best of his ability, that he and his family will be financially secure.

There have been numerous times when people have come into my office and I've told them they don't require my services because they already have a balanced, thoughtful plan of action that has been implemented. Though I can usually make some suggestions for fine tuning, I tell them they would not gain enough value from the dollars they would have to spend. Most of the time they don't believe me. But it's true. And you, too, are undoubtedly much smarter about money matters than you think you are. Still, there may be gray areas. You may have more questions than answers, or more answers than questions. You may have been tempted to step outside your "comfort zone" to achieve some investment goal. You may feel you should consider financial areas with which you are unfamiliar. Or no matter how much you know, you may lack self-confidence, either afraid of losing money or afraid of not making the best use of what you have.

If you can't sleep at night for fear of the financial unknown, despite the fact you have spent considerable time planning your personal financial life, then yes, you need a financial planner. If you haven't the time or inclination to make a financial plan, or if you already have eight, twelve or fifteen different kinds of financial intermediaries (accountants, brokers, real estate or insurance salesmen, etc.) working your investments into their structures, then again, yes, you do need to hire a financial planner.

If you do require the services of a financial planner, how do you choose a reliable one? Because the financial planning field is now flooded with newcomers who claim to be the "Dear Abby" of personal finance, finding a good financial advisor is not easy. For that reason I must emphasize that even before you begin your search, you must already know a lot about yourself, your tolerance for risk, your investment objectives and the means by which you will best be able to achieve them. That way you have less chance of becoming a target for inept or product-oriented planners, brokers and other financial service people all calling themselves financial planners, who want to sell you something you might not need.

Stockbrokers must have a securities license, certified public accountants must have a four-year college degree and insurance agents must get state certification. But financial planners don't have to attend one class, pass a solitary exam or sign a single registration form to advise clients on how to invest their money. They can simply hang out a shingle and open for business.

What business should they be in? They are not in the same business as that of an investment counselor or money manager, with whom financial planners are often confused. Money managers or investment counselors (two names for the same business) will manage a client's money, usually on a discretionary basis (where they decide the best way to use the assets) and restrict their investments to the bond and/or stock market. I can't count the number of times people have come to me ready to write a check and leave the funds with me to handle as I saw fit. Oh yes, they did want a report from time to time. That is *not* what a financial planner does.

Instead, a financial planner's function should be to focus on all the psychological and financial factors that have an impact on your life. A planner is a financial physician of sorts—someone who should be looking after the overall well-being of your personal finances. Unlike certified public accountants, tax lawyers and securities brokers, financial planners study the larger picture, including investments, insurance, your estate and taxes.

A good financial planner should have a genuine concern for you and your money—and *you* come before your money. Otherwise you run the risk of losing it, while the planner pockets a handsome profit. For that reason alone, you should never abdicate personal financial responsibility when consulting with a professional financial advisor. Even if you find one who has experience, knowledge and integrity, you must understand it can take a number of years to develop a relationship based on mutual trust and confidence.

Choosing a good financial planner is much like choosing a family doctor or lawyer. Directories, phone books and seminars give you names but don't tell you about quality or integrity. So how do you locate a reliable financial planner? There's the traditional approach: Ask other professional advisors and friends to refer you to one. How were they treated? Did the planner spend a reasonable amount of time with them? Did the planner prepare a careful plan or just push products? Were they satisfied with the plan's—and the planner's—performance?

If you know no one who has used a financial planner, you can contact the following organizations for a reference:

Institute of Certified Financial Planners
Two Denver Highlands
10065 East Harvard Avenue, Suite 320
Denver, CO 80231

This organization will provide a state-by-state list of certified financial planners (CFPs) who graduated from the College for Financial Planning in Denver and who also participate in the ICFP annual continuing education program.

The International Association for Financial Planning
Two Concourse Parkway, Suite 800
Atlanta, GA 30328

This organization will give names of the financial planners nearest you who have met IAFP's professional requirements. Also, a growing number of financial planners are members of the Registry of Financial Planning Practitioners. In order to become a member of the Registry, three years of experience, submission of several financial plans and references are required, and a five-hour Practice Knowledge Exam must be passed. You can write the IAFP for a list of Registry planners in your area.

National Center for Financial Education
50 Fremont Street, 31st Floor
San Francisco, CA 94105

This nonprofit group provides financial education material as well as the names of qualified financial planners.

National Association of Personal Financial Advisors
8140 Knue Road, Suite 110
Indianapolis, IN 46250

This organization represents fee-only financial planners.

The Society for CPA Financial Planners
1700 Montgomery Street, Suite 225
San Francisco, CA 94111

Contact these people if you are looking for a CPA who also practices financial planning.

The American Association of Personal Financial Planners
21031 Ventura Boulevard, Suite 903
Woodland Hills, CA 91362

This is another organization that can give you helpful information.

The Krause Surefire Method for Finding a Good Financial Planner

Many planners advertise and list their credentials in the yellow pages under "Financial planning," and believe it or not, that's where my "surefire" method for finding a good financial planner begins. Call ten financial planners, asking each to recommend another financial planner, the best in your locale aside from himself or his or her own firm (within any such professional group, of course, the better people are "known"). Describe your general financial situation—your net worth, your income and the cash you have to invest—to allow the person you've called to refer you to an appropriate planner. If the planners you call are "too busy" to answer your question, well, there's a loud message right there.

From this list of ten, call the three names that have been recommended most often. Make appointments and meet with these financial planners face to face—that's essential. See if you get along personally, and discuss what he or she would do for you professionally and how much it will cost. If the planner has any written material, try to view it before you meet so you can ask good questions and can quickly compare services, fees and abilities.

Don't be shy with your questions. Financial planning is about *your* life, after all. Ask about the planner's background. Credentials are important. Many financial planners have some sort of financial planning degree, either from the College for Financial Planning in Denver (CFP); the American College in Bryn Mawr, Pennsylvania (ChFC); Adelphi University in Garden City, New York; Brigham Young University in Provo, Utah; San Diego State University in San Diego, California; and Golden Gate University in San Francisco, California. A degree is no guarantee of competence, but if you don't have much else to go on, it's a good place to start.

Ask how long the planner has been counseling clients. Your advisor should have at least five years' experience in the business. Ten years is even better. While it's nice to give new people a chance, the fact remains that it's impossible to get a feel for a track record when it has yet to be established. And avoid any advisor who floats from firm to firm with regularity. A few changes are fine but changing firms every year and a half is disruptive.

Ask for references. Tell the planner you want to talk with a client

"Your guess is as good as mine. That'll be $350."

From The Wall Street Journal, by permission of Cartoon Features Syndicate

whose situation and objectives are similar to yours. He or she should be happy to give you a name or two. The planner also should be able to show you a sample financial plan for someone with circumstances similar to yours. (Actual client information, of course, is held in confidence.)

Also ask:

- How does the planner select investment solutions?
- Does he or she do independent analyses or depend on other companies' research?
- What is the planner's area of expertise and the breadth of his or her knowledge outside this area?
- Does he or she understand taxation, tax strategies and investments?
- Where was that knowledge acquired?
- Does the planner understand about estate planning and the different types of insurance?
- Is the planner willing to explain his or her advice thoroughly? If you don't understand it, you may not know if you are getting incompetent advice until it's too late.
- Does he or she appear to be able to work closely with accountants, attorneys and other professionals?
- How does the planner keep clients informed?
- How often does he or she meet with clients?

- How often does the advisor review a client's situation? Weekly may be too often, but yearly isn't often enough. There may be some additional charges for these reviews, so make sure to ask.
- What is the extent of the services he or she will provide, and how much will it cost?

As with so many other things in life, you often get what you pay for. When you choose a financial planner, fees can range from as little as free to more than $10,000. The financial planner who charges at the low end of the spectrum is usually providing the service in the hope that the client will buy an investment package. Those who charge more are often providing a higher level of individualized service and fewer products. Some planners will help you implement your plan on an ongoing basis, others will simply prepare a plan and the rest is up to you.

"This Is Your Life."

A financial plan, whether you have prepared it yourself or in consultation with a financial planner, is almost a living thing. It's a blueprint of your life, a very personal analysis of your heart and mind. If it doesn't grow with you, you'll make decisions based on outdated, outmoded desires and feelings. If you never sit back and think again about the major objectives and goals in your life, you never will be able to see the forest for the trees. Forget about keeping up with the Joneses. Keep in touch with yourself.

Believe in yourself. Many financial barriers are self-imposed. Look around you at the people who seem to have "made it"—the head of your company, the politicians who run the country, the people you read about in the newspapers or see on television. Are they any smarter than you? Luckier? Better-looking? Sexier? Chances are they're not. The one thing successful people have in common is *confidence,* the belief that their abilities or expertise are at least as good as anyone else's. If you believe you won't succeed, you won't; if you believe you can succeed, you probably will. If you also follow a custom-tailored financial plan, you almost certainly will. By using your untapped resources, by developing good financial habits and improving old ones, you will be well on your way to gaining financial control of your life. And when experience is coupled with self-confidence, your financial future will be secure.

Let me repeat: Act now. Drop this book—on second thought, please put it back on your financial reference shelf—and think about what you want out of life. Your life is indeed what you make of it; and you alone make the ultimate decisions about its direction. You can't avoid life, you don't want to avoid life; so why not enjoy it as best you can? That means setting goals, and the best way to achieve them is to map out an efficient, comfortable path. The sooner you get going, the sooner you'll get where you want to be—financially independent, your mind at peace, enjoying your life and the satisfaction and happiness it brings. I know change can be difficult. But the longer you wait, the less time you will have. So, change you must. And act you must. Remember the last words of a dying business always are "But that's the way we've always done it."

At the beginning of this book I said that financial planning was nothing less than life planning. I'm sure that some of you were skeptical, but by now I hope you'll see what I mean. Your finances, though probably not the most important thing in your life, affect your life in untold ways, and those effects can be turned to your advantage. You don't need to be an expert. You don't even want to be. You just want to gain control of your finances, to help in gaining control of your life. That, in this day and age, is nothing to sneeze at.

The self-control you gain through financial planning is one of the most important and significant things you can give yourself. It's something no one can take away from you. In fact, it *is* you, the *real* you. The best I can wish you is many days of happiness and financial security, and just as many peaceful, sleep-filled nights. That's what this book is all about. But only you can make that dream come true.

Index